D1649960

CCIE® Self-Study

CCIE Routing and Switching Flash Cards
and Exam Practice Pack

Anthony Sequeira
Kevin Wallace, CCIE No. 7945

Cisco Press

800 East 96th Street
Indianapolis, IN 46240 USA

CCIE Routing and Switching Flash Cards
and Exam Practice Pack

Anthony Sequeira

Kevin Wallace

Copyright© 2005 Cisco Systems, Inc.

Published by:
Cisco Press
800 East 96th Street
Indianapolis, IN 46240 USA

All rights reserved. No part of this book may be reproduced or transmitted in any form or by any means, electronic or mechanical, including photocopying, recording, or by any information storage and retrieval system, without written permission from the publisher, except for the inclusion of brief quotations in a review.

Printed in the United States of America   1 2 3 4 5 6 7 8 9 0

Library of Congress Cataloging-in-Publication Number: 2004105945

ISBN: 1-58720-129-1

First Printing   November 2004

Trademark Acknowledgments

Warning and Disclaimer

Corporate and Government Sales

Cisco Press offers excellent discounts on this book when ordered in quantity for bulk purchases or special sales.

For more information please contact: U.S. Corporate and Government Sales 1-800-382-3419 corpsales@pearsontechgroup.com

For sales outside the U.S., please contact: International Sales international@pearsoned.com

Feedback Information

At Cisco Press, our goal is to create in-depth technical books of the highest quality and value. Each book is crafted with care and precision, undergoing rigorous development that involves the unique expertise of members from the professional technical community.

Readers' feedback is a natural continuation of this process. If you have any comments regarding how we could improve the quality of this book, or otherwise alter it to better suit your needs, you can contact us through e-mail at feedback@ciscopress.com. Please make sure to include the book title and ISBN in your message.

We greatly appreciate your assistance.

Publisher	John Wait
Editor-in-Chief	John Kane
Executive Editor	Brett Bartow
Acquisitions Editor	Michelle Grandin
Cisco Representative	Anthony Wolfenden
Cisco Press Program Manager	Nannette M. Noble
Production Manager	Patrick Kanouse
Project Editor	Marc Fowler
Copy Editor	Kevin Kent
Technical Editors	Maurilio Gorito
	Tim Sammut
Media Developer	Brandon Penticuff
	Boson Software
Team Coordinator	Tammi Barnett
Cover Designer	Louisa Adair
Compositor	Mark Shirar

CISCO SYSTEMS

Corporate Headquarters	**European Headquarters**	**Americas Headquarters**	**Asia Pacific Headquarters**
Cisco Systems, Inc.	Cisco Systems International BV	Cisco Systems, Inc.	Cisco Systems, Inc.
170 West Tasman Drive	Haarlerbergpark	170 West Tasman Drive	Capital Tower
San Jose, CA 95134-1706	Haarlerbergweg 13-19	San Jose, CA 95134-1706	168 Robinson Road
USA	1101 CH Amsterdam	USA	#22-01 to #29-01
www.cisco.com	The Netherlands	www.cisco.com	Singapore 068912
Tel: 408 526-4000	www.europe.cisco.com	Tel: 408 526-7660	www.cisco.com
800 553-NETS (6387)	Tel: 31 0 20 357 1000	Fax: 408 527-0883	Tel: +65 6317 7777
Fax: 408 526-4100	Fax: 31 0 20 357 1100		Fax: +65 6317 7799

Cisco Systems has more than 200 offices in the following countries and regions. Addresses, phone numbers, and fax numbers are listed on the **Cisco.com Web site at www.cisco.com/go/offices.**

Argentina • Australia • Austria • Belgium • Brazil • Bulgaria • Canada • Chile • China PRC • Colombia • Costa Rica • Croatia • Czech Republic Denmark • Dubai, UAE • Finland • France • Germany • Greece • Hong Kong SAR • Hungary • India • Indonesia • Ireland • Israel • Italy Japan • Korea • Luxembourg • Malaysia • Mexico • The Netherlands • New Zealand • Norway • Peru • Philippines • Poland • Portugal Puerto Rico • Romania • Russia • Saudi Arabia • Scotland • Singapore • Slovakia • Slovenia • South Africa • Spain • Sweden Switzerland • Taiwan • Thailand • Turkey • Ukraine • United Kingdom • United States • Venezuela • Vietnam • Zimbabwe

About the Authors

Anthony Sequeira holds almost every major Microsoft and Cisco professional certification. For the past 10 years, he has written and lectured to massive audiences about the latest in networking technologies. Anthony is currently a senior technical instructor and certified Cisco Systems instructor for KnowledgeNet. Anthony lives with his wife and daughter in Massachusetts. When he is not reading about the latest Cisco innovations, he is training for the World Series of Poker.

Kevin Wallace, CCIE No. 7945, CCSI, CCNP, CCDP, MCSE 4, CNE 4/5, is a full-time instructor for KnowledgeNet, a pioneer of next-generation e-learning. With 15 years of Cisco internetworking experience, Kevin has been a network design specialist for The Walt Disney World Resort and a network manager for Eastern Kentucky University. Kevin holds a BS in electrical engineering from the University of Kentucky. Among Kevin's other publication credits are the *CCDA/CCDP Flash Cards and Exam Practice Pack* (also coauthored with Anthony Sequeria) and the *Cisco IP Telephony Flash Cards and Exam Practice Pack*, both available from Cisco Press. Additionally, Kevin authored Cisco Enterprise Voice over Data Design (EVoDD) 3.3 course and has written for the Cisco Packet magazine. Kevin also holds the IP Telephony Design Specialist and IP Telephony Support Specialist CQS certifications.

About the Technical Reviewers

Tim Sammut, CCIE No. 6642, is a senior network consultant for Northrop Grumman Information Technology. Tim has served in key project roles involving technologies from LAN switching to Security to SNA integration. He has helped many organizations, ranging from 100 to 130,000 users, make the most of their network investment. Tim holds the CISSP, CCIE Security, and CCIE Service Provider certifications.

Maurilio de Paula Gorito, CCIE No. 3807, is a triple CCIE, having certified in Routing and Switching in 1998, WAN Switching in 2001, and Security in 2003. Maurilio has more than 18 years of experience in networking, including Cisco networks and IBM/SNA environment. Maurilio's experience includes the planning, designing, implementation, and troubleshooting of large IP networks running RIP, IGRP, EIGRP, BGP, OSPF, QoS, and SNA worldwide, including Brazil and the United States. He also has more than seven years of experience in teaching technical classes at schools and companies. Maurilio currently works for Cisco Systems as part of the CCIE Team. As a Content Lead, Maurilio is responsible for managing the content development process for the CCIE Routing and Switching Labs and Written Exams, being in touch with candidates as part of CCIE Customer Service, and proctoring CCIE Routing and Switching and CCIE Security Lab Exams at the CCIE Lab in San Jose, California. Maurilio has also presented Power Sessions at Cisco Seminars. He holds degrees in mathematics and pedagogy. Maurilio is coauthor of the Cisco Press book, *CCIE Routing and Switching Practice Labs*.

Dedication

Kevin Wallace

This book is dedicated to my mother, Joyce Wallace. Her tierless support and prayers over the years provided the foundation for my career.

Anthony Sequeira

This book is dedicated to my brother, John Sequeira. He is wicked smart.

Acknowledgments

Kevin Wallace

My family's understanding and support made my contribution to this book possible. To my wife Vivian, the commitment and love for our family that you demonstrate each day inspires me to be more. To my daughter Sabrina, your energy and excitement for life keeps me young. To my daughter Stacie, your faith and immagination remind me to dream bigger dreams. I love you all.

The instructor team at KnowledgeNet, lead by Tom Warrick, fosters an environment of continual growth. What a priviledge it is to work with you. Michelle Grandin and the whole team at Cisco Press, you are the best in the business, and I consider it a privaledge to be associated with you. And as always, I acknowledge my Heavenly Father for His guiding hand.

Anthony Sequeira

As always, I must thank my incredible wife Joette– without her, these projects simply would not happen. Thank you also to my beuatiful daughter Annabella who provided such a valuable distraction during the writing of this book. She also tried to help with a flash card – but I could not use it because it was just a smiley face.

Thanks to all my peers at KnowledgeNet for helping me to master Cisco technologies—most especially Keith Barker.

This book also would not have happened without the tireless efforts of Michelle Grandin at Cisco Press. Michelle is the best I have ever met in the publishing business.

Finally, thanks also to God for all of my many blessings.

Table of Contents

Introduction

Since the Cisco Systems, Inc., career certification programs were announced in 1998, they have been the most sought-after and prestigious certifications in the networking industry. Achieving one's CCIE certification demonstrates an expert level of experience and understanding regarding the most advanced Cisco technologies.

Notorious as being some of the most difficult certifications in the networking industry, Cisco exams can cause much stress to the ill-prepared. Unlike other certification exams, the Cisco exams require that students truly understand the material instead of just memorizing answers. This pack has been designed to help you assess whether you are prepared to pass the CCIE – Routing/Switching written exam. This pack contains flash cards that assist in memorization, quick reference sheets that provide condensed exam information, and a powerful exam engine to help you determine if you are prepared for the actual exam.

The Purpose of Flash Cards

For years, flash cards have been recognized as a quick and effective study aid. They have been used to complement classroom training and significantly boost memory retention.

The flash cards in this pack serve as a final preparation tool for the CCIE-R/S written exam.

These flash cards work best when used in conjunction with official study aids for the CCIE-R/S exam. Note that these cards and quick reference sheets can be used in conjunction with any other CCIE-R/S written exam preparation book or course of study. They might also be useful to you as a quick desk or field reference guide. Finally, these flash cards and quick reference sheets can also help you dramatically in your preparations for the CCIE – Routing/Switching practical lab exam.

Who These Flash Cards Are For

These flash cards are designed for network administrators, network designers, and any professional or student looking to advance his or her career through achieving Cisco CCIE certifications.

How To Use These Flash Cards

Review one section at a time, reading each flash card until you can answer it correctly on your own. When you can correctly answer every card in a given section, move on to the next.

These flash cards are a condensed form of study and review. Don't rush to move through each section. The amount of time you spend reviewing the cards directly affects how long you'll be able to retain the information needed to pass the test. The couple of days before your exam, review each section as a final refresher.

Although these flash cards are designed to be used as a final-stage study aid (30 days before the exam), they can also be used in the following situations:

Pre-study evaluation—Before charting out your course of study, read one or two questions at the beginning and end of every section to gauge your competence in the specific areas.

Reinforcement of key topics—After you complete your study in each area, read through the answer cards (on the left side of the pages) to identify key topics and reinforce concepts.

Identifying areas for last-minute review—In the days before an exam, review the study cards and carefully note your areas of weakness. Concentrate your remaining study time on these areas.

Post-study quiz—By flipping through this book at random and viewing the questions on the right side of the pages, you can randomize your self-quiz to be sure you're prepared in all areas.

Desk reference or field guide to core concepts (quick reference sheets section only)—Networking professionals, sales representatives, and help-desk technicians alike can benefit from a handy, simple-to-navigate book that outlines the major topics aligned with networking principles and CCIE certifications.

Quick Reference Sheets

Following each flash card section, you will find quick reference sheets. These sheets serve as both a study guide for the CCIE written exam and as a companion reference to the text. For readers who seek the CCIE certification, these quick reference sheets are well suited to reinforce the concepts learned in the text rather than as a sole source of information. For readers who have either already obtained CCIE certification or simply need a basic overview, these sheets can serve as a standalone reference. A complete set of the notes can also be printed from the enclosed CD-ROM.

What Is Included on the CD-ROM

The CD-ROM includes copies of the 500+ flash cards and quick reference sheets presented in the physical set. Also included is an electronic version of the flash cards that runs on all Windows and Palm platforms. The CD-ROM allows you to shuffle the flash cards so that you can randomize your study. The CD-ROM also includes a powerful practice test engine designed to simulate the CCIE written exam. The practice test engine will help you become familiar with the format of the exams and reinforce the knowledge needed to pass them.

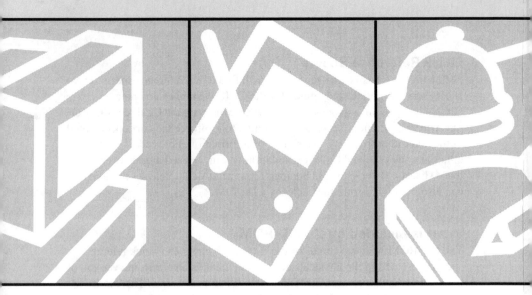

Section 1
General Networking Theory

This chapter ensures you are prepared for questions in the Cisco Certified Internetwork Expert (CCIE) written exam that deal with general networking theories. General networking theories include Open System Interconnection (OSI) models, routing concepts, networking standards, and protocol mechanics.

As you might expect, many of the concepts reviewed in this chapter receive additional and more specific coverage elsewhere in this text. It is critical that you review the topics at this level as well, however. The information contained here is not repeated later at all.

The CCIE—Routing/Switching candidate should have several years of hands-on experience with Cisco gear. Therefore, this section also ensures you are well-versed in Cisco device operations. This section focuses on general **show** and **debug** commands and their usage, as well as physical structures within almost all Cisco equipment. It also reviews basic device operational characteristics including device access, password recovery, Simple Network Management Protocol (SNMP), and Switched Port Analyzer (SPAN).

Question 1

Name the seven layers of the OSI model in order from top to bottom.

Question 2

Name the four layers of the Department of Defense (DoD) TCP/IP model in order from top to bottom.

Question 3

The Process/Application layer of the TCP/IP reference model encompasses the functionality of which OSI reference model layers?

Question 1 Answer

The seven layers of the OSI model from top to bottom are:

Application

Presentation

Session

Transport

Network

Data link

Physical

Question 2 Answer

The four layers from top to bottom are:

Process/Application

Host to Host

Internet

Network Access

Question 3 Answer

The Process/Application layer incorporates the functionality of the application, presentation, and session layers.

Question 4

The Host to Host layer of the TCP/IP reference model incorporates the functionality of which OSI layer?

Question 5

The network layer of the OSI reference model incorporates the functionality of which TCP/IP reference model layer?

Question 6

The Network Access layer of the TCP/IP reference model incorporates the functionality of which OSI reference model layers?

Question 4 Answer

The Host to Host layer incorporates the functionality of the transport layer.

Question 5 Answer

The Internet layer of the TCP/IP model is the equivalent of the OSI model's network layer.

Question 6 Answer

The Network Access layer is associated with the physical and data link layers of the OSI model.

Question 7

The IEEE 802.2 specification defines which sublayer of the data link layer of the OSI reference model?

Question 8

Which layer of the OSI reference model is responsible for path selection through an internetwork?

Question 9

Name four distance vector routing protocols.

Question 7 Answer

The IEEE 802.2 specification defines the logical link control (LLC) sublayer of the data link layer. IEEE 802.2 defines a number of fields in data link layer frames that enable multiple higher-layer protocols to share a single physical data link.

Question 8 Answer

The Network layer is responsible for path selection through the internetwork.

Question 9 Answer

Distance vector routing protocols include:

RIP version 1

RIP version 2

IGRP

EIGRP (Advanced Distance Vector)

BGP (Advanced Distance Vector)

Question 10

Name two link state routing protocols.

Question 11

Name three attributes typical of classic distance vector routing protocols.

Question 12

Name at least three attributes of link state routing protocols.

Question 10 Answer

Link state routing protocols include:

OSPF

IS-IS

Question 11 Answer

Classic distance vector routing protocols exhibit these attributes:

Defined finite hop count

Convergence tends to be slower

Periodic broadcast of routing tables

Many loop prevention mechanisms

Communication of routing table information with directly connected neighbors

Question 12 Answer

The following are all attributes of link state routing protocols:

More scalable because of no hop count limitations

Convergence tends to be quicker

Triggered multicast of routing information changes

Fewer loop prevention mechanisms required typically

Flooding of link information to all devices in the routing domain

Local databases used to derive best route information using the shortest path first algorithm

Question 13

What is the default administrative distance of a directly connected route?

Question 14

What is the default administrative distance of a static route that points to a next hop router?

Question 15

What is the default administrative distance of an Enhanced Interior Gateway Routing Protocol (EIGRP) summary route?

Question 13 Answer

0

Question 14 Answer

1

Question 15 Answer

5

Question 16

What is the default administrative distance of External Border Gateway Protocol (BGP)?

Question 17

What is the default administrative distance of Internal EIGRP?

Question 18

What is the default administrative distance of Interior Gateway Routing Protocol (IGRP)?

Question 16 Answer

20

Question 17 Answer

90

Question 18 Answer

100

Question 19

What is the default administrative distance of Open Shortest Path First (OSPF)?

Question 20

What is the default administrative distance of Intermediate System-to-Intermediate System (IS-IS)?

Question 21

What is the default administrative distance of Routing Information Protocol (RIP)?

Question 19 Answer

110

Question 20 Answer

115

Question 21 Answer

120

Question 22

What is the default administrative distance of External EIGRP?

Question 23

What is the default administrative distance of Internal BGP?

Question 24

What is a floating static route?

Question 22 Answer

170

Question 23 Answer

200

Question 24 Answer

A floating static route is a static route with an administrative distance assigned that is higher than the administrative distance of the dynamic routing protocol in use. This allows the static route to act as a backup route in the event of a link failure.

Question 25

Define split horizon.

Question 26

What is poison reverse?

Question 27

Name at least three advantages of route summarization.

Question 25 Answer

Split horizon refers to a routing protocol's not sending updates out an interface where the updates were originally received.

Question 26 Answer

Poison reverse is an exception to the split horizon rule. Poisoned routes are sent out an interface from where the update was originally received.

Question 27 Answer

Route summarization provides the following advantages:

Smaller routing tables (less memory required)

Less overhead for routers performing lookups

Causes fewer routing updates by hiding details of subnet status

Promotes the use of variable-length subnet mask (VLSM)

Enables classless interdomain routing (CIDR)

Question 28

If a router contains a route entry for the specific host address, a route entry for the subnet, and a summarized route entry for the major classful network, which route entry does the router use?

Question 29

What is tunneling?

Question 30

100BASE-TX requires what type of physical media?

Question 28 Answer

The router relies upon the longest match (of subnet mask) principle when evaluating routes. In this case—the host entry has the longest subnet mask and, therefore, is the route that is selected.

Question 29 Answer

Tunneling refers to further encapsulating header, data, and trailer information to carry this private information securely across a public network. The original packet with its encapsulation information appears as data in the tunnel.

Question 30 Answer

100BASE-TX requires Cat 5 unshielded twisted-pair (UTP) or Type 1 shielded twisted-pair (STP) wire.

Question 31

Is the TCP "handshake" process one way, two way, or three way?

Question 32

Which of the TCP hosts (sender or receiver) sets the SYN bit in the communication?

Question 33

Under the concept of "sliding windows" in TCP/IP, does the sender or receiver specify the window size?

Question 31 Answer

The TCP handshake process is three way. The TCP handshake is made up of three TCP segments exchanged between two devices; the initial SYN, a SYN/ACK, and an ACK.

Question 32 Answer

The sender sets the SYN bit to indicate that a connection request is being made. The receiver sets the SYN bit in its SYN/ACK response to the SYN packet.

Question 33 Answer

With TCP/IP sliding windows, the receiver specifies the current window size in every packet. The window is the number of data bytes that the sender is allowed to send before waiting for an acknowledgment.

Question 34

How does a receiver indicate to the sender not to send any data (using sliding windows)?

Question 35

If a TCP/IP sender transmits bytes 6 through 11 and these bytes are received successfully by the receiver, what acknowledgment number should be sent back to the sender?

Question 36

What does MTU refer to?

Question 34 Answer

The receiver indicates a window size of 0.

Question 35 Answer

The receiver should send an ACK = 12 to indicate that the next byte expected is 12.

Question 36 Answer

MTU refers to maximum transmission unit. MTU is the largest size packet or frame that can be sent in a network.

Question 37

Name two possible issues that can be caused by fragmentation.

Question 38

Which bit in the FLAGS field of the TCP/IP header indicates that the connection should be terminated?

Question 39

What is Q-in-Q tunneling and when might it be used?

Question 37 Answer

Possible issues include:

Overhead due to reassembly

Lost fragments

Firewalls permitting or denying non-initial fragments

Question 38 Answer

The FIN bit resides in the FLAGS field and is used for termination.

Question 39 Answer

Q-in-Q tunneling refers to tunneling an 802.1q packet inside another 802.1q packet to distinguish different customer's virtual LANs (VLANs). Providers might use this mechanism if they are providing Metro Ethernet service to multiple customers for high speed metropolitan-area network (MAN) connectivity.

Question 40

What is the default hop count limit used in RIP v2 networks?

Question 41

The use of keepalives on a serial interface can cause interface failures. What common show command checks to see if keepalives are set on the interface?

Question 42

What field in the show interface command output for a Fast Ethernet interface might indicate that cable runs are too long?

Question 40 Answer

The default is 15.

Question 41 Answer

The **show interface** command output features a Keepalive field used to indicate whether keepalives are set or not. If keepalives are set too low and considerable congestion exists on an opposing interface, keepalives might not be returned in time—causing interface failures.

Question 42 Answer

The Late Collisions field indicates the number of collisions that occur after transmitting the preamble; large numbers of late collisions often indicate that cable runs are too long or a duplex mismatch exists.

Question 43

Considering the show interface command—what field allows the analysis of the error rates reported to determine the true volume of damaged frames sent or received?

Question 44

What does the Overrun field indicate in a show interface command result?

Question 45

What command permits the determination of the type of interface processors installed in a Cisco 7500 series router?

Question 43 Answer

Use the Last Cleared field to see how long the counters have been tracking error conditions. The **clear counters** command allows you to reset the counters in these **show** commands.

Question 44 Answer

The Overrun field indicates the number of times the receiver hardware was unable to hand received data to a hardware buffer because the input rate exceeded the receiver's ability to handle the data.

Question 45 Answer

The **show diag** command permits the evaluation of interface types in the 7500 series.

Question 46

You can identify the feature set loaded on a particular router with the show version command. What does a jk8s in the image name typically indicate?

Question 47

A Cisco 7200 series router possesses an image name that contains the following portion:

c7200-ajs40-mz

What does the mz portion of this image name indicate?

Question 48

Cisco releases software in trains. This allows them to introduce new features in some software, while just fixing bugs in other releases. What is the purpose of an E train?

Question 46 Answer

This typically indicates the Enterprise Plus IPSec 56 feature set is in use. Common naming conventions for feature sets include:

IP Plus—is

IP—i

Enterprise Plus IPSec 56—jk8s

Enterprise Plus—js

Enterprise—j

Question 47 Answer

This portion of the name indicates the run-time memory in use and compression format. Here are common examples:

F—Image runs in Flash

m—Image runs in RAM

R—Image runs in ROM

L—Image is located at run time

z—Image is Zip compressed

x—Image is Mzip compressed

w—Image is STAC compressed

Question 48 Answer

The E train targets enterprise core and SP edge devices. This train supports advanced quality of service (QoS), voice, security, and firewall capabilities. This train fixes defects found in previous versions.

Other trains include:

mainline—Consolidates releases and fixes defects. Inherits features from the parent T train and does not add additional features.

T—Introduces new features and fixes defects.

S—Consolidates 12.1E, 12.2 mainline, and 12.0S, which supports high-end backbone routing and fixes defects.

E—Targets enterprise core and SP edge, supports advanced QoS, voice, security, and firewall, and fixes defects.

Question 49

How many images are required for the supervisor engine and the MSFC daughter card in a Cat 6500 series router running native IOS?

Question 50

Debug messages are sent to the console port by default. What command allows these messages to appear on a Telnet session?

Question 51

What is the most efficient method for logging on a Cisco device?

Question 49 Answer

One image is required in this case because of the use of native IOS. CatOS actually uses two images. The image naming convention used in the case of native IOS is:

c6sup{Supervisor Engine Model}{MSFCModel}.<features>.<version>.bin

Question 50 Answer

The **terminal monitor** command permits **debug** output to appear on a telnet client.

Question 51 Answer

Logging to an internal buffer is the most efficient method. This is configured with the **logging buffered** command.

Question 52

A show flash command depicts many files that possess a deleted flag. How can these files be removed from Flash memory?

Question 53

What are the three options for file transfers to and from your Cisco device from rommon mode?

Question 54

When the Enter key is pressed following the command copy tftp flash, what is the prompt that appears?

Question 52 Answer

The **squeeze** command removes deleted files from Flash memory.

Question 53 Answer

Xmodem , Ymodem, and TFTP are options from rommon mode on most Cisco devices.

Question 54 Answer

Address or name of remote host []?

Question 55

You are working on a Cisco device that features access to two different PCMCIA Flash cards. How can you move from one to another in the operating system?

Question 56

What is the default password set on a Cat 5000 for the first 30 seconds following boot?

Question 57

Describe the key steps for recovering the password on most Cisco routers?

Question 55 Answer

You use the **cd** command to move from card to card. For example, **cd slot0** moves you to the card in slot 0.

Question 56 Answer

The default password for 30 seconds following boot is none — simply press the Enter key at the password prompt.

Question 57 Answer

The most common password recovery procedures involve the following steps:

Access the console port and use the Break sequence during reboot.

Change the configuration register and have the router ignore the startup configuration on the subsequent boot.

Log in to the device and enter privileged mode.

Copy the startup configuration into RAM.

Reset the configuration register.

Set the new password.

Copy the configuration to startup.

Question 58

What do the bit numbers 0–3 control in the configuration register of a Cisco router?

Question 59

What does bit number 6 control in the configuration register?

Question 60

If the configuration register is set to 0x2101, where is the Cisco IOS image booted from?

Question 58 Answer

Bits 0–3 control the boot characteristics. These bits are often referred to as the boot field.

Question 59 Answer

Bit 6 causes the system to ignore the configuration in nonvolatile random-access memory (NVRAM).

Question 60 Answer

If the boot field is set to 0x1 as in the example here, the router boots the ROM image.

Question 61

What command disables SNMP agent functionality on a Cisco device?

Question 62

You are interested in permitting a CiscoWorks server to obtain performance and configuration information from a Cisco router in your network. At a minimum, what command must be in place on the Cisco device?

Question 63

How does RSPAN carried mirrored traffic to the destination port?

Question 61 Answer

The command **no snmp-server** disables SNMP functionality.

Question 62 Answer

At a minimum, the device must have a read-only SNMP community string set. This is accomplished on most devices using the following command:

```
snmp-server community [string] ro
```

Question 63 Answer

RSPAN uses a special RSPAN VLAN to transport the mirrored frames to the destination port.

Question 64

What is the default spanning-tree configuration of a Switched Port Analyzer (SPAN) destination port?

Question 65

You are configuring a Catalyst 3550 switch. You have made several VLAN configurations including the creation of several VLANs and the renaming of several others. Where (specifically) are these VLAN configurations stored on the switch?

Question 64 Answer

Spanning tree is disabled for SPAN destinations. This is one reason why it is very important to reverse the configuration of SPAN once you are done analyzing traffic. Plugging a switch into a SPAN destination port can introduce switching loops.

Question 65 Answer

Configurations for VLAN IDs 1 to 1005 are written to the file vlan.dat (VLAN database), and you can display them by entering the **show vlan** privileged EXEC command. The vlan.dat file is stored in Flash memory.

General Networking Theory Quick Reference Sheets

OSI Models

This figure shows the classic Open System Interconnection model and compares the model to the Department of Defense oD) TCP/IP model:

Networking Communications Models

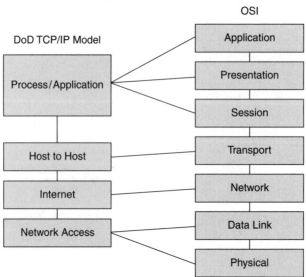

General Routing Concepts

Link State Versus Distance Vector

Distance Vector

- Examples: RIPv1, RIPv2, IGRP
- Features periodic transmission of entire routing tables to directly connected neighbors
- Mathematically compares routes using some measurement of distance
- Features hop count limitation

Link State

- Examples: OSPF, IS-IS
- Sends local connection information to all nodes in the internetwork

Hybrid

- Example: EIGRP
- Features properties of both distance vector and link-state routing protocols

Administrative Distance

If a router learns of a network from multiple sources (routing protocols or static configurations), it uses the administrative distance value to determine which route to install in the routing (forwarding) table. The default administrative distance values are listed here:

Source	Administrative Distance
Connected Interface	0
Static Route	1
EIGRP Summary Route	5
External BGP	20
Internal EIGRP	90
IGRP	100
OSPF	110
IS-IS	115
RIP	120
Exterior Gateway Protocol	140
On Demand Routing	160
External EIGRP	170
Internal BGP	200
Unknown	255

Administrators can create static routes that float. A floating static route means the administrator increases the administrative distance of the static route to be greater than the administrative distance of the dynamic routing protocol in use. This means the static route is relied upon only when the dynamic route does not exist.

Split Horizon

Split horizon is a technique used by routing protocols to help prevent routing loops. The split horizon rule states that an interface will not send routing information out an interface from which the routing information was originally received. Split horizon can cause problems in some topologies, such as hub and spoke Frame Relay configurations.

Loops

Routing loops are disastrous to the health of the network. They can lead to lost packets—or even worse consequences. Many mechanisms exist to prevent routing loops. These include the following:

- **Split horizon**—An interface will not send routing information out an interface from which the routing information was originally received.

- **Route poisoning**—A directly connected network failure is advertised as unreachable by the local router.

- **Poison reverse**—An exception to split horizon; the poisoned route can be sent out an interface from which the route was originally learned.

- **Hold-down timer**—A router will not listen to route updates regarding a network whose reachability has been reported as down.

- **Maximum metric**—There is a metric value that is considered unreachable—for example, Routing Information Protocol (RIP) uses a maximum metric of 15 hops.

Summarization

Summarization is the process in which the administrator collapses many routes with a long mask to form another route with a shorter mask. Route summarization reduces the size of routing tables and makes routing function more efficiently. Route summarization also helps to make networks more stable by reducing the number of updates that are sent when subnets change state. Route summarization makes classless interdomain routing (CIDR) possible. Variable-length subnet masking (VLSM) promotes the use of route summarization. Some dynamic routing protocols engage in route summarization automatically for changes in major classful network—while others do not and require manual route summarization.

To engage in route summarization, find all of the leftmost bits that are in common and create a mask that encompasses them. Here is an example:

The following routes exist in the routing table—all routes use a 24-bit mask:

    10.108.48.0 = 00001010 01101100 00110000 00000000

    10.108.49.0 = 00001010 01101100 00110001 00000000

10.108.50.0 = 00001010 01101100 00110010 00000000

10.108.51.0 = 00001010 01101100 00110011 00000000

10.108.52.0 = 00001010 01101100 00110100 00000000

10.108.53.0 = 00001010 01101100 00110101 00000000

10.108.54.0 = 00001010 01101100 00110110 00000000

10.108.55.0 = 00001010 01101100 00110111 00000000

Notice that the first 21 bits of the subnetwork IDs are all common. These can be masked off. The single route entry you can use for all of these subnetworks is as follows:

10.108.48.0/21

Tunneling

Tunneling refers to encapsulating header, trailer, and data information inside another protocol so that all of that information appears to be just data. Tunneling often involves security — allowing a company to transmit data intended for use in the private network across a public network. Two popular security tunneling protocols include Point-to-Point Tunneling Protocol (PPTP) and generic routing encapsulation (GRE).

IPSec also supports the operation of Tunnel mode as opposed to Transport mode. The more secure Tunnel mode has the ability to secure both the header and the payload of data as it travels on the network.

Tunneling is also used in Metro Ethernet environments in order to separate traffic from customers in the ISP network. Q-in-Q tunneling refers to further encapsulating 802.1Q packets in an additional 802.1Q header to distinguish the traffic.

Networking Standards

Cable Specifications

10BASE5 (Thicknet)

- 0.4 inch, 50 ohm cable

- max. segment length is 500 m

- max. attachments per segment is 100

- max. network length is 5 segments

- max. number of stations on network 1024

10BASE2 (Thinnet)

- 0.2 inch, 50 ohm cable

- max. segment length is 185 m

- max. attachments per segment is 30

10BASE-T

- 24 AWG UTP 0.4/0.6 mm cable
- max. segment length is 100 m
- 1 device per cable

100BASE-TX

- 100 Mbps technology
- Uses Category 5 UTP or Type 1 STP wire

100BASE-T4

- Not widely deployed
- Uses Category 3, 4, or 5 UTP wiring
- Full duplex not possible

100BASE-FX

- Operates over multimode or single-mode fiber cabling
- Greater distances supported compared to copper
- Uses MIC, ST, or SC fiber connectors

1000BASE-LX (Long Wavelength GE)

- Uses long wave (1300 nm)
- Operates over multimode or single-mode fiber cabling
- max. lengths 62.5 um fiber = 440 m; 50 um fiber = 550 m
- max. length for single-mode fiber is 10 km

1000BASE-SX (Short Wave GE)

- Uses short wave (850 nm)
- Operates over multimode fiber cabling
- max. lengths 62.5 um fiber = 260 m; 50 um fiber = 550 m

1000BASE-CX (GE over Coaxial Cable)

- Used on short run copper
- Used over a pair of 150-ohm balanced coaxial (twinax)
- max. length 25 m
- Typically used for server connections

1000BASE-T (GE over UTP)

- Uses Category 5 4-pair UTP

- max. length is 100 m

Protocol Mechanics

Handshaking

Handshaking often refers to the process of establishing a connection between two network entities that want to communicate with each other. Consider the following example on TCP/IP.

TCP/IP uses a "three-way handshake" mechanism to establish a connection. Each host randomly chooses a sequence number used to track bytes within the stream it is sending and receiving. The first host (Host A) initiates a connection by sending a packet with the initial sequence number (X) and SYN bit set to indicate a connection request. The second host (Host B) receives the SYN, records the sequence number X, and replies by acknowledging the SYN (with an ACK = X + 1).Host B also sets the SYN indication. Host B includes its own initial sequence number (SEQ = Y). An ACK = 20 means the host has received bytes 0 through 19 and expects byte 20 next. This technique is called forward acknowledgment. Host A then acknowledges all bytes Host B sent with a forward acknowledgment indicating the next byte Host A expects to receive (ACK = Y + 1). Data transfer can then begin.

Windowing/ACK

Windowing refers to a protocol's ability to send more data than just a single packet at a time. In the case of TCP/IP, a concept called sliding windows is used.

With TCP/IP sliding windows, the receiver specifies the current window size in every packet. The window is the number of data bytes that the sender is allowed to send before waiting for an acknowledgment. Initial window sizes are indicated at connection setup, but might vary throughout the data transfer to provide flow control. A window size of 0, for example, means, "Send no data." This variation during communication is set because the TCP header of every outgoing TCP segment indicates to the receiver the window size of the sender.

In a TCP sliding-window operation, for example, the sender might have a sequence of 10 bytes to send (numbered 1 to 10) to a receiver who has a window size of 5. Notice the receiver has set the initial window size to 5, therefore. The sender then would place a window around the first 5 bytes and transmit them together. It would then wait for an acknowledgment.

The receiver would respond with an ACK = 6, indicating that it has received bytes 1 to 5 and is expecting byte 6 next. In the same packet, the receiver would indicate that its window size is 5. The sender then would move the sliding window 5 bytes to the right and transmit bytes 6 to 10. The receiver would respond with an ACK = 11, indicating that it is expecting sequenced byte 11 next.

MTU

A maximum transmission unit (MTU) is the largest size packet or frame that can be sent in a network. TCP/IP uses the MTU to determine the maximum size of each packet in any transmission. Too large an MTU might mean retransmissions if the packet encounters a router that cannot handle that large a packet. Too small an MTU size means relatively more header overhead and more acknowledgements that have to be sent and processed.

Fragmentation

To support different MTUs in the network, TCP/IP and other protocols engage in fragmentation—the process of dividing the data into smaller packets for transmission. When you are discussing this process in terms of the OSI reference model, the process is known as segmentation. IP fragmentation involves breaking a datagram into a number of pieces that can be reassembled later. The IP source, destination, identification, total length, and fragment offset fields, along with the "more fragments" and "don't fragment" flags in the IP header, are used for IP fragmentation and reassembly.

Excessive fragmentation can become an issue due to the overhead that is involved with fragmenting and reassembly. Also, lost fragments necessitate a complete retransmission—including a refragmenting of the data. Also, firewalls that filter or manipulate packets based on Layer 4 through Layer 7 information in the packet might have trouble processing IP fragments correctly. If the IP fragments are out of order, a firewall might block the noninitial fragments because they do not carry the information that would match the packet filter. This would mean that the original IP datagram could not be reassembled by the receiving host. If the firewall is configured to allow noninitial fragments with insufficient information to properly match the filter, a noninitial fragment attack through the firewall could occur. Also, some network devices (such as Content Switch Engines) direct packets based on Layer 4 through Layer 7 information, and if a packet spans multiple fragments, the device might have trouble enforcing its policies.

Termination

Just as the handshaking process begins a communication session between two TCP/IP speakers, a termination process must also be used. The FLAGS field of the TCP/IP packet header carries a FIN bit used for connection termination. When the send has finished sending data, it sets this bit to indicate this fact.

Commands

show Commands

show commands provide you with a snapshot of performance statistics or router/switch settings at the time that the command is executed. If you need to see processes as they occur, you should use debug commands instead. **debug** commands place more overhead on the router or switch, however. As a result, you will find that almost all troubleshooting can be accomplished with **show** commands.

Some key show commands you should be familiar with are:

show interfaces—This command displays information about interfaces on the device. It includes the following information:

Field	Description
Is Up...Is Down	Indicates the physical layer status of the interface; administratively down indicates that the administrator has downed the interface
Line Protocol Is	Indicates whether or not software processes (above Layer 1) consider the line usable or not
Hardware	Indicates the hardware type and address
Internet Address	IP address and mask
MTU	Maximum transmission unit of the interface
BW	Bandwidth of the interface
DLY	Delay of the interface
Rely	Reliability of the interface
Load	Load on the interface
Encapsulation	Encapsulation used by the interface
ARP Type	Type of ARP resolution in use
Loopback	Indicates whether loopback is set or not
Keepalive	Indicates whether keepalives are set or not
Last Input	Time since the last packet was successfully received by an interface and processed locally on the router
Output	Time since the last packet was successfully transmitted
Output Hang	Time since the interface was last reset because of a transmission that took too long
Last Clearing	Time at which the counters used for the show interface command were last cleared
Output Queue, Input Queue, Drops	Number of packets in output and input queues; each number is followed by a slash, the maximum size of the queue, and the number of packets dropped because of a full queue
5 Minute Input Rate, 5 Minute Output Rate	Average number of bits and packets transmitted per second in the last 5 minutes
Packets Input	Total number of error-free packets received by the system
Bytes	Total number of bytes in the error-free packets received
No Buffer	Number of received packets discarded because there was no buffer space in the main system
Received Broadcasts	Total number of broadcast or multicast packets received by the interface
Runts	Number of packets that are discarded because they are smaller than the minimum packet size of the medium

Field	Description
Giants	Number of packets that are discarded because they exceed the maximum packet size of the medium
Input Errors	Includes runts, giants, no buffer, CRC, frame, overrun, and ignored counts
CRC	CRC failed; usually indicates noise or transmission problems on the LAN interface or the LAN bus itself; a high number of CRCs is usually the result of collisions or a station transmitting bad data
Frame	Number of packets received incorrectly due to CRC error
Overrun	Number of times the receiver hardware was unable to hand received data to a hardware buffer because the input rate exceeded the receiver's ability to handle the data
Ignored	Number of received packets ignored by the interface because the interface hardware ran low on internal buffers
Abort	Number of packets whose receipt was aborted
Watchdog	Number of times a packet was receiving with length greater than 2048
Multicast	Number of multicast packets received
Input Packets with Dribble Condition Detected	Indicates that frame was received that is slightly too long
Packets Output	Total number of packets sent by the system
Bytes	Total number of bytes transmitted by the system
Underruns	Number of times that the transmitter has been running faster than the router can handle
Output Errors	Sum of all errors that prevented the final transmission of datagrams out of the interface being examined
Collisions	Number of messages retransmitted because of an Ethernet collision
Interface resets	Number of times an interface has been completely reset; often this occurs because packets were queued for transmission but were not sent within several seconds; for serial lines, this can be caused by a malfunctioning modem that is not supplying the transmit clock signal, or by a cable problem
Restarts	Number of times a Type 2 Ethernet controller was restarted because of errors
Babbles	The transmit jabber timer expired
Late Collisions	Number of collisions that occur after transmitting the preamble; often indicates that cable runs are too long
Deferred	Deferred indicates that the chip had to defer while ready to transmit a frame because the carrier was asserted
Lost Carrier	Number of times the carrier was lost during transmission
No Carrier	Number of times the carrier was not present during the transmission
Output Buffer Failures	Number of failed buffers and number of buffers swapped out

show line—to display parameters of a terminal line, you should use the show line command. It displays the following information:

Field	Description
Tty	Line number
Typ	Type of line
Tx/Rx	Transmit/receive rate
A	Indicates whether autobaud is configured
Modem	Types of modem signals configured
Roty	Rotary group configured
AccO, AccI	Access list configured
Uses	Number of connections established to or from the line since the system was restarted
Noise	Number of times noise has been detected on the line since the system restarted
Overruns	Hardware Universal Asynchronous Receiver/Transmitter (UART) overruns or software buffer overflows
A (or I or *)	Indicates that the user is running an asynchronous interface; an I indicates that the line has an asynchronous interface available; an asterisk (*) indicates that the line is otherwise active (in character mode)
Line	Definition of the specified protocol and address of the line
Location	Location of the current line
Type	Type of line
Length	Length of the terminal or screen display
Width	Width of the terminal or screen display
Baud rate (TX/RX)	Transmit rate/receive rate of the line
Status	State of the line
Capabilities	Current terminal capabilities
Modem state	Modem control state
Special chars	Current settings of special characters that were input by the user (or taken by default) from the following global configuration commands
Timeouts	Current settings that were input by the user
Session limit	Maximum number of sessions
Time since activation	Last time start_process was run
Editing	Whether command-line editing is enabled
History	Current history list size
DNS resolution in **show** commands is	Whether Open Shortest Path First (OSPF) is configured to look up Domain Name System NS) names for use in show EXEC command displays

Field	Description
Full user help	Whether full user help has been set by the user with the terminal **full-help** EXEC command or by the administrator with the **full-help** line configuration command
Allowed input transports are	Current set transport method
Allowed output transports are	Current set transport method
Preferred transport is	Current set transport method
...characters are padded	Current set padding
...data dispatching characters	Current dispatch character

show diag—Use this command to display hardware information including dynamic RAM RAM) and static RAM (SRAM) on line cards.

show version—The **show version** command allows you to verify the specific Cisco device in use; verify the uptime of the device; determine the amount of RAM and Flash memory in the device; and also verify the image in use. When examining system image filenames, here are some common naming conventions:

IOS Feature	Filename Component
IP Plus	is
IP	i
Enterprise Plus IPSec 56	jk8s
Enterprise Plus	js
Enterprise	j

show module—This important **show** command details the hardware installed in a modular device—for example, a 6500 series switch.

Debug Commands

While **debug** commands require a lot of overhead, they can provide you with important data about activity on your router or switch as it occurs.

You execute most **debug** commands from privileged mode. To easily turn off the command, use the **no** keyword before the command or use the **undebug** keyword as opposed to **debug**. To view the status of debugging on a system, use the **show debugging** command. To turn off all possible debugging you can use the commands no debug all or **undebug all.**

By default, debug messages are sent to the console. Use the **terminal monitor** command to also display the output on Telnet lines.

You can use the **logging** command to direct syslog and debug messages to other destinations. For example, to direct this output to an internal buffer (the most efficient logging mechanism), you can use the command **logging buffered**.

Cisco Device Infrastructures

NVRAM

The nonvolatile RAM (NVRAM) is an important storage location on the router or the switch. This area is typically used to store the startup configuration used when the router or switch boots.

The commands used to interact with NVRAM include show nvram:startup-config to view the startup configuration in NVRAM. You can easily replace the contents of **startup-config** with a new file—use the copy command to do this—for example, copy source-url nvram:startup-config. If you want to save the configuration to a new location, this also uses the copy command as follows—**copy nvram:startup-config destination-url.** *Erasing the NVRAM is as simple as using the* erase **nvram**: *command.*

Flash

Flash is a critical area of memory on routers and switches. This area is often used to store the operating system and other important files.

There are currently three different Flash memory file system types—Class A, Class B, and Class C systems. Commands that you use to work with these different file systems might vary. Several of the file system types use the **delete** and **undelete** commands to delete and undelete files, respectively. The squeeze command can be used to permanently delete files from Flash memory. Often times, the erase command can be used to delete all files from the Flash file system. To view the contents of Flash memory, remember you can use the **show flash** command.

Memory and CPU

Memory and the CPU resources that are available are very important on the router or switch. You can obtain memory and CPU usage statistics of running processes, including the maximum amount of memory used by the process (in bytes) and the average amount of CPU resources demanded by the process (in percent).

First, generate a list of currently running processes, using the **show processes** command. This command not only lists the running processes on the device, but also lists the PID (Process ID) for each running process.

Once you have the PID, you can display memory and CPU utilization for a specific process. Use the command **show processes pid**.

To display detailed CPU utilization statistics (CPU use per process), use the **show processes cpu** command. To show memory used, use the **show processes memory** command.

Cisco IOS File System

The Cisco IOS file system provides a single interface for all of the file systems available on the device including:

- Flash
- NVRAM
- Network file systems (TFTP)
- ROM

The IOS file system (IFS) allows for command standardization across platforms. Also, commands can be entered in a single line and prompting can be minimized. If prompting is desired, this method is still available.

Files can now be copied using URLs. This is accomplished easily using the following syntax:

```
copy source-url destination-url
```

To specify a file on a network server, use one of the following forms:

- **ftp:[[//[username[:password]@]location]/directory]/filename**
- **rcp:[[//[username@]location]/directory]/filename**
- **tftp:[[//location]/directory]/filename**

The following example specifies the file named c7200-j-mz.112-current on the Trivial File Transport Protocol (TFTP) server named server.abc-company.com. The file is located in the directory named /images.

```
tftp://server.abc-company.com/images/c7200-j-mz.112-current
```

To specify a local file, use the prefix:[directory/]filename syntax. For example, this is how easy it is to refer to the **startup-config** file in NVRAM:

```
nvram:startup-config
```

Here are some common local prefixes you should be aware of:

- **flash:**
- **bootflash:**
- **nvram:**
- **system:**
- **slot0:**
- **slot1:**

For partitioned devices, the URL prefix includes the partition number. The syntax is **device:partition-number:** for the prefix on a partitioned device. For example, **flash:2:** refers to the second partition in Flash memory.

You should use context-sensitive help to determine which file systems are supported on your particular device. For example, using the **copy ?** command allows you to see the possible file systems for sourcing a copy operation.

On some systems you can use the **show file systems** command to view the available file systems.

For most commands, if no file system is specified, the file is assumed to be in the default directory, as specified by the **cd** command. If you use the **cd** command to change the default file system, you can check the default file system with the **pwd** command.

You can use the following commands to obtain information about files:

* **dir [/all] [filesystem:][filename]**—Displays a list of files on a file system

* **show file information file-url**—Displays information about a specific file

* **show file descriptors**—Displays a list of open file descriptors

To display the contents of any readable file, including a file on a remote file system, use the following command:

```
more [/ascii | /binary | /ebcdic] file-url
```

File Transfers

The Cisco IOS File System section of the study sheets revealed the use of the copy command to transfer images or files. But what about transferring a system image to a device that does not have network access? You can use the Xmodem or Ymodem protocols to download an image from a local or remote computer through the console port. Xmodem and Ymodem are common protocols used to transfer files and are included in applications such as Windows 3.1 (TERMINAL.EXE), Windows 95 (HyperTerminal), Windows NT 3.5x (TERMINAL.EXE), Windows NT 4.0 (HyperTerminal), and Linux UNIX freeware (minicom).

Xmodem and Ymodem file transfers are performed from ROM monitor with the following command:

```
xmodem [-y] [-c] [-s data-rate]
```

The **-y** option uses the Ymodem protocol, **-c** provides CRC-16 checksumming, and **-s** sets the console port data rate.

Configuration Register

The common uses of the configuration register value on a router are as follows:

* Password recovery

* Enable/disable the console Break key

* Change boot behavior to allow boot from Flash or ROM

* Maintenance testing

To display the current value of the configuration register, use the **show version** command.

The configuration register value is actually a 16-bit boot register; it is displayed in hexadecimal.

The default settings of the 16 bits of the boot register are as follows:

15	14	13	12	11	10	9	8	7	6	5	4	3	2	1	0
0	0	1	0	0	0	0	1	0	0	0	0	0	0	1	0
2				1				0				2			

Notice the default hex display in **show version** is 0x2102 as shown in the preceding example.

The uses of the bits are as follows:

- Bits 0–3—Boot Field—0x0 = boot ROM monitor; 0x1 = boot from ROM; 0x2 through 0xF = boot from Flash, boot using boot system commands, or boot from system image
- Bit 4—Fast Boot—Force load through the boot system commands
- Bit 5—High Speed Console—1 = console operates at 19.2 or 38.4 kbps; works with bits 11 and 12
- Bit 6—Ignore Startup Config File—1 = ignore NVRAM
- Bit 7—OEM Bit—1 = disables Cisco banner display
- Bit 8—Break Key—1 = disable
- Bit 9—Not Used
- Bit 10—Netboot Broadcast Format—1 = all zeros broadcast
- Bits 11-12—Console Baud Rate—See documentation for combinations and resultant rates
- Bit 13—Response to Netboot Failure—1 = boot to ROM after failure; 0 = continue to netboot
- Bit 14—Netboot Subnet Broadcast—1 = force subnet broadcast
- Bit 15—Enable Diagnostic Messages—1 = ignore NVRAM and display diagnostic messages

To change the configuration register settings on a router, use the following command:

`config-register`

To determine if the settings have taken effect, use the following command to view the register:

`show version`

Basic Device Operations

Accessing the Device

Most routers and switches feature an asynchronous serial console port and auxiliary port for administrative access. The console port is for local access from a workstation, and the auxiliary port is for remote access via a modem.

Cisco Device Access

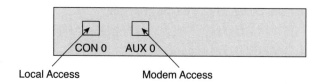

Cisco typically provides cables and adapters for accessing the device via these ports. These cables/adapters include one console adapter cable (RJ-45-to-DB-9, blue) and one modem adapter cable (RJ-45-to-DB-25, black).

To access the device from a workstation, connect the device to the console port using the appropriate cable and adapter. Configure your PC terminal emulation software (HyperTerminal) for 9600 baud, 8 data bits, no parity, and 2 stop bits.

For use of the auxiliary port with a modem, connect the modem to the AUX port using the correct cable and adapter. Make sure that your modem and the auxiliary port on the router are configured for the same transmission speed (up to 115200 bps) and hardware flow control with Data Carrier Detect CD) and data terminal ready TR) operations.

Most routers and switches present a Setup script following the initial boot output. This is a wizard-like series of prompts that aids in the basic configuration of the device.

Once you work through the Setup script or skip it, you can use the **enable** command to enter privileged mode. Additional configurations are made in global configuration mode. You can enter this mode for configurations from the terminal using the **configure terminal** command.

Password Recovery

Most Routers

Step 1   Connect via the console port.

Step 2   Power cycle the router.

Step 3   Press the Break key within 60 seconds of initialization.

Step 4   Run the configuration register utility by entering confreg.

Step 5   Answer **yes** to **ignore system** config info.

Step 6   Reload the router with the **reset** command.

Step 7   Abort the Setup script.

Step 8   Enter privileged mode and copy the config in NVRAM to RAM using the command **copy star run**.

Step 9   Run **confreg** and restore the default configuration register values.

Step 10 Issue **no shut** on interfaces.

Step 11 Set the privileged mode password to a new value.

Step 12 Save the new configuration with **copy run star**.

Most Switches

Step 1 Power cycle the switch.

Step 2 As soon as possible, enter enable to enter privileged mode.

Step 3 For the first 30 seconds the password is the Enter key.

Step 4 Use the appropriate command to set the new password.

Step 5 If prompted for the old password, use the Enter key.

SNMP

Simple Network Management Protocol (SNMP) is a part of the TCP/IP suite of protocols. It permits powerful monitoring capabilities for networking equipment. CiscoWorks relies upon SNMP and various other protocols to configure and monitor Cisco equipment.

CiscoWorks

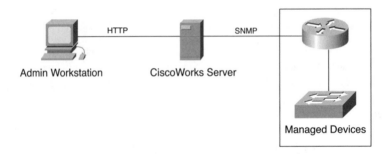

At a minimum, to configure a Cisco device for SNMP, you need to assign passwords—known as community strings in SNMP. Here are typical IOS commands for setting strings that permit configuration and monitoring, respectively:

```
snmp-server community [string] rw
snmp-server community [string] ro
```

Typically, you view information obtained by SNMP using a graphical user interface, like that provided by CiscoWorks.

You should be aware of several **show** commands for monitoring SNMP activities on the equipment. Here are some examples:

- **no snmp-server**—Disables SNMP agent operation

- **show snmp engineid**—Displays the identification of the local SNMP engine and all remote engines that have been configured on the router

- **show management event**—Displays the SNMP Event values that have been configured on your routing device through the use of the Event Management Information Base (MIB)

- **show snmp**—Checks the status of SNMP communications

- **show snmp group**—Displays the names of groups on the router and the security model, the status of the different views, and the storage type of each group

- **show snmp pending**—Displays the current set of pending SNMP requests

- **show snmp sessions**—Displays the current SNMP sessions

- **show snmp user**—Displays information on each SNMP username in the group username table

SPAN

Network analysis in a switched Cisco environment is handled using SPAN (Switched Port Analyzer). Traffic is mirrored from source ports to a destination port on the switch; a network analyzer should be located at the destination switch.

SPAN is available in several forms:

- **Local SPAN**—SPAN source port(s) and the destination port are located on the same device

- **VLAN-based SPAN (VSPAN)**—The source is a virtual LAN (VLAN) as opposed to one or more ports

- **Remote SPAN (RSPAN)**—The SPAN source and destination ports are located on different switches; a special purpose VLAN carries the mirrored frames to the destination port in the network

The following figure demonstrates a sample RSPAN configuration.

RSPAN: Configuration Example

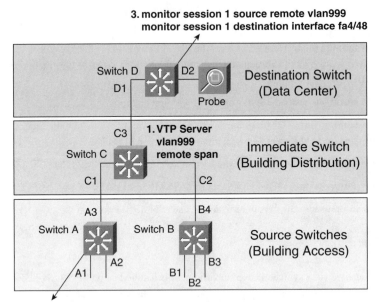

3. monitor session 1 source remote vlan999
monitor session 1 destination interface fa4/48

Switch D — D1, D2 — Probe — **Destination Switch (Data Center)**

Switch C — C3, C1, C2 — **1. VTP Server vlan999 remote span** — **Immediate Switch (Building Distribution)**

Switch A — A3, A2, A1 — Switch B — B4, B3, B1, B2 — **Source Switches (Building Access)**

2. monitor session 1 source interface fast ethernet 1/1 both
monitor session 1 destination remote vlan999

You should be aware of important guidelines regarding SPAN:

- You can configure destination ports as trunks to capture tagged traffic.

- A port specified as a destination port in one SPAN session cannot be a destination port for another SPAN session.

- A port channel interface (an EtherChannel) cannot be a destination.

- If you specify multiple ingress source ports, the ports can belong to different VLANs.

- Destination ports never participate in any spanning tree instance.

Section 2
Bridging and LAN Switching

Bridging and LAN switching technologies have helped to revolutionize modern
networks and bring about speeds and network efficiencies that have paved the
way for new services and transports on the network. This section helps prepare
you for the CCIE written exam areas of focus in the broad subject of bridging/
switching. You should ensure that you spend extra time mastering the complex
topic of Spanning Tree Protocol (STP). This is an area of particular exam focus,
and it is no surprise, because Cisco reports that the number one area of technical
issues with Catalyst switches comes from the area of Spanning Tree Protocol.

Question 1

The IEEE 802.2 Logical Link Control (LLC) protocol provides a link mechanism for upper layer protocols. Which LLC service provides a connection-oriented service at the data link layer?

Question 2

Which Ethernet standard uses all four wires in Cat 5 cable and a different modulation technique to transmit data at a higher rate of speed?

Question 3

According to the IEEE 802.3 standard, what is the maximum size of a packet and what is the maximum number of hosts permissible on a network?

Question 1 Answer

LLC Type I service provides a data link connectionless mode service, while LLC Type II provides a connection-oriented service at the data link layer.

Question 2 Answer

1000BASE-T is a Gigabit Ethernet standard that uses all four wires in Cat 5 cable.

Question 3 Answer

The maximum packet size is 1518 bytes, and the maximum number of hosts on a network is 1024.

Question 4

What is the default STP priority value for a Cisco switch?

Question 5

Name the four steps in proper order that a switch running IEEE 802.1d STP uses to select the best bridge protocol data unit (BPDU) seen on every port.

Question 6

What are the three steps (in order) of the initial convergence process in 802.1d STP?

Question 4 Answer

The default priority value in STP for Cisco switches is 32,768.

Question 5 Answer

The four steps used by the switch are as follows:

Step 6	Lowest root BID
Step 7	Lowest path cost to root bridge
Step 8	Lowest sender BID
Step 9	Lowest port ID

Question 6 Answer

The initial convergence process takes place in three steps:

Step 1	Elect a root bridge—Lowest BID wins
Step 2	Elect root ports—Every non-root bridge selects 1 root port
Step 3	Elect designated ports—Each segment has one designated port (the bridge with the designated port is the designated bridge for that segment); all active ports on the root bridge are designated (unless you connect two ports to each other).

Question 7

What are the five possible port states in 802.1d STP?

Question 8

What are the three timer values used in 802.1d STP to control convergence and what are their values?

Question 9

What are the timer and its value used by the Listening and Learning states?

Question 7 Answer

The five possible port states include:

Disabled

Blocking

Listening

Learning

Forwarding

Question 8 Answer

The timers and their values are:

Hello—2 sec

Forward Delay—15 sec

Max Age—20 sec

Question 9 Answer

The Forward Delay timer (15 seconds) is used for the Listening and Learning states.

Question 10

When a switch is brought up for the first time on a network, it could take up to how long for a port to enter the Forwarding state from the Blocking state? How is this value arrived at?

Question 11

What occurs during the 802.1d Listening state?

Question 12

You are interested in manipulating the 802.1d timers in your switched infrastructure. From where should you make this change?

Question 10 Answer

It could take as long as 50 seconds for the port to enter the Forwarding state. This value is from the addition of the Max Age and twice the Forward Delay.

Question 11 Answer

BPDUs are sent and received during this state of transition.

Question 12 Answer

This change should be made on the root bridge in your network.

Question 13

What value appears in the Type field for a Topology Change Notification (TCN) BPDU?

Question 14

In 802.1d STP, what are the two possible cases that result in the sending of a TCN BPDU?

Question 15

Out which port does an 802.1d switch send TCN BPDUs and on what interval?

Question 13 Answer

The value of 0x80 appears in the Type field.

Question 14 Answer

A bridge sends a TCN BPDU in two cases:

The bridge takes a port into forwarding state and it has at least one designated port

The bridge takes a port from Forwarding/Learning to Blocking

Question 15 Answer

The switch sends these special TCN BPDUs out the root port, and it does so each Hello interval.

Question 16

How does an upstream switch stop the sending of TCN BPDUs in an 802.1d switched infrastructure?

Question 17

You are configuring a Catalyst 3550 switch and you issue the following command:

```
Switch(config)# spanning-tree vlan 10 root primary
```

Each switch in the infrastructure is configured with the default STP settings. What priority value does this switch possess for VLAN 10?

Question 18

You are configuring a Catalyst 3550 switch and you issue the following command:

```
Switch(config)# spanning-tree vlan 10 root secondary
```

Each switch in the infrastructure is configured with the default STP settings. What priority value does this switch possess for VLAN 10?

Question 16 Answer

The upstream switch sets the Topology Change Acknowledgement (TCA) field of the next config BPDU it receives and sends downstream.

Question 17 Answer

When you enter the **spanning-tree vlan vlan-id root** command, the software checks the switch priority of the current root switch for each VLAN. Because of the extended system ID support, the switch sets the switch priority for the specified VLAN to 24576 if this value will cause this switch to become the root for the specified VLAN.

Question 18 Answer

When you enter the **spanning-tree vlan vlan-id root secondary** command, because of support for the extended system ID, the software changes the switch priority from the default value (32768) to 28672.

Question 19

If you manipulate the default timers for Max Age, Forward time, and the Hello time, and then use the spanning-tree vlan vlan-id root command, what happens to your custom values?

Question 20

One method of load balancing with 802.1d Spanning Tree Protocol is to place the root for different VLANs on different switches. What is another method of configuring load balancing?

Question 21

What are the two effects that PortFast has on a switch port in 802.1d STP?

Question 19 Answer

When you enter the **spanning-tree vlan vlan-id root primary** command, the switch recalculates the **forward-time**, **hello-time**, **max-age**, and **priority** settings. If you previously configured these parameters, the switch overrides and recalculates them.

Question 20 Answer

You can also configure load balancing by manipulating the port priority or port cost.

Question 21 Answer

PortFast has two effects:

Ports coming up are put directly into the forwarding STP mode.

The switch does not generate a Topology Change Notification when a port configured for PortFast is going up or down—for example, when a workstation power cycles.

Question 22

Where should you configure UplinkFast in your Catalyst switch infrastructure?

Question 23

What happens to the priority value on a switch that has UplinkFast configured?

Question 24

Where should BackboneFast be configured in a switched infrastructure?

Question 22 Answer

UplinkFast detects a directly connected failure and allows for a new root port to come up almost immediately. You should configure this enhancement on wiring closet switches.

Question 23 Answer

When configuring UplinkFast, the local switch has a priority set to 49,152, and it adds 3000 to the cost of all links.

Question 24 Answer

BackboneFast should be configured on all switches in the infrastructure.

Question 25

What is the purpose of the following command:

```
instance int vlan range
```

Question 26

In Multi-Instance Spanning Tree Protocol (MISTP), what is an Internal Spanning Tree and what is its purpose?

Question 27

What two properties are needed to properly configure a MISTP domain?

Question 25 Answer

This command maps VLANs to a particular Multiple Spanning Tree (MST) instance.

Question 26 Answer

With MISTP, you have an Internal Spanning Tree that is capable of representing the entire MST region as a Common Spanning Tree (CST) for backward compatibility with earlier IEEE implementations.

Question 27 Answer

A region name and configuration revision number are required in the configuration.

Question 28

What is the the Tag Protocol Identifier value for a frame carrying an IEEE 802.1Q/802.1P tag?

Question 29

What is the default native VLAN setting for a port on a Catalyst switch?

Question 30

Name at least two characteristics for the native VLAN in 802.1Q trunking.

Question 28 Answer

The Tag Protocol Identifier has a defined value of 8100 in hex; with the EtherType set at 8100, this frame is identified as carrying the IEEE 802.1Q/ 802.1P tag.

Question 29 Answer

The default native VLAN setting on all ports is VLAN 1.

Question 30 Answer

Here are native VLAN characteristics that you should be familiar with:

The VLAN a port is in when not trunking

The VLAN from which frames are sent untagged on an 802.1Q port

The VLAN to which frames are forwarded if received untagged on an 802.1Q port

Question 31

You are using the Dynamic Trunking Protocol (DTP) to ease the administrative burden associated with the creation of your trunk links. What is the trunk status that results from an ON-AUTO combination?

Question 32

You are using the DTP to ease the administrative burden associated with the creation of your trunk links. What is the trunk status that results from a NONEGOTIATE-AUTO combination?

Question 33

DTP negotiations can fail based on VLAN Trunking Protocol (VTP) configurations. What specific condition must be met regarding DTP and VTP configurations?

Question 31 Answer

A trunk is formed when the ON-AUTO combination is configured.

Question 32 Answer

No trunk is formed with the NONEGOTIATE-AUTO combination.

Question 33 Answer

Both ports must participate in the same VTP domain for DTP negotiations to succeed.

Question 34

You would like to ensure that two of your switches can participate in VTP with each other to share VLAN information dynamically. Name at least two conditions that must be met.

Question 35

Name at least two items that are typically found in all VTP messages.

Question 36

Name at least two VTP message types.

Question 34 Answer

To enjoy the benefits of VTP, your switches must meet the following requirements:

You must configure the VTP domain name identically on each device; domain names are case sensitive.

The switches must be adjacent.

The switches must be connected with trunk links.

The VTP password must match if set.

Question 35 Answer

Generally, four items are found in all VTP messages:

VTP protocol version (either 1 or 2)

VTP message type

Management domain name length

Management domain name

Question 36 Answer

Four possible message types exist:

Summary advertisements

Subset advertisements

Advertisement requests

VTP join messages (used for pruning)

Question 37

In VTP, what ultimately determines if your switch updates its VLAN information with the information from another switch?

Question 38

You want to ensure that a switch you are introducing into your network does not overwrite the VLAN database of other systems because of VTP. What VTP mode would ensure this, yet still allow you to create VLANs on the switch?

Question 39

You are considering the configuration of VTP pruning in your switched infrastructure. Can you prohibit this behavior for certain VLANs, and if so, what is the correct Cisco IOS command for such a configuration?

Question 37 Answer

The VTP configuration revision number determines if a switch has stale information regarding VLANs, and ultimately controls whether or not the switch overwrites its VLAN database with new information. The revision number increments each time a change is made to the VLAN database on a Server mode VTP system. The number is one from 0 to 4,294,967,295.

Question 38 Answer

VTP Transparent mode allows you to create and modify VLANs on the switch, but the switch does not update the VLAN configurations of other switches. It does not generate VTP messages; it only passes them on.

Question 39 Answer

You can choose which VLANs are prune eligible when you configure VTP pruning in your environment. This is done with the following command:

```
switchport trunk pruning vlan {none |{{add | except | remove}
   vlan[,vlan[,vlan[,...]]}}
```

Question 40

What is the default VTP mode for a Catalyst switch?

Question 41

Name at least three guidelines that must be met when you are configuring an EtherChannel in your Cisco switched network.

Question 42

What technology aids an administrator in the creation of EtherChannel links between Catalyst switches?

Question 40 Answer

The default VTP mode for a Catalyst switch is Server mode.

Question 41 Answer

Be aware of the following guidelines regarding EtherChannel:

You have a maximum of eight interfaces per EtherChannel.

The ports do not need to be contiguous or on the same module.

All ports in the EtherChannel must be set for the same speed and duplex.

An EtherChannel does not form if one of the ports is a SPAN destination.

Assign all EtherChannel ports to the same VLAN or ensure they are all set to the same trunk encapsulation and trunk mode.

The same allowed range of VLANs must be configured on all ports in an EtherChannel.

Question 42 Answer

Port aggregation protocol (PAgP) aids in the automatic creation of EtherChannel links.

Question 43

Name at least three options for load balancing criteria within an EtherChannel on your Cisco switches.

Question 44

What technology disables a port when traffic transmitted from the local switch is received by the neighbor, but traffic sent from the neighbor is not received by the local switch?

Question 45

Name the three actions that are supported in a VLAN Access Control List (VACL).

Question 43 Answer

You can specify exactly how load balancing should occur across an EtherChannel. Options include:

- MAC addresses
- IP addresses
- Layer 4 port numbers
- Source address
- Destination address
- Both source and destination addresses

Question 44 Answer

Unidirectional Link Detection (UDLD) detects and disables unidirectional links. To perform UDLD, packets are sent to neighbor devices on interfaces with UDLD enabled. Both sides of the link must support UDLD, therefore. By default, UDLD is locally disabled on copper interfaces and is locally enabled on all Ethernet fiber-optic interfaces.

Question 45 Answer

VACLs support three actions:

- Permit
- Redirect
- Deny

Question 46

What are the two options for the configuration of the secondary VLAN in a private VLAN design?

Question 47

Ports in a private VLAN structure can be configured in one of two modes—what are these two modes?

Question 48

What are the three regions found in the ternary content addressable memory (TCAM)?

Question 46 Answer

Secondary VLANs can be set up as:

Isolated VLANs—A port within an isolated VLAN can reach only the primary VLAN.

Community VLANs—Ports in a community VLAN can communicate with other ports in the community VLAN and the primary VLAN; these ports cannot communicate with another secondary VLAN.

Question 47 Answer

Ports must be defined with one of the following roles:

Promiscuous—This port can communicate with anything in the primary and secondary VLANs (it is typically for the gateway device).

Host—This port is in the isolated or community VLAN—it communicates with only the promiscuous port (isolated port)—or with other hosts in the community and the promiscuous port (community port).

Question 48 Answer

The three regions found in the TCAM are:

- Exact-match
- Longest-match
- First-match

Question 49

In topology-based multilayer switching, what is the structure in hardware that provides for fast lookups of forwarding information.

Question 50

You would like to configure the duplex setting for ports 0/1 through 0/10 on your Catalyst 3550. What command should you use to enter the most appropriate configuration mode?

Question 49 Answer

The Forwarding Information Base (FIB) is a structure in hardware that is built from the routing table stored in software.

Question 50 Answer

You should use the **interface range** configuration command.

Bridging and LAN Switching Quick Reference Sheets

Data Link Layer

The data link layer provides reliable transit of data across a physical network link. Different data link layer specifications define different network and protocol characteristics. These characteristics include the following:

- **Physical addressing**—Defines how devices are addressed at the data link layer

- **Network topology**—Consists of the data link layer specifications that often define how devices are to be physically connected, such as in a bus or a ring topology

- **Error notification**—Alerts upper-layer protocols that a transmission error has occurred

- **Sequencing of frames**—Reorders frames that are transmitted out of sequence

- **Flow control**—Moderates the transmission of data so that the receiving device is not overwhelmed with more traffic than it can handle at one time

The Institute of Electrical and Electronic Engineers (IEEE) has subdivided the data link layer into two sublayers:

- Logical Link Control (LLC)

- Media Access Control (MAC)

Sublayers of the Data Link Layer

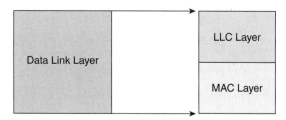

The Logical Link Control (LLC) sublayer of the data link layer manages communications between devices over a single link of a network. LLC is defined in the IEEE 802.2 specification and supports both connectionless and connection-oriented services used by higher-layer protocols. IEEE 802.2 defines a number of fields in data link layer frames that enable multiple higher-layer protocols to share a single physical data link.

The Media Access Control (MAC) sublayer of the data link layer manages protocol access to the physical network medium. The IEEE MAC specification defines MAC addresses. MAC addresses enable multiple devices to uniquely identify one another at the data link layer.

Examples of data link protocols are Ethernet for local area networks and PPP, High-Level Data Link Control (HDLC), and Advanced Data Communications Control Protocol (ADCCP) for point-to-point connections.

Ethernet

Ethernet refers to the family of local-area network (LAN) products covered by the IEEE 802.3 standard. This standard defines the carrier sense multiple access collision detect (CSMA/CD) protocol. Four data rates are currently defined for operation over optical fiber and twisted-pair cables:

- **10 Mbps**—10BASE-T Ethernet
- **100 Mbps**—Fast Ethernet
- **1000 Mbps**—Gigabit Ethernet
- **10,000 Mbps**—10 Gigabit Ethernet

Ethernet has replaced just about every other LAN technology because of the following reasons:

- It is easy to understand, implement, manage, and maintain.
- It features relatively low costs.
- It provides extensive topological flexibility.
- It is a standards-compliant technology.

802.3

802.3 defines the original shared media LAN technology. This early Ethernet specification runs at 10 Mbps.

Ethernet possesses the capability to run over various media such as twisted pair and coaxial. You often see 802.3 Ethernet referred to as different terms because of the differences in the underlying media. Here are examples:

- **10BASE-T**—Ethernet over Twisted Pair Media
- **10BASE-F**—Ethernet over Fiber Media
- **10BASE2**—Ethernet over Thin Coaxial Media
- **10BASE5**—Ethernet over Thick Coaxial Media

802.3U (Fast Ethernet)

Fast Ethernet refers to any one of a number of 100-Mbps Ethernet specifications. As its name implies, Fast Ethernet offers speeds ten times that of the 10BASE-T Ethernet specification.

While Fast Ethernet is a much faster technology, it still preserves such qualities as frame format, MAC mechanisms, and maximum transmission unit (MTU). These similarities permit you to use existing 10BASE-T applications and network management tools on Fast Ethernet networks.

802.3Z (Gigabit Ethernet)

Once again, this Ethernet technology builds upon the foundations of the old, but increases speeds tenfold over Fast Ethernet to 1000 Mbps, or 1 gigabit per second (Gbps).

802.3AB (Gigabit Ethernet over Copper)

Gigabit Ethernet over Copper (also known as 1000BASE-T) is yet another extension of the existing Fast Ethernet standard. 802.3AB specifies Gigabit Ethernet operation over the Category 5e/6 cabling systems already installed. This reuse of the existing infrastructure helps to make 802.3AB a highly cost-effective solution.

10 Gigabit Ethernet

The latest in Ethernet technologies, 10 Gigabit Ethernet provides the following features:

- High bandwidth
- Low cost of ownership
- Scalability from 10 Mbps to 10,000 Mbps

Long Reach Ethernet (LRE)

The Cisco Long Reach Ethernet (LRE) networking solution delivers 5–15 Mbps speeds over existing Category 1/2/3 wiring. As the name conveys, this Ethernet-like performance extends to 3500–5000 feet.

Gigabit Interface Converter (GBIC)

The Gigabit Interface Converter (GBIC) is a Cisco standards-based hot-swappable input/output device that plugs into a Gigabit Ethernet slot on a Cisco network device. This flexibility allows you to inexpensively adapt your network equipment to any changes in the physical media that might be introduced.

You can intermix GBICs in a Cisco device to support any combination of 802.3z-compliant 1000BASE-SX, 1000BASE-LX/LH, or 1000BASE-ZX interfaces. Upgrading to the latest interface technologies is simple thanks to these Gigabit Interface Converters.

Transparent Bridging

IEEE/DEC Spanning Tree

Spanning Tree Protocol (STP) is a Layer 2 loop prevention mechanism. Layer 2 loops are terrible because of no Time to Live (TTL) value in frame. Loop can cause broadcast storm, MAC table corruption, and multiple-frame copies.

The STP Process

The Bridge ID is a critical element for the creation of the spanning-tree loop free topology. The Bridge ID consists of a 2-byte bridge priority and a 6-byte MAC address. The default priority is 32,768.

Bridge ID

2 Byte Priority Field Default 32,768	6 Byte MAC Address

Path cost is the measure of distance from one bridge to another. Greater bandwidth features lower cost.

Configuration bridge protocol data units (BPDUs) are sent between switches for each port. Switches use a four-step process to save a copy of the best BPDU seen on every port. When a port receives a better BPDU, it stops sending them. If the BPDUs stop arriving for 20 seconds (default), it begins sending them again.

Step 1   Lowest Root Bridge ID (BID)

Step 2   Lowest Path Cost to Root Bridge

Step 3   Lowest Sender BID

Step 4   Lowest Port ID

The initial convergence process takes place in three steps:

Step 1 Elect a Root Bridge—Lowest BID wins

Step 2 Elect Root Ports—Every nonroot bridge selects one root port

Step 3 Elect Designated Ports—Each segment has one designated port (the bridge with the designated port is the designated bridge for that segment); all active ports on the root bridge are designated (unless you connect two ports to each other).

Once convergence occurs, BPDUs radiate out from the root bridge over loop-free paths.

Ports have a port state under 802.1D STP. They have more than just forwarding or blocking stated in reality:

- **Disabled**—Administratively down
- **Blocking**—BPDUs received only (20 sec)
- **Listening** —BPDUs sent and received (15 sec)
- **Learning**—Bridging table is built (15 sec)
- **Forwarding**—Sending/receiving data

Timers are used in the process to control convergence.

- **Hello**—2 sec—Time between each configuration BPDU
- **Forward Delay**—15 sec—List/learning states
- **Max Age**—20 sec—Time BPDU stored

Default convergence time is 30 to 50 seconds. Timer modification is possible from the root bridge.

Topology Changes

Topology Change Notification (TCN) BPDU is used. Type Field of BPDU signifies this BPDU—0x80 in Type field used for TCN BPDU. TCN BPDU improves convergence time when failure in network occurs—primarily because it helps in a rapid updating of MAC address tables.

1 A bridge sends a TCN BPDU in two cases:

  a It takes a port into forwarding, and it has at least one designated port (DP).

  b A port goes from Forwarding/Learning to Blocking.

  TCNs go out the root port; sends them each Hello interval until they are acknowledged.

3 Upstream bridges process TCN on DPs.

4 Upstream switch sets the Topology Change Acknowledgement (TCA) field of next config BPDU it receives and sends downstream. This causes the downstream switch to stop sending TCN BPDUs.

5 Upstream switch sends TCN further upstream.

6 This continues until the root receives the TCN.

7 Root sets TCA and Topology Change flags in the next config BPDU.

8 Root sets TC flag in all BPDUs sent for Forward Delay + Max Age. This instructs all switches to age MAC table address entries faster.

Root Bridge Placement

You should set the root bridge location in your network using the appropriate CatOS or Cisco IOS command. You should also select a secondary root in the event the primary root fails.

set spantree priority allows you to modify the priority value and "rig" the root election. For example, **set spantree priority 100 1** sets the priority to 100 for VLAN 1 on the local switch. If all switches are at the default priority value of 32,768, the bridge becomes the root. If you do not specify a VLAN with the **set spantree** command, VLAN 1 is assumed. You can use the priority value of 200 in this case on another switch to elect it as the secondary root bridge.

set spantree root is actually a macro command that examines the priority of the existing root and sets the priority on the local switch to be one less. If the default is used on the root, the priority is set to 8,192. To create a secondary root, you can use the following command:

```
set spantree secondary
```

This command sets the priority value to 16,384.

Remember, in a Cisco environment, all spanning-tree mechanisms occur on a VLAN-by-VLAN basis. This is called Per-VLAN Spanning Tree (PVST+).

In the Cisco IOS environment, the following commands are available:

```
spanning-tree vlan vlan_ID root primary
 [diameter hops [hello-time seconds]]
spanning-tree vlan vlan_ID root secondary
 [diameter hops [hello-time seconds]]
```

Load Balancing

One method of load balancing with Spanning Tree Protocol is to place the root for different VLANs on different switches.

Another technique is to use the following command:

```
set spantree portvlanpri
```

This command allows you to configure load balancing by setting the port priority for a subset of VLANs in the trunk port.

Finally, set **spantree portvlancost** can be utilized. This is the most flexible option; it allows the command to be entered and observed on the switch where the load balancing is to be performed.

The equivalent Cisco IOS commands include:

```
spanning-tree port-priority port_priority
spanning-tree vlan vlan_ID cost port_cost
```

Fast STP Convergence

PortFast   PortFast is a Cisco proprietary enhancement to the 802.1D STP implementation. You apply the command to specific ports, and that application has two effects:

- Ports coming up are put directly into the forwarding STP mode.

- The switch does not generate a Topology Change Notification when a port configured for PortFast is going up or down—for example, when a workstation power cycles.

Therefore, consider enabling PortFast on ports that are connected to end user workstations.

UplinkFast   Configure UplinkFast on wiring closet switches. It detects a directly connected failure and allows for a new root port to come up almost immediately.

When you are configuring UplinkFast, the local switch has a priority set to 49,152, and it adds 3000 to the cost of all links. Finally, a mechanism is included that causes the manipulation of MAC address tables for other bridges.

BackboneFast   Configure BackboneFast on all switches. It speeds convergence when the failure occurs and is indirectly located, such as in the core of the backbone. Reduces convergence from about 50 seconds to about 30 seconds.

MISTP

MISTP (802.1s) is an IEEE standard that allows several VLANs to be mapped to a reduced number of spanning-tree instances. This provides advantages over PVST+ since typical topologies need only a few spanning-tree topologies to be optimized.

You configure a set of switches with the same MISTP parameters, and this becomes a Multiple Spanning Tree (MST) region. With MISTP, you have an Internal Spanning Tree that is capable of representing the entire MST region as a Common Spanning Tree for backward compatibility with earlier IEEE implementations.

Follow these steps to configure MISTP:

Step 1   Globally enable MISTP (MSTP) on your switches:

```
spanning-tree mode mst
```

Step 2   Enter MST configuration submode:

```
spanning-tree mst configuration
```

Step 3   Set the MST region name:

```
name name
```

Step 4   Set a configuration revision number:

```
revision rev_num
```

Step 5   Map your VLANs to MST instances:

```
instance int vlan range
```

You can easily verify an MISTP configuration using the following commands:

```
show spanning-tree mst configuration
show spanning-tree mst vlan_id
```

LAN Switching

VLAN Trunking

802.1Q

The IEEE 802.1Q standard trunking protocol uses an extra tag in the MAC header to identify the VLAN membership of a frame across bridges. This tag is used for VLAN and quality of Service (QoS) priority identification.

802.1Q

The VLAN ID (VID) associates a frame with a specific VLAN and provides the information that switches need to process the frame across the network. Notice that a tagged frame is four bytes longer than an untagged frame and contains two bytes of TPID (Tag Protocol Identifier) and two bytes of TCI (Tag Control Information). These components of an 802.1Q tagged frame are described in more detail here:

- **TPID**—The Tag Protocol Identifier has a defined value of 8100 in hex; with the Ether-Type set at 8100, this frame is identified as carrying the IEEE 802.1Q/802.1P tag.

- **Priority**—The first 3 bits of the Tag Control Information define user priority; notice the eight (2^3) possible priority levels. IEEE 802.1P defines the operation for these 3 user priority bits.

- **CFI**—The Canonical Format Indicator is a single-bit flag, always set to zero for Ethernet switches. CFI is used for compatibility reasons between Ethernet networks and Token Ring.

- **VID**—VLAN ID identifies the VLAN; notice it allows the identification of 4096 (2^{12}) VLANs. Two of these identifications are reserved, permitting the creation of 4094 VLANs.

On most set-based (CatOS) Catalyst switches, ISL trunk encapsulation is the default; therefore, you must use the **set trunk dot1q** command to use 802.1Q as your trunk protocol.

802.1Q trunks feature a concept called the native VLAN. The native VLAN is a VLAN for which frames are not tagged. Here are all aspects of the native VLAN:

- The VLAN a port is in when not trunking
- The VLAN from which frames are sent untagged on an 802.1Q port
- The VLAN to which frames are forwarded if received untagged on an 802.1Q port

To successfully trunk between two devices using 802.1Q, the native VLAN setting must match. The default native VLAN in Cisco devices is VLAN 1.

You can control the 802.1Q VLAN traffic that is sent over a trunk; this is possible for security purposes or load balancing.

802.1Q trunks can be dynamically formed using the Dynamic Trunking Protocol (DTP).

ISL

Cisco features its own proprietary trunking protocol called Inter-Switch Link (ISL). ISL does not modify the frame with tagging as 802.1Q does; it instead encapsulates the frame with new information and is, therefore, protocol-independent.

ISL

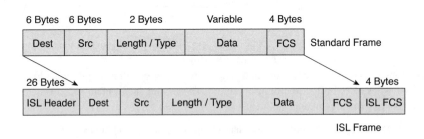

The 26-byte ISL header contains the following fields in an Ethernet environment:

- **DA**—Destination address—It is a 40-bit multicast address
- **TYPE**—4-bit descriptor of the encapsulated frame type—0000 for Ethernet
- **USER**—4-bit descriptor used to define Ethernet priority value
- **SA**—Source address—48-bit source MAC address
- **LEN**—16-bit frame length descriptor

- **AAAA03**—SNAP 802.2 LLC header
- **HSA**—First 3 bytes of the SA
- **VLAN** ID—15-bit VID in which only the low 10 bits are used for 1024 possible VLANs
- **BPDU**—1-bit descriptor that identifies the frame as a BPDU or a Cisco Discovery Protocol (CDP) frame
- **INDX**—16-bit value that indicates the port index
- **ENCAP FRAME**—The encapsulated data packet including its cyclic redundancy check (CRC)
- **FCS**—4-byte frame check sequence including a 32-bit CRC
- **RES**—16-bit reserved field for additional information

Just as with 802.1Q, ISL supports the assignment of VLANs to trunk links for security and/or load balancing.

DISL

Dynamic Inter-Switch Link Protocol (DISL) allows the creation of an ISL trunk from two interconnected Fast Ethernet devices with the administrator only configuring one link of the trunk pair. This technology was Cisco's first attempt at a trunk negotiation protocol. It was used to negotiate trunks for ISL only. DISL has been replaced with Dynamic Trunk Protocol (DTP), which functions for both ISL and 802.1Q on the latest switch operating systems.

DISL is a Layer 2 protocol that uses a multicast destination address used by several Cisco protocols. The Subnetwork Access Protocol (SNAP) value distinguishes the frame purpose.

DISL offers one of five trunk modes (very similar to DTP):

- **Off**—Locally disables trunk and negotiates other side to disable as well
- **On**—Locally enables trunk and negotiates other side to enable if possible
- **Desirable**—Negotiates with other side to enable and locally enables if the other side is in appropriate mode
- **Auto**—Port configured to receive a request to trunk and does so when requested
- **Nonegotiate**—Causes local trunk, but no request is sent for trunking

Note that the following combinations are possible resulting in the trunk status shown:

	OFF	ON	AUTO	DESIR.	NONEG.
OFF	No Trunk	No Trunk	No Trunk	No Trunk	No Trunk
ON	No Trunk	Trunk	Trunk	Trunk	Trunk
AUTO	No Trunk	Trunk	No Trunk	Trunk	No Trunk
DESIR.	No Trunk	Trunk	Trunk	Trunk	Trunk
NONEG.	No Trunk	Trunk	No Trunk	Trunk	Trunk

Dynamic trunk negotiations are not recommended in high security and/or critical/core areas of the network. Also, remember that dynamic negotiations fail if the links participate in different VLAN Trunking Protocol (VTP) domains.

VTP

VTP is a Cisco proprietary Layer 2 multicast messaging protocol that synchronizes VLAN information across all media types and tagging methods on your switches. To enjoy the benefits of VTP, your switches must meet the following requirements:

- You must configure the VTP domain name identically on each device; domain names are case sensitive.
- The switches must be adjacent.
- The switches must be connected with trunk links.
- The same VTP password must be configured if used in the domain.

Generally, you find four items in all VTP messages:

- VTP protocol version (either 1 or 2)
- VTP message type
- Management domain name length
- Management domain name

VTP has four possible message types:

- Summary advertisements
- Subset advertisements
- Advertisement requests
- VTP join messages (used for pruning)

The VTP configuration revision number is extremely important. This value is used to determine if a switch has stale information regarding VLANs and ultimately controls whether or not the switch overwrites its VLAN database with new information. The revision number increments each time a change is made to the VLAN database on a Server mode VTP system. The number is one from 0 to 4,294,967,295. You must ensure when introducing new Server mode switches that you do not inadvertently overwrite the VLAN database because of a higher configuration revision number on the new switch. Introducing new switches in Transparent mode helps to ensure this problem never results.

You have three possible modes your VTP servers. These modes are as follows:

- **Server**—This mode enables you to create, modify, and delete VLANs; these changes are advertised to VTP Client mode systems; Catalyst switches default to this mode.
- **Client**—This mode does not allow for the creation, modification, or deletion of VLANs on the local device ; VLAN configurations are synchronized from Server mode system(s).

- **Transparent**—This mode permits the addition, deletion, and modification of VLAN information, but the information resides only locally on the Transparent device; these systems forward advertisements from Servers, but do not process these advertisements

Here is an example configuration of VTP for a Server mode system in CatOS mode:

```
Console> (enable) set vtp domain Lab_Network
VTP domain Lab_Network modified
Console> (enable) set vtp mode server
Changing VTP mode for all features
VTP domain Lab_Network modified
```

Here is an example configuration of VTP for a Server mode system in IOS mode:

```
Router# configure terminal
Router(config)# vtp mode server
Setting device to VTP SERVER mode.
Router(config)# vtp domain Lab_Network
Setting VTP domain name to Lab_Network
Router(config)# end
Router#
```

VTP Pruning

VTP pruning allows you to limit the amount of traffic sent on trunk ports. It limits the distribution of flooded frames to only switches that have members of the particular VLAN. You can enable VTP pruning in CatOS with this command:

```
set vtp pruning enable
```

When you enable pruning on the switch, all VLANs are pruned by default (with the exception of VLAN 1). You need to configure pruning on only one VTP server, and the setting automatically propagates. You can change this behavior by making select VLANs you choose prune ineligible. This is done in CatOS with the following commands:

```
clear vtp pruneeligible
set vtp pruneeligible
```

The Cisco IOS commands are as follows:

```
vtp pruning
switchport trunk pruning vlan {none I {{add I except I remove}
  vlan[,vlan[,vlan[,...]]}}
```

EtherChannel

EtherChannels allow you to bundle redundant links and treat them as a single link, thus achieving substantial bandwidth benefits. It is often advisable to use an EtherChannel for key trunks in your campus design. EtherChannel is actually a Spanning Tree Protocol enhancement, because ordinarily one or more of the links would be disabled to prevent a loop.

Be aware of the following guidelines regarding EtherChannel:

- All Ethernet interfaces on all modules must support EtherChannel.
- You have a maximum of eight interfaces per EtherChannel.

- The ports do not need to be contiguous or on the same module.

- All ports in the EtherChannel must be set for the same speed and duplex.

- Enable all interfaces in the EtherChannel.

- An EtherChannel will not form if one of the ports is a SPAN destination.

- For Layer 3 EtherChannels, assign a Layer 3 address to the port-channel logical interface, not the physical interfaces.

- Assign all EtherChannel ports to the same VLAN or ensure they are all set to the same trunk encapsulation and trunk mode.

- The same allowed range of VLANs must be configured on all ports in an EtherChannel.

- Interfaces with different STP port path costs can form an EtherChannel.

- Once an EtherChannel is configured, a configuration made to the physical interfaces effects the physical interfaces only.

Port aggregation protocol (PAgP) aids in the automatic creation of EtherChannel links. PAgP packets are sent between EtherChannel-capable ports to negotiate the forming of a channel. Note this is very similar to DISL/DTP. Only one switch needs to be configured to fully configure the link.

EtherChannel load balancing can use MAC addresses, IP addresses, or Layer 4 port numbers; either source, destination, or both source and destination addresses.

Here is a CatOS EtherChannel configuration example:

```
Console> (enable) set port channel 2/2-8 mode desirable
Ports 2/2-8 left admin_group 1.
Ports 2/2-8 joined admin_group 2.
Console> (enable)
Here is an example from Cisco IOS:
Router# configure terminal
Router(config)# interface range fastethernet 2/2 -8
Router(config-if)# channel-group 2 mode desirable
Router(config-if)# end
```

UDLD

Unidirectional Link Detection (UDLD) detects and disables unidirectional links. A unidirectional link occurs when traffic transmitted from the local switch is received by the neighbor, but traffic sent from the neighbor is not. Unidirectional links can cause a variety of problems, including spanning-tree loops. UDLD performs tasks that autonegotiation cannot perform.

To perform UDLD, packets are sent to neighbor devices on interfaces with UDLD enabled. Both sides of the link must support UDLD, therefore. By default, UDLD is locally disabled on copper interfaces and is locally enabled on all Ethernet fiber-optic interfaces.

The CatOS command to enable UDLD on an interface is as follows:

```
set udld enable mod/port
```

The Cisco IOS command to enable UDLD on an interface is simply this:

```
udld enable
```

Security

VACL

Cisco multilayer switches support three types of access control lists (ACLs):

- **Router access control lists (RACLs)**—Supported in the TCAM (ternary content-addressable memory) hardware

- **Quality of Service (QoS) access control lists**—Supported in the TCAM

- **VLAN access control lists (VACLs)**—Supported in software and hardware on some platforms

Catalyst switches, therefore, support four ACL lookups per packet—input/output, security, and QoS ACLs. VACLs follow route map conventions. In fact, they are referred to as VLAN access maps. If a match clause for that type of packet (IP or MAC) exists in the VLAN map, the default action is to drop the packet if the packet does not match any of the entries within the map. If no match clause exists for that type of packet, the default is to forward the packet. VACLs have no direction. To filter traffic in a specific direction by using a VACL, you need to include an ACL with specific source or destination addresses.

VACLs support three actions:

- Permit

- Redirect

- Deny

Here is an example from CatOS:

```
Console> (enable) set security acl ip IPACL1 permit any
IPACL1 editbuffer modified. Use 'commit' command to apply changes.
Console> (enable)
Console> (enable) set security acl ip IPACL1 deny host 171.3.8.2
IPACL1 editbuffer modified.  Use 'commit' command to apply changes.
Console> (enable)
Console> (enable) commit security acl all
ACL commit in progress.
ACL IPACL1 is committed to hardware.
Console> (enable)
```

Here is an example from the Cisco IOS that uses an ACL, as well:

```
Switch(config)# ip access-list extended ip1
Switch(config-ext-nacl)# permit tcp any any
Switch(config-ext-nacl)# exit
Switch(config)# vlan access-map map_1 10
Switch(config-access-map)# match ip address ip1
Switch(config-access-map)# action drop
```

Private VLANs

Private VLANs allow you to segment traffic within a VLAN—for example, an Internet service provider (ISP) can create a VLAN for a server farm that consists of servers from various organizations. These servers can be isolated from each other in the VLAN, but they can all still communicate with a gateway to reach clients beyond the local network.

Private VLANs function by associating a primary VLAN with special secondary VLANs. Hosts that reside in the secondary VLAN can communicate with ports in the primary VLAN (the gateway, for example), but they cannot communicate with hosts of another secondary VLAN. Secondary VLANs can be set up as follows:

- **Isolated VLANs**—A port within an isolated VLAN can reach only the primary VLAN.

- **Community VLANs**—Ports in a community VLAN can communicate with other ports in the community VLAN and the primary VLAN; these ports cannot communicate with another secondary VLAN, however.

The following guidelines apply to the creation of private VLANs:

- All secondary VLANs must be associated with one primary VLAN.

- Private VLANs are created using special cases of regular VLANs.

- VLAN Trunking Protocol (VTP) does not pass any information about private VLANs.

- Each switch port that uses a private VLAN must be configured with a VLAN association.

- Ports must be defined with one of the following roles:

  - **Promiscuous**—This port can communicate with anything in the primary and secondary VLANs (it is typically for the gateway device).

  - **Host**—This port is in the isolated or community VLAN; it communicates with only the promiscuous port (isolated port)—or with other hosts in the community and the promiscuous port (community port).

Here is an example configuration of private VLANs in the Cisco IOS:

```
Switch(config)# vlan 10
Switch(config-vlan)# private-vlan community
Switch(config-vlan)# vlan 20
Switch(config-vlan)# private-vlan community
Switch(config-vlan)# vlan 30
Switch(config-vlan)# private-vlan isolated
Switch(config-vlan)# vlan 100
Switch(config-vlan)# private-vlan primary
Switch(config-vlan)# private-vlan association 10,20,30
```

```
Switch(config-vlan)# exit
Switch(config)# interface range fastethernet 1/1 - 2
Switch(config-if-range)# switchport private-vlan host-association 100 10
Switch(config-if-range)# interface range fastethernet 1/4 - 5
Switch(config-if-range)# switchport private-vlan host-association 100 20
Switch(config-if-range)# interface fastethernet 1/3
Switch(config-if)# switchport private-vlan host-association 100 30
Switch(config-if)# interface fastethernet 2/1
Switch(config-if)# switchport mode private-vlan promiscuous
Switch(config-if)# switchport private-vlan mapping 100 10,20,30
```

MLS

Switching Table Architectures

Both a content-addressable memory (CAM) and a TCAM can be used with modern multilayer switch equipment.

Content-Addressable Memory Table

The CAM is useful whenever the switch needs to do a lookup and needs to be an exact match. An excellent example is a Layer 2 lookup. The switch needs to match on a MAC address and the match must be an exact match. Examples of CAM table usage include the following:

Cat 6500—Layer 2 tables and NetFlow tables

Cat 4000—Layer 2 tables

With CAM table technology, the destination MAC address is the key, and this key is fed into a hashing algorithm. This hash produces a pointer into a table. This allows for fast lookups in the table without producing a table scan.

Notice that the CAM approach does not help when you are interested only in a certain portion of the address as a match. For example, perhaps you want to match on only the first 16 bits of a 32-bit address. The CAM does not help because it uses an exact match approach. The TCAM is used in this case.

Ternary Content-Addressable Memory Table

The TCAM table has a limited number of entries that are populated with pattern values and mask values, each with an associated result. These entries are referred to as VMR entries. The "value" in VMR refers to the pattern that is to be matched. The "mask" refers to the mask bits associated with the pattern. The "result" refers to the result or action that occurs in the case of a match on pattern and mask. This result might be a simple "permit" or "deny," or it might be a pointer to other more complex information.

Currently three platforms rely on the TCAM for Layer 3 switching:

- Catalyst 6500
- Catalyst 4000
- Catalyst 3550

The TCAM table consists of these types of regions:

- **Exact-match region**—Used anytime an exact match entry is required – for example, a host entry.
- **Longest-match region**—Used for routing decisions.
- **First-match region**—Consists of ACL entries; lookup stops after first match of the entry.

You can configure the size of your TCAM based on your network requirements.

Multilayer Switching Architectures

Two main multilayer switching architectures are used today.

NetFlow-Based Switching

NetFlow-based switching is also known as flow-based, route caching, or demand-based switching. The first packet in a flow is switched in software; subsequent packets are switched in the hardware forwarding table. This is "classic" multilayer switching that is often known by the term "route once-switch many."

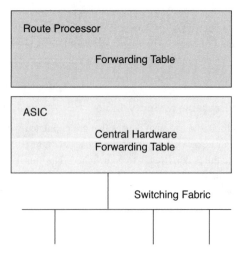

NetFlow-based Switching

Topology-Based Switching

With the latest topology-based switching, a route cache approach is not used. The forwarding structures required in hardware are built in advance without waiting for traffic flows.

The Cisco implementation of topology-based multilayer switching is called CEF (Cisco Express Forwarding). The two main components of CEF operation are the following:

- **FIB (Forwarding Information Base)**—CEF uses an FIB to make IP destination prefix-based switching decisions. The FIB is conceptually similar to a routing table or information base. The FIB maintains a mirror image of the forwarding information contained in the IP routing table.

- **Adjacency tables**—Network nodes in the network are said to be adjacent if they can reach each other with a single hop across a link layer. In addition to the FIB, CEF uses adjacency tables to prepend Layer 2 addressing information. The adjacency table maintains Layer 2 next-hop addresses for all FIB entries. This structure is built from the ARP table.

Topology-based Switching

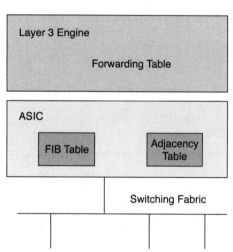

Configuring CEF

CEF switching is permanently enabled on the Catalyst 6500 series switches when they are equipped with the following hardware:

- Supervisor Engine 2
- Policy Feature Card 2 (PFC2)
- Multilayer Switch Feature Card 2 (MSFC2)
- Distributed Forwarding Card (DFC)

You can use the **no ip cef** command to disable CEF on the Catalyst 4000.

The default configuration on devices with CEF enabled is for CEF to be functional on all Layer 3 interfaces. If you disable CEF on an interface, you can enable CEF as follows:

- On the Catalyst 3550 switch, use the **ip route-cache** `cef` interface configuration command to enable CEF on an interface.

- On the Catalyst 4000 switch, use the **ip cef interface** configuration command to enable CEF on an interface after it has been disabled.

- On the Catalyst 6500 with PFC2, DFCs, and MSFC2, you cannot disable CEF.

Per-destination load balancing is enabled by default when you enable CEF.

Configuring CEF

You can use the following command to display a summary of IP unicast traffic on an interface:

```
show interface type slot/interface | begin L3
```

Another option for viewing this information on some platforms, such as the 6500, is to use the following command:

```
show interfaces type slot/interface | include Switched
```

To view all of the FIB entries on a multilayer switch, use the following command:

```
show ip cef
```

To view details from all of the FIB entries, use the following command:

```
show ip cef detail
```

Use the following command to view adjacency table information:

```
show adjacency [{{type1 slot/port} | {port-channel number}} | detail | internal |
summary]
```

Debugging commands for CEF are also available. These include the following:

```
debug ip cef {drops [access-list] | receive [access-list] | events [access-list] |
prefix-ipc [access-list] | table [access-list]} debug ip cef accounting non-
recursive
```

Catalyst IOS Configuration Commands

Cisco is attempting to standardize on a single base operations system for its broad line of Catalyst switches. Thanks to the acquisition of several different switch vendors, Catalyst switches of the past might run the CatOS (set-based) operation system or an entirely unique OS.

This standardization on an Cisco IOS-based operating system is a welcome switch for many engineers that are already very familiar with the operating systems found on modern routers.

While the appropriate sections of these study sheets demonstrate specific commands that a CCIE candidate should be familiar with, this section covers three important Cisco IOS-based configuration modes and associated commands that are not covered elsewhere.

Command Modes

The configuration modes from a router-based environment are present on the switch. In addition to those, you also have the following modes:

- **(config-vlan)**—Use this mode to configure VLAN parameters; enter this mode by entering **vlan number** in global configuration mode.

- **(vlan)**—This is an alternative to VLAN configuration mode; you enter this mode using the **vlan database** command.

- **(if-range)**—Use the mode to apply a configuration to a range of interfaces on the switch; enter this mode using the **interface range** command.

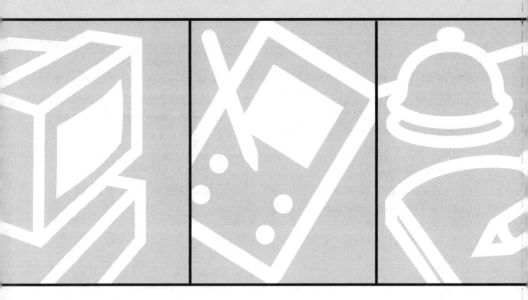

Section 3
IP

TCP/IP offers many robust services and applications that any CCIE candidate should be very familiar with. These flash cards demonstrate the types of facts that you should be aware of regarding IP and its related components, and they also review key points of Cisco router configurations that you should fully comprehend.

You should also note that while it is not fully implemented at the time of this writing, Cisco expects the CCIE candidate to have at least a basic, working knowledge of IPv6.

Question 1

What technology causes a router to generate an Address Resolution Protocol (ARP) reply to an ARP request for a host that is not on the same network as the ARP request sender?

Question 2

What form of address resolution was created by Hewlett-Packard Company for use on IEEE-802.3 networks?

Question 3

What is the default address resolution that is enabled on a Cisco router IP interface?

Question 1 Answer

Proxy ARP allows a router to respond to such an ARP query.

Question 2 Answer

Probe is a protocol developed by the Hewlett-Packard Company (HP) for use on IEEE 802.3 networks.

Question 3 Answer

ARP is the default address resolution method. It is identified by the keyword **arpa**.

Question 4

What is the EtherType field entry for an ARP frame?

Question 5

What is the name of the address that is for an outside host as seen by the inside network in a Network Address Translation (NAT) configuration?

Question 6

What is the name of the address that is assigned to a host in the inside network in a NAT configuration as it appears to the inside network?

Question 4 Answer

0x806 is the EtherType setting for an ARP frame.

Question 5 Answer

An address of an outside host as seen by the inside network is called an outside local address.

Question 6 Answer

The address that is assigned to a host in the inside network is called the inside local address.

Question 7

What is the name of the address that is assigned to a host in the outside network in a NAT configuration as it is seen from another host on the outside network?

Question 8

What is the name of the address that represents one or more inside local addresses to the outside world in a NAT configuration?

Question 9

What is the correct command to establish a static translation between an inside local address and an inside global address when configuring NAT?

Question 7 Answer

The address that is assigned to a host in the outside network in a NAT configuration is called an outside global address.

Question 8 Answer

The address used to represent one or more inside local addresses to the outside world is called an inside global address.

Question 9 Answer

To establish a static translation between an inside local address and an inside global address, use the following command:

```
Router(config)# ip nat inside source static local-ip global-ip
```

Question 10

When configuring NAT on a Cisco router, what is the keyword that permits many different inside local addresses to use a single inside global address?

Question 11

What is the correct command to clear all dynamic address translation entries from the NAT translation table?

Question 12

What command do you use to enable Hot Standby Router Protocol (HSRP) on an interface?

Question 10 Answer

The **overload** keyword allows you to use few inside global addresses for many more inside local addresses. This keyword causes the use of port address translation (PAT) on the router.

Question 11 Answer

To clear all dynamic address translation entries from the NAT translation table use the following command:

```
Router# clear ip nat translation *
```

Question 12 Answer

To enable HSRP on an interface, use the following command:

```
Router(config-if)# standby [group-number] ip [ip-address [secondary]]
```

Question 13

You want to configure your HSRP-speaking device so that if it fails, it regains the role of active router upon repair. What command allows you to configure this?

Question 14

What is the correct HSRP command to cause your router to lower its HSRP priority value based on the failure of another interface on the device?

Question 15

What are the four record types that form the basic infrastructure of DNS?

Question 13 Answer

You can configure this behavior with the following command:

```
Router(config-if)# standby [group-number] preempt [delay {minimum
  delay | reload delay | sync delay}]
```

Question 14 Answer

The following command allows HSRP to track an interface and adjust priority based on the status of the interface:

```
Router(config-if)# standby [group-number] track type number
  [interface-priority]
```

Question 15 Answer

The record types NS, SOA, CNAME, and PTR form the basic infrastructure of DNS. These record types exist in all classes.

Question 16

What command prohibits your router from using Domain Name System (DNS) for name resolution?

Question 17

Which two Dynamic Host Configuration Protocol (DHCP) message types are sent as unicast packets?

Question 18

Which two DHCP message types are sent as broadcast packets?

Question 16 Answer

If you do not want to enable your router to use DNS for name resolution, you can use the following command to disable this default behavior:

```
Router(config)# no ip domain-lookup
```

Question 17 Answer

The DHCPOFFER and DHCPACK are sent as unicast packets.

Question 18 Answer

The DHCPREQUEST and DHCPDISCOVER message types are sent as broadcast packets.

Question 19

What is the correct command to configure a DHCP pool name and enter DHCP pool configuration mode?

Question 20

What is the purpose of an Internet Control Message Protocol (ICMP) Source Quench message and what triggers these messages?

Question 21

In a typical implementation of FTP, what is the port number that the server listens to for control connection requests?

Question 19 Answer

The correct command to enter DHCP pool configuration mode is the following:

```
Router(config)# ip dhcp pool name
```

Question 20 Answer

ICMP Source Quench messages instruct a sender to slow down the rate of transmission. These messages are triggered when a router no longer has buffer space for packets.

Question 21 Answer

Typically, the server listens on TCP port 21 for FTP control connection request.

Question 22

In a typical implementation of FTP, does the client or server indicate the port number for an incoming data connection?

Question 23

Name at least two differences between TFTP and FTP?

Question 24

What is the correct command to set the maximum transmission unit (MTU) of an interface?

Question 22 Answer

Conventionally, the client sends a control message that indicates the port number on which the client is prepared to accept an incoming data connection request.

Question 23 Answer

FTP uses TCP and is reliable. TFTP uses UDP and is, therefore, unreliable. TFTP also does not provide the security features found in FTP.

Question 24 Answer

To set the MTU of an interface, use the command:

```
Router(config-if)# ip mtu bytes
```

Question 25

What Cisco IOS technology allows a router to dynamically discover and adapt to differences in the maximum allowable MTU size of the various links along a path?

Question 26

An IPv4 address is 32 bits in size, how large is an IPv6 address?

Question 27

In what format is an IPv6 address?

Question 25 Answer

IP Path MTU Discovery allows a router to dynamically discover and adapt to differences in the maximum allowable MTU size of the various links along a path.

Question 26 Answer

An IPv6 address is 128 bits long.

Question 27 Answer

IPv6 addresses are shown in hexadecimal as a series of 16-bit fields separated by colons.

Question 28

What are techniques that can be used to write IPv6 addresses in "shorthand"?

Question 29

List at least three benefits achieved through the use of IPv6.

Question 30

Which field of the IPv6 packet header is 20 bits in length and labels sequences of packets for special handling by IPv6 routers?

Question 28 Answer

To shorten the writing of IPv6 addresses, the following techniques can be used:

The leading zeros in a field are optional.

Two colons (::) can be used to compress successive hexadecimal fields of zeros at the beginning, middle, or end of an IPv6 address; this can be done once in an address.

Question 29 Answer

The main benefits of IPv6 include the following:

Larger IP address space
Elimination of need for NAT
Allows hosts to have multiple IPv6 addresses and networks to have multiple IPv6 prefixes (Site Multihoming)
A fixed header size makes processing more efficient
Introduces optional security headers
Increased mobility and multicast capabilities
A new capability enables packet labeling to belong to particular traffic "flows" so the sender can request special handling

Question 30 Answer

The Flow Label field of the IPv6 header is 20 bits in length and labels sequences of packets for special handling.

Question 31

What field of the IPv6 header is roughly equivalent to the Time to Live (TTL) field of the IPv4 header?

Question 32

No broadcast packets are used in IPv6. What type of packet replaces them?

Question 33

What is the new scope type in IPv6 and how does it function?

Question 31 Answer

The Hop Limit field is an 8-bit field that is roughly equivalent to the TTL field.

Question 32 Answer

Broadcasts are replaced with multicasts in IPv6.

Question 33 Answer

The anycast scope type is new. An anycast address is an identifier for a set of interfaces that typically belong to different nodes. A packet sent to an anycast address is delivered to the closest interface, as defined by the routing protocols in use, identified by the anycast address.

Question 34

What IPv6 address type is similar to the concept of Automatic Private IP Addressing (APIPA)?

Question 35

What IPv6 address type is similar to the private IP address space of IPv4?

Question 34 Answer

Link-local addresses are similar to APIPA.

Question 35 Answer

Site-local addresses are similar to the private IP address space of IPv4.

IP Quick Reference Sheets

Addressing

IPv4 Addresses

IPv4 addresses consist of 32 bits. These 32 bits are divided into four sections of 8 bits, each called octets. Addresses are typically represented in dotted decimal notation. For example:

10.200.34.201

Subnet masks identify which portion of the address identifies a particular network and which portion identifies a host on the network.

The address classes defined for public and private networks consist of the following subnet masks:

Class A   255.0.0.0 (8 bits)

Class B   255.255.0.0 (16 bits)

Class C   255.255.255.0 (24 bits)

Class A addresses begin with 0 and have a first octet in decimal of 1–127. Class B addresses begin with 10 and range from 128–191. Class C addresses begin with 110 and range from 192–223.

ARP

Address Resolution Protocol (ARP) is used to resolve IP addresses to MAC addresses in an Ethernet network. A host wanting to obtain a physical address broadcasts an ARP request onto the TCP/IP network. The host on the network that has the IP address in the request then replies with its physical hardware address. Once a MAC address is determined, the IP address association is stored in an ARP cache for rapid retrieval. Then the IP datagram is encapsulated in a link-layer frame and sent over the network. Encapsulation of IP datagrams and ARP requests and replies on IEEE (Institute of Electrical and Electronic Engineers) 802 networks other than Ethernet is specified by the Subnetwork Access Protocol (SNAP).

Reverse Address Resolution Protocol (RARP) works the same way as ARP, except that the RARP request packet requests an IP address instead of a MAC address. Use of RARP requires a RARP server on the same network segment as the router interface. RARP often is used by diskless nodes that do not know their IP addresses when they boot. The Cisco IOS software attempts to use RARP if it does not know the IP address of an interface at startup. Also, Cisco routers can act as RARP servers by responding to RARP requests that they can answer.

Defining Static ARP Cache Entries

To configure static mappings, use the following command:

```
Router(config)# arp ip-address hardware-address type
```

Use the following command to set the length of time an ARP cache entry stays in the cache:

```
Router(config-if)# arp timeout seconds
```

Setting ARP Encapsulations

Cisco routers can actually use three forms of address resolution: Address Resolution Protocol (ARP), proxy ARP, and Probe (similar to ARP). Probe is a protocol developed by the Hewlett-Packard Company (HP) for use on IEEE 802.3 networks.

By default, standard Ethernet-style ARP encapsulation (represented by the **arpa** keyword) is enabled on the IP interface. You can change this encapsulation method to SNAP or HP Probe, as required by your network, to control the interface-specific handling of IP address resolution into 48-bit Ethernet hardware addresses.

To specify the ARP encapsulation type, use the following command:

```
Router(config-if)# arp {arpa | probe | snap}
```

Enabling Proxy ARP

Cisco routers use proxy ARP to help hosts with no knowledge of routing determine the MAC addresses of hosts on other networks. If the router receives an ARP request for a host that is not on the same network as the ARP request sender, and if the router has all of its routes to that host through other interfaces, it generates a proxy ARP reply packet, giving its own local MAC address. The host that sent the ARP request then sends its packets to the router, which forwards them to the intended host. Proxy ARP is enabled by default.

To enable proxy ARP if it has been disabled, use the following command:

```
Router(config-if)# ip proxy-arp
```

NAT

Network Address Translation (NAT) allows an organization to use private IP address space inside their organization (or any other IP address they might require) and present this IP address differently to the outside networks. Organizations might use NAT for the following purposes:

- To connect private IP internetworks that use nonregistered IP addresses to the Internet. NAT translates the internal local addresses to globally unique IP addresses before sending packets to the outside network.

- Internal addresses must be changed, and this requires a large administrative burden. NAT is used instead to translate addresses.

- To do basic load sharing of TCP traffic. A single global IP address is mapped to many local IP addresses by using the TCP load distribution feature.

NAT uses the following definitions:

- **Inside local address**—The IP address that is assigned to a host on the inside network. Often times this is a nonregistered IP address.

- **Inside global address**—A legitimate IP address that represents one or more inside local IP addresses to the outside world.

- **Outside local address**—The IP address of an outside host as it appears to the inside network.

- **Outside global address**—The IP address assigned to a host on the outside network by the owner of the host.

NAT Terminology

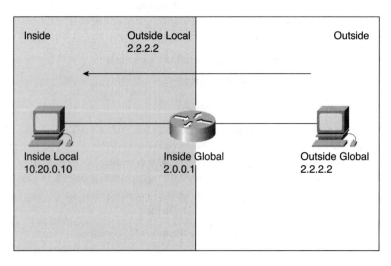

Translating Inside Source Addresses

You can configure static or dynamic inside source translation:

- Static translation establishes a one-to-one mapping between your inside local address and an inside global address. Static translation is useful when a host on the inside must be accessible by a fixed address from the outside.

- Dynamic translation establishes a mapping between an inside local address and a pool of global addresses.

Configuring Static Translations   To establish a static translation between an inside local address and an inside global address, use the following command:

```
Router(config)# ip nat inside source static local-ip global-ip
```

To mark the appropriate interface as connected to the inside, use the following command:

```
Router(config-if)# ip nat inside
```

To mark the appropriate interface as connected to the outside, use the following command:

```
Router(config-if)# ip nat outside
```

Configuring Dynamic Translations   To define a pool of global addresses to be allocated as needed, use the following command:

```
Router(config)# ip nat pool name start-ip end-ip {netmask netmask | prefix-length
  prefix-length}
```

To define a standard access list permitting those addresses that are to be translated, use the following command:

```
Router(config)# access-list access-list-number permit source [source-wildcard]
```

Next, establish dynamic source translation, specifying the access list defined in the prior step, using the following command:

```
Router(config)# ip nat inside source list access-list-number pool name
```

To mark the appropriate interface as connected to the inside, use the following command:

```
Router(config-if)# ip nat inside
```

To mark the appropriate interface as connected to the outside, use the following command:

```
Router(config-if)# ip nat outside
```

Overloading an Inside Global Address

You can conserve addresses in the inside global address pool by allowing the router to use one global address for many local addresses. When multiple local addresses map to one global address, the TCP or User Datagram Protocol (UDP) port numbers of each inside host distinguish between the local addresses.

To permit this behavior, use the dynamic translations configuration from the previous section and include the `overload` **keyword as follows:**

```
Router(config)# ip nat inside source list access-list-number pool name overload
```

Translating Overlapping Addresses

You can use NAT to translate inside addresses that overlap with outside addresses. Use this feature if your IP addresses in the stub network are legitimate IP addresses belonging to another network, and you want to communicate with those hosts or routers.

You can configure the translations using static or dynamic means. To do so, use the same commands from the "Translating Inside Source Addresses" section, but use the **ip nat outside source syntax.**

TCP Load Distribution

If your organization has multiple hosts that must communicate with a heavily used host, you can establish a virtual host on the inside network that coordinates load sharing among real hosts. Destination addresses that match an access list are replaced with addresses from a rotary pool. Allocation is done on a round-robin basis, and only when a new connection is opened from the outside to the inside.

First, define a pool of addresses containing the addresses of the real hosts:

```
Router(config)# ip nat pool name start-ip end-ip {netmask netmask | prefix-length
    prefix-length} type rotary
```

Next, define an access list permitting the address of the virtual host:

```
Router(config)# access-list access-list-number permit source [source-wildcard]
```

Next, establish dynamic inside destination translation, specifying the access list defined in the prior step:

```
Router(config)# ip nat inside destination list access-list-number pool name
```

To mark the appropriate interface as connected to the inside, use the following command:

```
Router(config-if)# ip nat inside
```

To mark the appropriate interface as connected to the outside, use the following command:

```
Router(config-if)# ip nat outside
```

Monitoring and Maintaining NAT

To clear all dynamic address translation entries from the NAT translation table, use the following command:

```
Router# clear ip nat translation *
```

To clear a simple dynamic translation entry containing an inside translation, or both inside and outside translation, use the following command:

```
Router# clear ip nat translation inside global-ip local-ip [outside local-ip
  global-ip]
```

To clear a simple dynamic translation entry containing an outside translation, use the following command:

```
Router# clear ip nat translation outside local-ip global-ip
```

To clear an extended dynamic translation entry, use the following command:

```
Router# clear ip nat translation protocol inside global-ip global-port local-ip
  local-port [outside local-ip local-port global-ip global-port]
```

To display active translations, use the following command:

```
Router# show ip nat translations [verbose]
```

To display translation statistics, use the following command:

```
Router# show ip nat statistics
```

HSRP

The Hot Standby Router Protocol (HSRP) provides high network availability by routing IP traffic from hosts without relying on the availability of any single router. HSRP is used in a group of routers for selecting an active router and a standby router. The active router is the router of choice for routing packets; a standby router is a router that takes over the routing duties when an active router fails, or when other preset conditions are met.

HSRP is useful for hosts that do not support a router discovery protocol (such as ICMP Router Discovery Protocol [IRDP]) and cannot switch to a new router when their selected router reloads or loses power.

When the HSRP is configured on a network segment, it provides a virtual MAC address and an IP address that is shared among a group of routers running HSRP. The address of this HSRP group is referred to as the virtual IP address. One of these devices is selected by the protocol to be the active router.

HSRP detects when the designated active router fails, at which point a selected standby router assumes control of the MAC and IP addresses of the Hot Standby group. A new standby router is also selected at that time. Devices that are running HSRP send and receive multicast UDP-based Hello packets to detect router failure and to designate active and standby routers.

HSRP

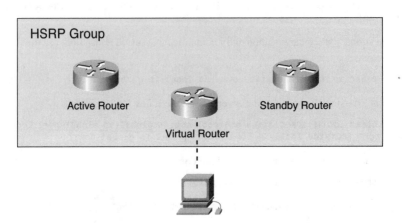

Devices that are running HSRP send and receive multicast UDP-based Hello packets to detect router failure and to designate active and standby routers.

You can configure multiple Hot Standby groups on an interface, thereby making fuller use of redundant routers and load sharing. To do so, specify a group number for each Hot Standby command you configure for the interface.

To enable the HSRP on an interface, use the following command:

```
Router(config-if)# standby [group-number] ip [ip-address [secondary]]
```

While the preceding represents the only required HSRP configuration commands, you should be familiar with many others for configuring additional HSRP behaviors:

To configure the time between Hello packets and the hold time before other routers declare the active router to be down, use the following command:

```
Router(config-if)# standby [group-number] timers [msec] hellotime [msec]
   holdtime
```

You can also set the Hot Standby priority used in choosing the active router. The priority value range is from 1 to 255, where 1 denotes the lowest priority and 255 denotes the highest priority:

```
Router(config-if)# standby [group-number] priority priority
```

You can also configure a router with higher priority to preempt the active router. In addition, you can configure a preemption delay, after which the Hot Standby router preempts and becomes the active router:

```
Router(config-if)# standby [group-number] preempt [delay {minimum delay | reload
   delay | sync delay}]
```

You can also configure the interface to track other interfaces, so that if one of the other interfaces goes down, the Hot Standby priority of the device is lowered:

```
Router(config-if)# standby [group-number] track type number [interface-priority]
```

You can also specify a virtual MAC address for the virtual router:

```
Router(config-if)# standby [group-number] mac-address macaddress
```

Finally, you can configure HSRP to use the burned-in address of an interface as its virtual MAC address instead of the preassigned MAC address (on Ethernet and FDDI) or the functional address (on Token Ring):

```
Router(config-if)# standby use-bia [scope interface]
```

Services

DNS

Cisco routers have the capability of participating in the Domain Name System (DNS). For example, you can specify a default domain name that the Cisco IOS software uses to complete domain name requests. You can specify either a single domain name or a list of domain names. Any IP host name that does not contain a domain name has the domain name you specify appended to it before being added to the host table. To specify this domain name, use the following command:

```
Router(config)# ip domain name name
```

To define a list of default domain names to complete unqualified host names, use the following command:

```
Router(config)# ip domain list name
```

You can also specify DNS name servers for the router or switch to call upon for name resolution. To do so, use the following command:

```
Router(config)# ip name-server server-address1 [server-address2...server-
    address6]
```

If you do not want to enable your router to use DNS for name resolution, you can use the following command to disable this default behavior:

```
Router(config)# no ip domain-lookup
```

DHCP

Cisco devices can function as Dynamic Host Configuration Protocol (DHCP) servers. They can be configured to forward requests onto secondary servers should the Cisco device be unable to satisfy the request. The following figure shows the four-step process that the router participates in to provide DHCP services.

DHCP

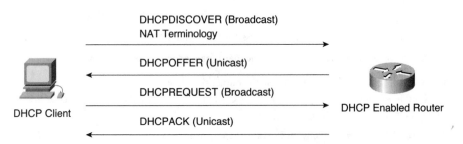

DHCPDISCOVER (Broadcast)
NAT Terminology

DHCPOFFER (Unicast)

DHCPREQUEST (Broadcast)

DHCP Client

DHCPACK (Unicast)

DHCP Enabled Router

Configuring a Cisco Device as a DHCP Server

To configure the DHCP address pool name and enter DHCP pool configuration mode, use the following command:

```
Router(config)# ip dhcp pool name
```

The DHCP server assumes that all IP addresses in a DHCP address pool subnet are available for assigning to DHCP clients. You must specify the IP address that the DHCP Server should not assign to clients. To do so, use the following command:

```
Router(config)# ip dhcp excluded-address low-address [high-address]
```

To configure a subnet and mask for the DHCP address pool, use the following command in DHCP pool configuration mode:

```
Router(config-dhcp)# network network-number [mask | /prefix-length]
```

Additional DHCP pool configuration mode commands allow you to configure additional parameters for the scope including domain name, DNS server addresses, Windows Internet Naming Service (WINS) server addresses, etc.

ICMP

Internet Control Message Protocol (ICMP) assists the operation of the IP network by delivering messages about the network's functionality—or lack thereof. ICMP includes functions for the following:

- **Communicating network errors**—Such as host or network unreachable.

- **Announcing network congestion**—An example is the ICMP Source Quench messages used to cause a sender to slow down transmission because of a router buffering too many packets.

- **Provide troubleshooting tools**—The Echo function is used by the ping utility to test connectivity between two systems.

- **Communicate timeouts in the network**—If a packet's Time to Live (TTL) reaches zero, an ICMP message can be sent announcing this fact.

ICMP Protocol Unreachable Messages

If the Cisco device receives a nonbroadcast packet destined for itself that uses an unknown protocol, it sends an ICMP protocol unreachable message back to the source. Similarly, if the device receives a packet that it is unable to deliver to the ultimate destination because it knows of no route to the destination address, it sends an ICMP host unreachable message to the source. This feature is enabled by default. To enable it, if disabled, use the following command:

```
Router(config-if)# ip unreachables
```

ICMP Redirects

If the router resends a packet through the same interface on which it was received, the Cisco IOS software sends an ICMP redirect message to the originator of the packet telling the originator that the router is on a subnet directly connected to the receiving device and that it must forward the packet to another system on the same subnet.

To enable the sending of ICMP redirect messages if this feature was disabled, use the following command:

```
Router(config-if)# ip redirects
```

Applications

Telnet

A Telnet TCP connection is established between a user's port and a server's port. The server listens on its well-known port (port 23) for such connections. Since a TCP connection is full-duplex and identified by the pair of ports, the server can engage in many simultaneous connections involving its port and different user ports.

FTP

An FTP session normally involves the interaction of five software elements:

- **User Interface**—This provides a user interface and drives the client protocol interpreter.
- **Client PI**—This is the client protocol interpreter; it issues commands to the remote server protocol interpreter and it also drives the client data transfer process.
- **Server PI**—This is the server protocol interpreter, which responds to commands issued by the client protocol interpreter and drives the server data transfer process.
- **Client DTP**—This is the client data transfer process responsible for communicating with the server data transfer process and the local file system.
- **Server DTP**—This is the server data transfer process responsible for communicating with the client data transfer process and the remote file system.

Two separate network connections are present during an FTP session. One of these is between the PIs, and one is between the DTPs. The connection between the PIs is known as the control connection. The connection between the DTPs is known as the data connection. Both connections use TCP.

In normal Internet operation the FTP server listens on the well-known port number 21 for control connection requests. The choice of port numbers for the data connection depends on the commands issued on the control connection. Conventionally, the client sends a control message that indicates the port number on which the client is prepared to accept an incoming data connection request.

The use of separate connections for control and data offers the advantages that the two connections can select different appropriate qualities of service. It also avoids problems of providing escape and transparency for commands embedded within the data stream.

When a transfer is being set up, it always initiated by the client, but keep in mind either the client or the server can be the sender of data. As well as transferring user requested files, the data transfer mechanism is also used for transferring directory listings from server to client.

FTP also has a mode known as Passive mode. In Passive mode FTP, the client initiates both connections to the server. When opening an FTP connection, the client opens two random unprivileged ports locally. The first port contacts the server on port 21, but instead of then issuing a **PORT** command and allowing the server to connect back to its data port, the client issues the **PASV** command. This results in the server opening a random unprivileged port and sending the **PORT P** command back to the client. The client then initiates the connection to transfer data.

TFTP

Trivial File Transfer Protocol (TFTP) uses the User Datagram Protocol (UDP) and provides no security features. It is often used by servers to boot diskless workstations, X terminals, and routers.

Transport

Path MTU Discovery

Cisco IOS devices support the IP Path MTU Discovery mechanism. IP Path MTU Discovery allows a host to dynamically discover and adapt to differences in the maximum allowable maximum transmission unit (MTU) size of the various links along a path.

A router might be unable to forward a datagram because it requires fragmentation, but the "don't fragment" (DF) bit is set. The Cisco IOS software sends a message to the sending host, alerting it to the problem. The host needs to fragment packets for the destination so that they fit the smallest packet size of all the links along the path.

IP Path MTU Discovery is useful when a link in a network goes down, forcing the use of another, different MTU-sized link. Suppose a router is sending IP packets over a network where the MTU in the first router is set to 1500 bytes, but the second router is set to 512 bytes. If the "don't fragment" bit of the datagram is set, the datagram would be dropped because the 512-byte router is unable to forward it. All packets larger than 512 bytes are dropped in this case. The second router returns an ICMP destination unreachable message to the source of the datagram with its Code field indicating, "Fragmentation needed and DF set." To support IP Path MTU Discovery, it would also include the MTU of the next hop network link in the low-order bits of an unused header field.

IP Path MTU Discovery is also useful when a connection is being established and the sender has no information about the intervening links. It is always advisable to use the largest MTU that the links can bear; the larger the MTU, the fewer packets the host must send.

Setting MTU

To set the MTU packet size for a specified interface, use the following command:

```
Router(config-if)# ip mtu bytes
```

IPv6

Address Structure

An IPv6 address is 128 bits long, a much larger address space than the address space in IPv4. It can provide approximately $3.40 * 10^{38}$ addresses.

IPv6 addresses are represented as a series of 16-bit fields presented as a hexadecimal number and separated by colons (:). The format uses is x:x:x:x:x:x:x:x.

To shorten the writing of IPv6 addresses, you can use the following techniques:

- The leading zeros in a field are optional.

- You can use two colons (::) to compress successive hexadecimal fields of zeros at the beginning, middle, or end of an IPv6 address; this can be done once in an address.

IP Addresses

IPv4 Address 32-bit

10.100.34.123

IPv6 Address 128-bit

2031:0000:130F:0000:0000:09C0:876A:130B

or

2031:0:130F::9C0:876A:130B

Benefits

The main benefits of IPv6 include the following:

- Has larger IP address space

- Eliminates of need for NAT

- Allows hosts to have multiple IPv6 addresses and networks to have multiple IPv6 prefixes (Site Multihoming)

- A fixed header size makes processing more efficient

- Optional security headers

- Has increased mobility and multicast capabilities

- A new capability enables packet labeling to belong to particular traffic "flows" so the sender can request special handling

Datagram Structure

The header has eight fields:

- **Version**—A 4-bit field that indicates the IP version

- **Traffic Class**—An 8-bit field that tags packets with a traffic class that is used in differentiated services

- **Flow Label**—A 20-bit field that a source uses to label sequences of packets for which the source requests special handling by the IPv6 routers

- **Payload Length**—A 16-bit field similar to the Total Length field in the IPv4 packet header

- **Next Header**—An 8-bit field similar to the Protocol field in the IPv4 packet header

- **Hop Limit**—This 8-bit field specifies the maximum number of hops an IP packet can traverse and is similar to the Time to Live (TTL) field in the IPv4 packet header

- **Source Address**—This 128-bit (16 octets) field contains the source address of the packet

- **Destination Address**—This 128-bit (16 octets) field contains the destination address

Address Scope Types

Scope types under version 6 include the following:

- **Unicast**

- **Anycast**—An identifier for a set of interfaces that typically belong to different nodes. A packet sent to an anycast address is delivered to the closest interface, as defined by the routing protocols in use, identified by the anycast address.

- **Multicast**

Address Types

- **Link-local address**—A link-local address is an IPv6 unicast address that you can automatically configure on any interface by using the link-local prefix FE80::/10 (1111 111010) and the interface identifier; link-local addresses are used in the neighbor discovery protocol and the stateless autoconfiguration process.

- **Site-local address**—Site-local addresses are IPv6 unicast addresses that use the prefix FEC0::/10 (1111 111011) and concatenate the subnet identifier (the 16-bit field) with the interface identifier.

- **Global aggregatable address**—Aggregatable global unicast addresses enable strict aggregation of routing prefixes that limits the number of routing table entries in the global routing table.

Routing Protocols

- Interior Gateway Protocols (IGPs):
    - Routing Information Protocol next generation (RIPng)
    - Open Shortest Path First (OSPF)
    - Integrated Intermediate System-to-Intermediate System (IS-IS)
- Exterior Gateway Protocols (EGPs):
    - BGP+

Deployment Strategies

Three primary mechanisms help with the transition from IPv4 to IPv6:

- **Dual stack**—Both the IPv4 and the IPv6 stacks run on a system; this system can communicate with both IPv6 and IPv4 devices.

- **Tunneling**—IPv6 packets are encapsulated to traverse IPv4 networks and vice versa.

- **Translation**—This mechanism translates one protocol to the other to facilitate communication between the two networks.

Section 4
IP Routing

As you might guess, this is the most important chapter of the book. IP routing questions make up the bulk of the CCIE—Routing and Switching written exam. A CCIE must be very proficient with Interior Gateway Protocols and Exterior Gateway Protocols. This chapter ensures that you know the major points and fine details of routing protocols from Routing Information Protocol (RIP) version 2 to Border Gateway Protocol (BGP).

Question 1

What IP protocol number is used by Open Shortest Path First (OSPF)?

Question 2

To what IP address does OSPF send packets destined for all OSPF routers in the LAN?

Question 3

To what IP address does OSPF send packets destined for the Designated Router (DR) and Backup Designated Router (BDR) in the LAN?

Question 1 Answer

OSPF uses IP protocol number 89.

Question 2 Answer

OSPF addresses packets to multicast address 224.0.0.5.

Question 3 Answer

OSPF addresses packets to multicast address 224.0.0.6.

Question 4

What is the purpose of the Type 2 DBD packet?

Question 5

In a LAN, with which router(s) does a DROTHER form an adjacency?

Question 6

In a LAN, to which router(s) does a DROTHER send an update?

Question 4 Answer

The Database Description (DBD) packet type checks for database synchronization between routers.

Question 5 Answer

DROTHERs form an adjacency with the DR and BDR.

Question 6 Answer

Updates are sent to the DR.

Question 7

What is the default link-state advertisement (LSA) aging timer?

Question 8

What is the default Hello interval for OSPF in a LAN?

Question 9

Regarding the establishment of OSPF adjacencies, which state follows the Exstart State?

Question 7 Answer

The default LSA aging timer is 30 minutes.

Question 8 Answer

10 seconds is the default Hello interval and the default Dead interval is 4 times that value.

Question 9 Answer

During the OSPF adjacency process, the Exchange State follows the Exstart State.

Question 10

Once adjacencies are established in the LAN and router information is being maintained, what step follows a router noticing a change and multicasting an LSU to 224.0.0.6?

Question 11

You have a serial point-to-point connection in your OSPF-enabled WAN environment. Is there a DR/BDR election process in this environment by default?

Question 12

For the nonbroadcast (NBMA) RFC-compliant mode of operation, fill in the following information:

Dynamic or manual neighbor configuration? _____

DR/BDR election required? _____

Question 10 Answer

The next step in the update process features the DR acknowledging the LSU and flooding it to all OSPF speakers using multicast 224.0.0.5.

Question 11 Answer

No DR/BDR election exists in a point-to-point environment by default.

Question 12 Answer

For the nonbroadcast (NBMA) RFC-compliant mode of operation:

Dynamic or manual neighbor configuration? Manual

DR/BDR election required? DR/BDR election

Question 13

For the Point-to-multipoint RFC-compliant mode of operation, fill in the following information:

Dynamic or manual neighbor configuration? _____

DR/BDR election required? _____

Question 14

For the Point-to-multipoint nonbroadcast Cisco mode of operation, fill in the following information:

Dynamic or manual neighbor configuration? _____

DR/BDR election required? _____

Question 15

For the Broadcast Cisco mode of operation, fill in the following information:

Dynamic or manual neighbor configuration? _____

DR/BDR election required? _____

Question 13 Answer

For the Point-to-multipoint RFC-compliant mode of operation:

Dynamic or manual neighbor configuration? <u>Dynamic</u>

DR/BDR election required? <u>Not required</u>

Question 14 Answer

For the Point-to-multipoint nonbroadcast Cisco mode of operation:

Dynamic or manual neighbor configuration? <u>Manual</u>

DR/BDR election required? <u>Not required</u>

Question 15 Answer

For the Broadcast Cisco mode of operation:

Dynamic or manual neighbor configuration? <u>Dynamic</u>

DR/BDR election required? <u>DR/BDR election</u>

Question 16

For the Point-to-point Cisco mode of operation, fill in the following information:

Dynamic or manual neighbor configuration? _____

DR/BDR election required? _____

Question 17

Which of the Cisco OSPF nonbroadcast multiaccess (NBMA) modes of operation requires a full mesh topology?

Question 18

Identify the command that can be used to manually configure a neighbor in a NBMA OSPF environment.

Question 16 Answer

For the Point-to-point Cisco mode of operation:

Dynamic or manual neighbor configuration? <u>Dynamic</u>

DR/BDR election required? <u>Not required</u>

Question 17 Answer

The Cisco mode of Broadcast requires a full mesh topology.

Question 18 Answer

The **neighbor** command can be used to manually configure a neighbor in a NBMA OSPF environment. The full syntax of the command is:

```
Router(config-router)# neighbor ip-address [priority number] [poll-
    interval seconds] [cost number] [database-filter all]
```

Question 19

What are five possible reasons that the OSPF neighbor list might be empty when troubleshooting OSPF?

Question 20

Name at least one reason that an OSPF neighbor can be stuck in the ATTEMPT state.

Question 21

Name at least two reasons that an OSPF neighbor can be stuck in the INIT state:

Question 19 Answer

The neighbor list might be empty because of any one of the following reasons:

Access list(s) blocking Hello packets in multiple directions

Error in IP address or subnet mask configuration

Hello or Dead interval mismatch

Authentication configuration error

Area ID mismatch

Stub flag mismatch

OSPF adjacency exists with secondary IP addressing or asynchronous interface

Incorrect configuration type for NBMA environment

Question 20 Answer

An OSPF neighbor can be stuck in the ATTEMPT state for one of the following reasons:

Misconfigured neighbor statement

Unicast non-functional in NBMA environment

Question 21 Answer

An OSPF neighbor can be stuck in the INIT state for any one of the following reasons:

Access list or L2 problem blocking Hellos in one direction

Multicast non-functional on one side

Authentication configured on only one side

broadcast keyword missing from the map command

Question 22

Why might an OSPF neighbor be stuck in the 2-WAY state?

Question 23

Name at least two reasons why an OSPF neighbor might be stuck in the EXSTART/EXCHANGE state.

Question 24

Name at least one reason why an OSPF neighbor might be stuck in the LOADING state.

Question 22 Answer

A Priority value of 0 is configured on all routers.

Question 23 Answer

An OSPF neighbor might be stuck in the EXSTART/EXCHANGE state for any one of the following reasons:

Mismatched interface MTU

Duplicate router IDs on routers

Broken unicast connectivity

Network type of point-to-point between PRI and BRI/dialer

Question 24 Answer

An OSPF neighbor might be stuck in the LOADING state for any one of the following reasons:

Mismatched MTU

Corrupted link-state request packet

Question 25

What does a Type 1 LSA describe and where is this LSA flooded?

Question 26

What does a Type 2 LSA describe, what router produces it, and where is it flooded?

Question 27

What does a Type 3 LSA describe, what router produces it, and where is it flooded by default?

Question 25 Answer

The Router LSA (Type 1) lists all of a router's links and their state. These LSAs are flooded within the area they originated.

Question 26 Answer

The Network LSA (Type 2) lists all attached routers. These LSAs are produced by the DR on every multi-access network. They are flooded within the originating area.

Question 27 Answer

The Network Summary (Type 3) LSA is sent into an area to advertise destinations outside the area. These LSAs are originated by Area Border Routers (ABRs). They flood throughout the autonomous system.

Question 28

What does a Type 4 LSA describe, what router produces it, and where is it flooded by default?

Question 29

What does a Type 5 LSA describe, what router produces it, and where is it flooded by default?

Question 30

What does a Type 7 LSA describe, what router produces it, and where is it flooded by default?

Question 28 Answer

The ASBR Summary (Type 4) LSA advertises an Autonomous System Boundary Router (ASBR) destination. This LSA is originated at an ABR. This LSA type is flooded throughout an autonomous system.

Question 29 Answer

The AS External (Type 5) LSAs advertise an external destination or a default route to an external destination. These LSAs are originated by ASBRs. They are flooded throughout the autonomous system.

Question 30 Answer

The NSSA External (Type 7) LSA is almost identical to a Type 5 AS External LSA, yet it is used to create Not-So-Stubby Areas. An NSSA ASBR generates this LSA, and an NSSA ABR translates it into a Type 5 LSA, which gets propagated into the OSPF domain. This LSA type exists only in a Not So Stubby Area.

Question 31

You are examining the results of the show ip route command, and you notice several OSPF routes bear an O route designator. What does this signify?

Question 32

You are examining the results of the show ip route command, and you notice several OSPF routes bear an O IA route designator. What does this signify?

Question 33

You are examining the results of the show ip route command, and you notice several OSPF routes bear an O E1 route designator. What does this signify?

Question 31 Answer

The O indicates the route is an OSPF intra-area route. The network destination is within the same area as the router on which this command is issued.

Question 32 Answer

These route types are OSPF inter-area routes. They define networks outside of the area of the router, but within the autonomous system. Type 3 LSAs are used to advertise these route types.

Question 33 Answer

These routes are Type-1 external routes. They define networks outside of the autonomous system and are advertised by Type 5 LSAs. The cost is calculated by adding the external cost to the internal cost of each link that the packet crosses. The use of Type-1 external routes is appropriate when multiple ASBRs are advertising the external route.

Question 34

You are examining the results of the show ip route command, and you notice several OSPF routes bear an O E2 route designator. What does this signify?

Question 35

You are considering designing an area as a stub area in OSPF. Which LSA types will still flow in this area?

Question 36

When an area is configured as Totally Stubby, what LSAs are flooded into the area?

Question 34 Answer

These are Type-2 external routes. Again, they define networks outside of the autonomous system and are advertised by Type 5 LSAs. In this case cost is always the external cost only. This is the default OSPF external route type on Cisco routers.

Question 35 Answer

An OSPF stub area is an area into which External LSAs are not flooded (Type 4 and 5 LSAs are blocked.) Type 1, 2, and 3 LSAs are still used in a stub area.

Question 36 Answer

The only LSA flooded into the area is a single Type 3 default LSA.

Question 37

What is the command that you use to configure an area as Totally Stubby?

Question 38

To configure an OSPF area as Totally Stubby, which systems need to have the no-summary keyword configured?

Question 39

What is the command to change the cost of the default route used within a Totally Stubby area?

Question 37 Answer

You use the following command to configure an area as Totally Stubby:

```
Router(config-router)# area area-id stub no-summary
```

Question 38 Answer

The **no-summary** keyword needs to be used on the ABR only.

Question 39 Answer

You can change the cost of the default route sent into the Totally Stubby area using the following command:

```
Router(config-router)# area area-id default-cost cost
```

Question 40

What is the default cost of the default route generated by the Totally Stubby configuration of OSPF area?

Question 41

What is the type number of the external routes permitted in a Not-So-Stubby OSPF area?

Question 42

In a Not-So-Stubby Area, what router translates the Type 7 LSA, and what is the LSA translated into?

Question 40 Answer

The default cost of the default route is 1.

Question 41 Answer

Type 7 LSAs are special external routes that you permit in a Not-So-Stubby area.

Question 42 Answer

The Type 7 LSA is translated into a Type 5 LSA by the ABR.

Question 43

What is the correct command to configure a Not-So-Stubby Area in OSPF?

Question 44

When configuring a Not-So-Stubby Area, where is the appropriate configuration command applied?

Question 45

How do you ensure the router ID is changed on a device following the use of the router-id command?

Question 43 Answer

The correct command to configure a Not-So-Stubby Area in OSPF is as follows:

```
Router(config-router)# area area-id nssa [no-redistribution] [default-
   information-originate]
```

Question 44 Answer

The command is applied on all routers in the area.

Question 45 Answer

Once using the command, you use the **clear ip ospf process** to reset the OSPF process and change the router ID.

Question 46

If you do not use the router-id command, how is the router ID selected on an OSPF speaking router?

Question 47

What command should you use to verify the router ID of an OSPF-speaking router?

Question 48

You want to improve the troubleshooting capabilities of your administration of an OSPF network. You plan to do this by making sure you can ping each router ID of each router. How can you accomplish this?

Question 46 Answer

The highest IP address of an active interface is selected; any loopback interface overrides this behavior. Therefore, if you have loopback interfaces, the highest IP address on an active loopback interface is selected.

Question 47 Answer

You can use the **show ip ospf** command to verify the router ID of an OSPF-speaking router.

Question 48 Answer

To ensure that the router ID can be pinged, be sure to advertise the address using the appropriate **network** command.

Question 49

What command do you use in OSPF to configure inter-area route summarization on the ABR?

Question 50

What command do you use to configure route summarization on an ASBR to summarize external routes?

Question 51

You need to advertise a default route into an area regardless of whether or not a default route exists on the router. What command do you use to configure this?

Question 49 Answer

Use the following command to configure inter-area route summarization on the ABR:

```
Router(config-router)# area area-id range address mask
```

Question 50 Answer

Use the following command to configure route summarization on an ASBR to summarize external routes:

```
Router(config-router)# summary-address address mask [not-advertise]
    [tag tag]
```

Question 51 Answer

For an OSPF router to advertise a default route into an area, the command **default-information originate** must be used. If the advertising router does not possess a default route in its routing table, you can use the always keyword to still generate the default route to 0.0.0.0. The complete command syntax for generating default routes is as follows:

```
Router(config-router)# default-information originate [always] [metric
    metric_value] [metric-type type-value] [route-map map-name]
```

Question 52

What is the correct router configuration command that must be issued on all routers in an OSPF area to use the strongest authentication method possible?

Question 53

What is the formula used by OSPF for the calculation of cost?

Question 54

What OSPF-related command allows you to reset the refbw value used in the formula for OSPF cost calculation?

Question 52 Answer

To enable message digest algorithm 5 (MD5) area authentication on all routers in an OSPF area, use the following command:

```
Router(config-router)# area area_id authentication message-digest
```

Note: Additional (interface configuration) commands are required for the configuration of authentication, but this is the router configuration command required.

Question 53 Answer

The Cisco implementation of OSPF calculates the metric using the following formula:

cost = refbw/bandwidth

The default refbw is 100 Mbps.

Question 54 Answer

To reset the value, use the following command on each router:

```
Router(config-router)# auto-cost reference-bandwidth refbw
```

Question 55

How do you override the cost value that is calculated for a particular interface?

Question 56

You can manipulate the administrative distance of three different types of OSPF routes. What are the three types?

Question 57

You can reduce the flooding of LSAs in a stable network topology with what command?

Question 55 Answer

Use the Router(config-if)# **ip ospf cost value** command to override the cost value that is calculated for a particular interface.

Question 56 Answer

Three different administrative distance values are possible for OSPF—intra-area routes, inter-area routes, and external routes. By default all are set to 110.

Question 57 Answer

Reduce the flooding of LSAs in stable topologies by setting LSAs to "do not age"—accomplished with the following command:

```
Router(config-if)# ip ospf flood-reduction
```

Question 58

You are considering the use of a virtual link to connect an OSPF area to the backbone. This link is configured between two ABRs. These ABRs must not be part of what type of area?

Question 59

You need to suppress the periodic Hellos so that an ISDN link is not constantly enabled in a dial-on-demand routing (DDR) environment. What feature of OSPF should you use?

Question 60

What are two possible causes for an ABR not to advertise a summary route?

Question 58 Answer

A virtual link is a link to the backbone through a non-backbone area. Virtual links are created between two ABRs, and the area cannot be stub.

Question 59 Answer

On-demand circuit is an enhancement that allows efficient operations over dialup, ISDN, and other on-demand circuits.

Question 60 Answer

An ABR might not advertise a summary route for the following reasons:

Area configured as Totally Stubby area

ABR lacks Area 0 connectivity

A discontiguous Area 0 exists

Summarization is not correctly configured

Question 61

You have configured the demand-circuit configuration in your OSPF network, but the link keeps coming up because of OSPF. Name at least three possible reasons for this.

Question 62

What is the port number used by BGP for neighbor establishment?

Question 63

Given the fact that the BGP route selection process begins by excluding any route with an inaccessible next hop, what is the next route selection criteria that is used?

Question 61 Answer

If the demand circuit keeps bringing up the link, possible causes include:

Link flapping

Network type being broadcast

PPP host route being redistributed

One router being not demand-circuit capable

Question 62 Answer

TCP port number 179 is used for the establishment of the BGP neighborship.

Question 63 Answer

The next route selection criteria is for the router to prefer the highest weight (local to router).

Question 64

What are the two methods by which BGP injects local routes into the BGP table?

Question 65

What is the Private autonomous system number range used in BGP?

Question 66

How can you temporarily disable a BGP neighborship?

Question 64 Answer

The BGP process injects local routes in two different ways—1) using the network configuration commands and 2) using redistribution by another routing protocol.

Question 65 Answer

The Private autonomous system number range is 64512–65535.

Question 66 Answer

Use the following command to temporarily disable a BGP neighborship:

```
Router(config-router)# neighbor ip-address shutdown
```

Question 67

If you want to modify parameters before inserting prefixes into the BGP table, you can use a route map. Name at least three reasons why this might be accomplished.

Question 68

What is the default origin code for BGP routes that you inject using redistribution?

Question 69

What technique can you use to ensure that a particular classless prefix is always advertised by a BGP-speaking router?

Question 67 Answer

This option might be used for one or more of the following:

Changing the weight of a locally sourced route

Tagging source routes with BGP communities

Setting the local preference

Changing the value of the MED

Question 68 Answer

The default origin code for BGP routes that you inject using redistribution is unknown.

Question 69 Answer

Place a static route pointing to NULL0 in the IP routing table.

Question 70

You are engaged in route filtering using regular expressions. How can you match any single character?

Question 71

What is the meaning of the following regular expression:

_200$

Question 72

You are interested in monitoring the use of your regular expressions for manipulating the BGP routing process. What command can you use to display routes matching the AS-path regular expression?

Question 70 Answer

String matching ranges and wildcards—brackets "[]" can be used for ranges, and the "." can match any single character.

Question 71 Answer

This regular expression matches routes that originated in autonomous system 200.

Question 72 Answer

To display routes matching the AS-path regular expression, use the **show ip bgp regexp** command.

Question 73

You need to distribute select BGP prefix information as specified in a prefix-list. What command do you use to enact this?

Question 74

What are the actions used by an Outbound Route Filter (ORF) type of Network Layer Reachability Information (NLRI)-based filtering (Type 1)?

Question 75

You are considering the use of route maps in BGP for filtering purposes. Name at least five options for match clause criteria.

Question 73 Answer

To distribute select BGP prefix information as specified in a prefix-list, use the following command:

```
Router(config-router)# neighbor {ip-address | peer-group-name} prefix-
   list prefix-listname {in | out}
```

Question 74 Answer

An ORF type of NLRI-based filtering (type 1) uses the following actions:

ADD—Adds a line to a prefix-list filter on the remote peer

DELETE—Removes a line from a filter that was previously installed on a remote peer

DELETE ALL—Removes all previously installed filters on the remote peer

Question 75 Answer

Match clauses in the BGP route map can be based on the following:

IP network numbers and subnet masks (prefix-list or access-list)

Route originator

Next hop

Origin code

Tag value attached to an Interior Gateway Protocol (IGP) route

AS-path

Community

IGP route type

Question 76

Name at least four BGP-related parameters that you can set with a route map.

Question 77

You need to apply a route map to updates that are received from a BGP neighbor. What is the command you use to configure this?

Question 78

You are utilizing the soft reconfiguration feature of Cisco IOS Release 12.x with BGP. You have completed the changes to filters and route maps that are applied on the outgoing information. What command should you execute?

Question 76 Answer

With a route map, the following can be set:

Origin

Next-hop

Weight

Community

Local preference

Multi Exit Discriminator (MED)

Question 77 Answer

You should use the following command:

```
Router(config-router)# neighbor ip-address route-map name in
```

Question 78 Answer

You should use the following command:

```
Router# clear ip bgp ip-address soft out
```

Question 79

You need to send a route refresh message to a specific BGP-speaking neighbor. What is the correct command syntax to do so?

Question 80

What are the three possible origin codes as specified by the origin attribute?

Question 81

Name three Mandatory Well-Known BGP attributes.

Question 79 Answer

Use the following command to send a refresh message to a specific router:

```
Router# clear ip bgp ip-address in
```

Question 80 Answer

The origin of the route is specified by the origin attribute. This attribute can have one of three values:

IGP

Exterior Gateway Protocol (EGP)

Unknown

Question 81 Answer

Three Mandatory Well-Known BGP attributes are as follows:

Origin

AS-Path

Next-Hop

Question 82

Name two Discretionary Well-Known BGP attributes.

Question 83

Name a Nontransitive BGP attribute.

Question 84

Name two Transitive BGP attributes.

Question 82 Answer

Two Discretionary Well-Known BGP attributes are as follows:

Local Preference

Atomic Aggregate

Question 83 Answer

A Nontransitive BGP attribute is Multi Exit Discriminator.

Question 84 Answer

Two Transitive BGP attributes are as follows:

Aggregator

Community

Question 85

You are considering the use of the weight attribute to influence route selection. Is a higher or lower weight preferred by Cisco routers?

Question 86

You have local BGP routing policies you can enact, and you have global autonomous system policies that you can implement. What is the purpose of local preference, local or global?

Question 87

You need to change the default local preference value applied to all updates coming from external neighbors or originating locally. What command should you use?

Question 85 Answer

Cisco routers prefer a higher weight value.

Question 86 Answer

Local preference can be used to enact global autonomous system routing policies.

Question 87 Answer

Use the **bgp default local-preference** command to change the default local preference value applied to all updates coming from external neighbors or originating locally.

Question 88

What is the command syntax that you should use inside a route map to configure manual manipulation of the AS-path attribute to control the choice of a return path?

Question 89

What is the default value of the MED attribute?

Question 90

You need all redistributed networks to have a specified MED value. What command should you use?

Question 88 Answer

You can configure manual manipulation of the AS-path attribute with the **set as-path prepend** command.

Question 89 Answer

The default value of the MED attribute is 0.

Question 90 Answer

Using the **default-metric** command in BGP configuration mode causes all redistributed networks to have the specified MED value.

Question 91

Name at least two standard filtering-oriented communities for use in BGP.

Question 92

What does a router do if that router does not support BGP communities and a route update appears with community information?

Question 93

Describe a typical form that your communities can take.

Question 91 Answer

The BGP standards define several filtering-oriented communities for your use:

no-export—Do not advertise routes to real External BGP (EBGP) peers

no-advertise—Do not advertise routes to any peer

local-as—Do not advertise routes to any EBGP peers

internet—Advertise this route to the Internet community

Question 92 Answer

The router passes the community information on unchanged.

Question 93 Answer

You can specify a 32-bit community value as

[AS-number]:[low-order-16-bits]

Question 94

How is route tagging with communities actually accomplished in BGP?

Question 95

What is the correct command to configure community propagation to BGP neighbors?

Question 96

You need to configure BGP community propagation for a large number of BGP neighbors. What is the ideal mechanism to use to assist with this configuration?

Question 94 Answer

Route tagging with communities is always done with a route map. You can specify any number of communities. Communities specified in the **set** keyword overwrite existing communities unless you specify the **additive** option.

Question 95 Answer

By default, communities are stripped in outgoing BGP updates; therefore, you must manually configure community propagation to BGP neighbors. You can do so using the following command:

```
Router(config-router)# neighbor ip-address send-community
```

Question 96 Answer

BGP peer groups would be ideal for this situation.

Question 97

What is the correct syntax to find community attributes in routing updates?

Question 98

What key design requirement of BGP does a BGP route reflector address?

Question 99

What is the command to configure a router as a BGP route reflector?

Question 97 Answer

Here is the syntax for the creation of the standard community list:

```
Router(config)# ip community-list 1-99 permit | deny value [ value … ]
```

Question 98 Answer

Route reflectors help address the fact that BGP requires that all BGP peers in the same autonomous system form an Internal BGP (IBGP) session with all peers in the autonomous system.

Question 99 Answer

The command used to configure the router as a BGP route reflector and configure the specified neighbor as its client is as follows:

```
Router(config-router)# neighbor ip-address route-reflector-client
```

Question 100

Another method is commonly used to solve the IBGP full mesh requirement. It involves the configuration of smaller sub-autonomous systems created within a primary autonomous system. What are these called?

Question 101

What is the effect of the network backdoor command in BGP?

Question 102

You are concerned that a flapping route is ruining the stability of your BGP network. What command allows the router to remove the update until it is proven to be more stable?

Question 100 Answer

Confederations are another method of solving the IBGP full mesh requirement. Confederations are smaller sub-autonomous systems created within the primary autonomous system to decrease the number of BGP peer connections.

Question 101 Answer

The **network backdoor** router configuration command causes the administrative distance assigned to the network to be forced to 200. The goal is to make Interior Gateway Protocol (IGP) learned routes preferred.

Question 102 Answer

Route dampening can make the network more stable. To enable route dampening, use the **bgp dampening** command.

Question 103

What is the correct command to view the BGP table on the local router?

Question 104

What is the IP protocol number used by Enhanced Interior Gateway Routing Protocol (EIGRP)?

Question 105

What is the multicast address used by EIGRP for the sending of Hellos and routing updates?

Question 103 Answer

The correct command is **show ip bgp**.

Question 104 Answer

EIGRP uses IP protocol number 88.

Question 105 Answer

EIGRP uses the multicast IP address of 224.0.0.10 for Hellos and routing updates.

Question 106

The metric of EIGRP is compatible with the metric of the earlier Interior Gateway Routing Protocol (IGRP). How do you convert the IGRP metric to the form of EIGRP?

Question 107

The metric of EIGRP contains a reliability component. What is the value that indicates a completely unreliable link?

Question 108

You are considering manipulating the K values on an EIGRP router. Which routers in the EIGRP domain must have this configuration made?

Question 106 Answer

Multiply the IGRP metric by 256.

Question 107 Answer

In EIGRP, a reliability of value 1 indicates a completely unreliable link.

Question 108 Answer

You must manipulate the K values on all routers if you plan to manipulate them on one.

Question 109

How often are Hello packets sent on a point-to-point subinterface in an EIGRP environment?

Question 110

How often are Hello packets sent on a multipoint circuit with bandwidth less than T1 in an EIGRP environment?

Question 111

What are the packets in an EIGRP environment that require an acknowledgement?

Question 109 Answer

Hellos are sent every 5 seconds on broadcast links, as well as p2p serial, p2p subinterface, and multipoint circuits greater than T1.

Question 110 Answer

Hellos are sent every 60 seconds on multipoint circuits with bandwidth less than T1.

Question 111 Answer

Packets that require acknowledgement are as follows:

Update

Query

Reply

Question 112

How does EIGRP deal with a router that is slow in responding to reliable packets with acknowledgements?

Question 113

When an EIGRP-speaking router receives Hello packets from a neighbor for the first time, how does the router respond if it has matching Hello parameters in the packet?

Question 114

What is the Advertised Distance (AD) in EIGRP?

Question 112 Answer

Slow neighbors are sent unicast packets in an attempt to resolve issues with slow neighbors.

Question 113 Answer

The router responds with an update of the routing information it possesses.

Question 114 Answer

The AD is the cost between that next hop router and the destination.

Question 115

What is the Feasible Distance (FD) value in EIGRP?

Question 116

What is the feasible successor in EIGRP?

Question 117

How can a router qualify as a feasible successor in EIGRP?

Question 115 Answer

Lowest cost route calculated by adding the cost between the next hop router and the destination (AD) and the cost between the local router and the next hop. This sum is referred to as the FD.

Question 116 Answer

The next hop router for a backup path is called the feasible successor.

Question 117 Answer

To qualify as a feasible successor, a next hop router must have an AD less than the FD of the current successor route. More than one feasible successor can exist.

Question 118

You want to propagate a default route to other EIGRP speakers in the autonomous system. What command do you used to accomplish this?

Question 119

You are using the show ip eigrp topology command to troubleshoot your EIGRP network. You notice an entry is marked as Active. What does this indicate?

Question 120

You are considering the usage of manual route summarization in your EIGRP network. How is the metric calculated for the summary route.

Question 118 Answer

Using the **default-network** command, you can configure a default route for the EIGRP process so that it propagates to other EIGRP routers within the same autonomous system.

Question 119 Answer

This network is currently unavailable and installation cannot occur in the routing table. The router is currently searching for a replacement route.

Question 120 Answer

The minimum metric of the specific routes is used as the metric of the summary route.

Question 121

What is the command that you use in EIGRP to control the load balancing across unequal cost paths?

Question 122

By default, how much bandwidth does EIGRP consume on an interface for its operan you change the amount of bandwidth that EIGRP consumes on an interface?

Question 123

How can you change the amount of bandwidth that EIGRP consumes on an interface?

Question 121 Answer

Use the **variance** command in EIGRP to control load balancing behavior—potentially across unequal bandwidth links.

Question 122 Answer

EIGRP uses up to 50 percent of the bandwidth (as set by the **bandwidth** command) for its operations.

Question 123 Answer

This percentage can be changed on a per-interface basis by using the **ip bandwidth-percent eigrp** interface configuration command.

Question 124

You have a hub and spoke topology, and you are using EIGRP as your IGP. You want only routes that you specify propagated from the spoke of your topology. What EIGRP feature allows you to configure this?

Question 125

What is it that makes up the backbone in an Intermediate System-to-Intermediate System (IS-IS) network?

Question 126

What is the equivalent of an ABR from OSPF in the IS-IS routing environment?

Question 124 Answer

EIGRP stub routing is a feature that allows you to specify the routes that are propagated from the spoke.

Question 125 Answer

The backbone is the path of L2 and L1/2 routers in the IS-IS network. This is much more flexible when compared to the structure of OSPF.

Question 126 Answer

An ABR is very similar to the Level 1/2 router in IS-IS.

Question 127

What is the default metric value used for interfaces in IS-IS on Cisco routers?

Question 128

What is the Network Selector (NSEL) value for a Network Entity Title in IS-IS?

Question 129

How long is the System ID portion of a network service access point (NSAP) address on Cisco routers?

Question 127 Answer

Cisco routers use a metric of 10 for all interfaces by default. Note this is essentially hop count.

Question 128 Answer

An NSEL of 0 is used for routers and is called the Network Entity Title or NET. This identifies a network service.

Question 129 Answer

The System ID is a fixed length of 6 octets in Cisco implementations of IS-IS.

Question 130

What is the AFI byte value that indicates a locally administered area?

Question 131

What protocol data unit (PDU) type does IS-IS use to request missing pieces of link-state information?

Question 132

What is the approximate equivalent of the DR in an IS-IS broadcast environment?

Question 130 Answer

49 is the most common setting and indicates a locally administered area.

Question 131 Answer

IS-IS uses the partial sequence number PDU (PSNP) to acknowledge and request missing pieces of link state information.

Question 132 Answer

The Designated Intermediate System (DIS) is roughly the equivalent of the DR.

Question 133

What is the command required to configure the NSAP address on a Cisco router?

Question 134

What command configures an interface to participate in IS-IS routing in an IS-IS environment?

Question 135

What command can you use to configure the type of adjacency that is to form over an interface?

Question 133 Answer

Use the **net** command to configure the NSAP address on a router. In this case, the NSAP address is also the network entity title address. The **net** command is a router configuration command and is a requirement for IS-IS to function.

Question 134 Answer

To configure the interfaces that are to participate in IS-IS use the **ip router isis** interface configuration mode command.

Question 135 Answer

You can use the interface configuration command **isis circuit-type {level-1 | level-1-2 | level-2-only}**. This command allows you to specify the type of adjacency to form over an interface; this reduces the bandwidth waste when IS-IS attempts to form adjacencies that do not exist.

Question 136

You are using RIP version 2 and you would like to configure manual summarization on an interface. What command accomplishes this?

Question 137

What mechanism helps prevent route feedback during redistribution?

Question 138

Name at least three common uses for a route-map.

Question 136 Answer

This can be accomplished with the **ip summary-address** command.

Question 137 Answer

A distribute list can help prevent route feedback during redistribution.

Question 138 Answer

Several of the more common applications for route maps are as follows:

Route filtering during redistribution

Policy-based routing (PBR)

Network Address Translation (NAT)

Implementing Border Gateway Protocol (BGP) policies

Question 139

What is the correct command to identify a route map to use for PBR on an interface?

Question 140

When redistributing routes into OSPF, what is the meaning of the subnets keyword?

Question 139 Answer

To identify a route map to use for PBR on an interface, use the following command:

```
Router(config-if)# ip policy route-map map-tag
```

Question 140 Answer

The **subnets** keyword allows the redistribution of subnets of major classful networks into the area.

IP Routing
Quick Reference Sheets

OSPF

Open Shortest Path First (OSPF) link-state routing protocol is designed to be more scalable and efficient than Routing Information Protocol (RIP). Some OSPF features you should be aware of are as follows:

- Runs on IP and uses protocol 89

- Classless with variable-length subnet mask (VLSM) support

- Uses multicasts (224.0.0.5—all shortest path first [SPF] routers; 224.0.0.6—Designated Router [DR]/Backup Designated Router [BDR]) for Hellos and updates

- Plain text and message digest algorithm 5 (MD5) authentication available

- Dijkstra'a algorithm is used to produce Shortest Path Tree for each destination; link-state advertisements are used to build a database of the topology

OSPF Packet Types

Type 1—Hello—These packets are used to build adjacencies

Type 2—Database Description (DBD)—Checks for database synchronization between routers

Type 3—Link-State Request (LSR)—Requests link state specifics from router

Type 4—Link-State Update (LSU)—Sends requested link-state records

Type 5—Link-State Acknowledgements (LSA)—Acknowledge the other packet types

OSPF Adjacencies

- Occurs through exchange of Hello packets

- After adjacency established, link-state databases (LSDBs) are synched

- Two OSPF neighbors on point-to-point link form full adjacency with each other

- In LANs, all routers form adjacency with the DR and BDR; updates need to be sent only to DR, which updates all other routers; all other routers on LAN are called DROTHERS and maintain a partial neighbor relationship with each other

Once adjacencies are established, LSAs are exchanged through a reliable mechanism. LSAs are flooded to ensure topological awareness. LSAs have a sequence number and a lifetime value. LSAs convey the cost of links used for the SPF calculation. The cost metric is based on interface bandwidth. The LSA aging timer is a 30-minute default.

Hello packets are sent periodically and contain the following fields:

- **Router ID**—Identifies the router; highest IP chosen; loopback overrides all interfaces, however; can also be set with router-id command; this ID is used to break ties for DR election

- **Hello/Dead intervals**—Frequency that Hellos are sent and the amount of time that can elapse before router is declared dead; default is 10 seconds and the default dead interval is 4 times that for an Ethernet-type network; these defaults vary based on network type

- **Neighbors**—List of the adjacent routers

- **Area ID**—The area identifier (always 0 for backbone)

- **Router priority**—Priority value used for DR and BDR election

- **DR/BDR addresses**—The IP addresses of the DR and BDR if known

- **Authentication password**—This password must match on routers configured for authentication

- **Stub area flag**—Routers must agree on this setting to form a stub area

Here are the details of the exchange process between two routers on a LAN (Router 1 and Router 2) and the OSPF adjacency states involved:

Step 1   Router 1 begins in the down state because it is not exchanging OSPF information with any other router. It sends Hello packets via multicast address 224.0.0.5 (all SPF).

Step 2   Router 2 receives the OSPF Hello and adds Router 1 in its list of neighbors. This is the beginning of the init state.

Step 3   Router 2 sends a unicast Hello packet response to Router 1.

Step 4   Router 1 receives the Hello and notes that it is listed in the packet. It adds Router 2 to its list of neighbors. Router 1 knows that it has bidirectional communication with Router 2. This is known as the Two-Way State.

Step 5   In LAN environment, DR and BDR elected.

Step 6 In LAN environment, Hello packets function as keepalive mechanism every 10 seconds.

Once the DR and BDR are established, the routers are in Exstart State and they are ready to exchange database information. The exchange protocol functions as follows:

Step 1 In the Exstart State, the DR and BDR establish an adjacency with each router in the network; a master-slave relationship is formed with the router ID indicating the master in the relationship.

Step 2 The master and slave routers exchange DBD packets; this is called the Exchange State. The LSAs in the DBD include sequence numbers that are used to indicate "freshness."

Step 3 When a DBD is received, the router acknowledges the receipt and compares the information with its current database. If more recent information is described in the DBD, the router sends a LSR to request the information. This is called the Loading State. The router receiving the LSR responds with a LSU; this LSU is also acknowledged by the receiver.

Step 4 The router adds the new information to its LSDB.

Step 5 Once the exchange completes, the routers are in Full State.

Router information is later maintained using the following process:

Step 1 Router notices change and multicasts a LSU to the OSPF DR and BDR multicast address of 224.0.0.6.

Step 2 The DR acknowledges the LSU and floods to all using multicast 224.0.0.5. This process involves acknowledgements as well.

Step 3 The DR also sends the LSU to any other networks to which it is attached.

Step 4 Routers update their LSDB with the new information in the LSU.

Summaries are sent every 30 minutes to ensure synchronization, and link state entries have a Max Age of 60 minutes.

Point-to-Point Links

Typically a point-to-point link is a serial link, but it might also be a subinterface in a Frame Relay or Asynchronous Transfer Mode (ATM) network. No DR or BDR election exists in the point-to-point environment. Packets are multicast to 224.0.0.5.

NBMA Modes of Operation

RFC-compliant modes:

- Nonbroadcast (NBMA)
  - One IP subnet required
  - Must manually configure neighbors—neighbor address [priority number] [poll-interval number]

- — DR/BDR election
- — DR/BDR need full connectivity with all routers
- — Sometimes used in partial mesh
- — Frame Relay and ATM networks default to this type
- Point-to-multipoint
  - — One IP subnet required
  - — Hello packets used to discover neighbors
  - — DR/BDR not required
  - — Sometimes used in partial mesh

Modes from Cisco:

- Point-to-multipoint nonbroadcast
  - — Used if interface does not support multicast capabilities
  - — Neighbors must be manually configured
  - — DR/BDR election is not required
- Broadcast
  - — Makes WAN appear as LAN
  - — One IP subnet required
  - — Hellos discover neighbors
  - — DR/BDR elected
  - — Requires full mesh
- Point-to-point
  - — One IP subnet required
  - — No DR/BDR election
  - — Interfaces can be LAN or WAN

You can use the following command to define the OSPF network type:

```
Router(config-if)# ip ospf network [{broadcast I nonbroadcast I point-to-
  multipoint I point-to-multipoint nonbroadcast}]
```

Here is an example of statically defining adjacencies in a nonbroadcast multi-access environment:

```
RouterA(config)# router ospf 1
RouterA(config-router)# network 172.16.0.0 0.0.255.255 area 0
RouterA(config-router)# neighbor 172.16.0.5 priority 0
RouterA(config-router)# neighbor 172.16.0.10 priority 0
```

Priorities are set to 0 for the neighboring routers to ensure that RouterA becomes the DR. This is the only router with full connectivity.

Troubleshooting Neighbor Relationships

OSPF Neighbor List is Empty

- OSPF not enabled properly on appropriate interfaces

- Layer 1 or 2 not functional
- Passive interface configured
- Access list(s) blocking Hello packets in multiple directions
- Error in IP address or subnet mask configuration
- Hello or dead interval mismatch
- Authentication configuration error
- Area ID mismatch
- Stub flag mismatch
- OSPF adjacency exists with secondary IP addressing or asynchronous interface
- Incorrect configuration type for nonbroadcast multiaccess (NBMA) environment

OSPF Neighbor Stuck in Attempt

- Misconfigured **neighbor** statement
- Unicast nonfunctional in NBMA environment

OSPF Neighbor Stuck in init

- Access list or Layer 2 problem blocking Hellos in one direction
- Multicast nonfunctional on one side
- Authentication configured on only one side
- Broadcast keyword missing from the map command

OSPF Neighbor Stuck in Two-Way

- Priority 0 configured on all routers
- OSPF Neighbor Stuck in Exstart/Exchange
- Mismatched interface maximum transmission unit (MTU)
- Duplicate router IDs on routers
- Broken unicast connectivity
- Network type of point-to-point between Primary Rate Interface (PRI) and Basic Rate Interface (BRI)/dialer
- OSPF Neighbor Stuck in Loading
- Mismatched MTU
- Corrupted link-state request packet

LSA Types

Type	Description
1	Router
2	Network
3	Network Summary
4	ASBR Summary
5	AS External
6	Group Membership
7	NSSA External
8	External Attributes
9	Opaque (link-local scope)
10	Opaque (area-local scope)
11	Opaque (AS scope)

Router LSA (Type 1)—Lists all of a router's links and their state. These LSAs are flooded within the area they originated.

Network LSA (Type 2)—Produced by the DR on every multi-access network. These LSAs list all attached routers, including the DR itself; they are flooded within the originating area.

Network Summary (Type 3)—Originated by Area Border Routers (ABRs); sent into an area to advertise destinations outside the area; flood throughout the autonomous system.

ASBR Summary (Type 4)—Also originated by ABRs; the destination advertised is an ASBR; flood throughout the autonomous system.

AS External (Type 5)—Originated by ASBRs and advertise an external destination or a default route to an external destination; flooded throughout the autonomous system.

Group Membership (Type 6)—Used in Multicast OSPF (MOSPF), which is not supported in Cisco routers.

NSSA External (Type 7)—Originated by ASBRs in Not-So-Stubby Areas.

External Attribute (Type 8)—Proposed as an alternate to IBGP.

Opaque (Type 9–11)—Used for various application specific information.

Router Types

Internal routers—All interfaces belong within the same area; these routers have a single link-state database

Area Border Routers (ABRs)—Connect one or more areas to the backbone; act as gateway for interarea traffic; separate link-state database for each connected area

Backbone routers—At least one interface in the backbone area

Autonomous System Boundary Router (ASBR)—Inject routes into the OSPF network learned from another protocol; this router might be located anywhere (it might also be backbone, internal, or Area Border Router)

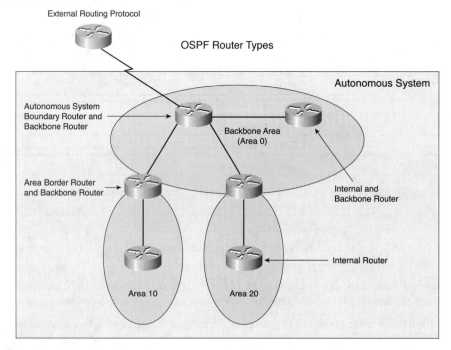

Type of Routes

OSPF uses routing designators in the routing table to distinguish between types of routes. Here are the designators used and their meaning:

O—OSPF intra-area (router LSA)—Networks from within the same area as the router; Type 1 LSAs are used to advertise.

O IA—OSPF interarea (summary LSA)—These are networks outside of the area of the router, but within the autonomous system; Type 3 LSAs are used to advertise.

O E1—Type 1 external routes—Networks outside of the autonomous system; advertised by Type 5 LSAs; calculate cost by adding the external cost to the internal cost of each link that the packet crosses; use when multiple ASBRs are advertising the external route.

O E2—Type 2 external routes—Networks outside of the autonomous system; advertised by Type 5 LSAs; cost is always the external cost only. This is the default type on Cisco routers.

Areas

Routers must share identical link-state database with other routers in same area. Area ID 0 is reserved for the backbone area. The backbone is responsible for summarizing each area to every other area. You configure a router for the backbone area by placing interface(s) in area 0 via the network command. For example:

```
Router(config)# router ospf 1
Router(config-router)# network 10.10.0.1 0.0.0.0 area 0
```

OSPF Areas

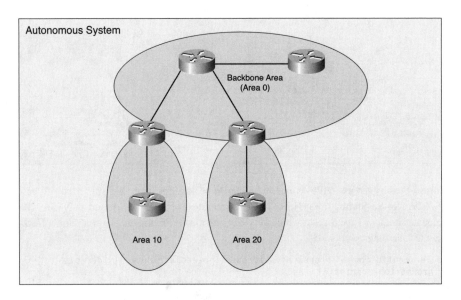

Stub Area—An area into which external LSAs are not flooded (Type 4 and 5 LSAs are blocked). Adjacencies do not form with any other router not marked as stub. Virtual links cannot be configured within a stub. To configure an area as stub, use the following command:

```
Router(config-router)# area area-id stub
```

Totally Stubby Area—Also block summary (Type 3 LSAs); the only exception is a single Type 3 default LSA. To configure an area as Totally Stubby use the following command:

```
Router(config-router)# area area-id stub [no-summary]
```

The no-summary keyword needs to be used on the ABR only. You can change the cost of the default route sent into the Totally Stubby Area using the following command (default cost is 1):

```
Router(config-router)# area area-id default-cost cost
```

Stub and Totally Stubby Areas

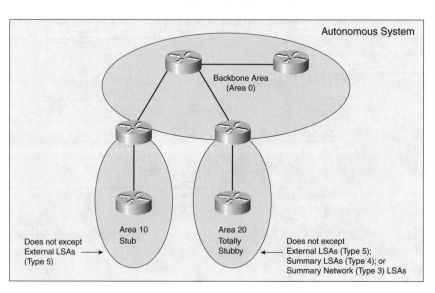

Not-So-Stubby Areas—Allows external routes to be advertised into the Stub Area—Type 7 LSAs. A Not-So-Stubby Area (NSSA) ASBR generates the Type 7 LSA, and an NSSA ABR translates it into a Type 5 LSA, which gets sent into the OSPF domain. To configure a NSSA, use the following command:

```
Router(config-router)# area area-id nssa [no-redistribution] [default-
  information-originate]
```

The **area area-id nssa** command is used on all routers in the area; it is used in place of the area stub command.

Not-So-Stubby Areas

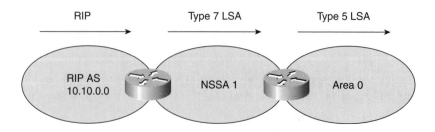

Here is a summary of the LSA types permitted in each area:

Area	1	2	3	4	5	7
Backbone	Yes	Yes	Yes	Yes	Yes	No
Non-backbone	Yes	Yes	Yes	Yes	Yes	No
Stub	Yes	Yes	Yes	Yes	No	No
Totally Stubby	Yes	Yes	No	No	No	No
NSSA	Yes	Yes	Yes	Yes	No	Yes

Configuring Basic Single-Area OSPF

First, you must enable the OSPF routing process on the router using the global configuration command:

```
Router(config)# router ospf process-id
```

Use the network command to identify those interfaces that are to participate in OSPF:

```
Router(config-router)# network address inverse-mask area [area-id]
```

Verification commands include the following:

- **show ip protocols**
- **show ip route ospf**
- **show ip ospf interface**
- **show ip ospf**
- **show ip ospf neighbor [detail]**

OSPF Router ID

The router ID is how the router is identified in OSPF. The router ID also is used to break a tie for DR/BDR if the administrator has not set the OSPF priority values on routers using the ip ospf priority command. The router with the highest router ID wins the election in that case. Here is the process for router ID selection (in order):

1 The router ID as set with the router-id address router configuration command. If you are using this command after OSPF has selected a router ID, you should use clear ip ospf process to reset.

2 The highest IP address on a loopback interface.

3 The highest IP address on an active interface.

You can choose to advertise the router ID if you like using an appropriate **network** command—this makes router ID ping-able. If you would like to save on address space, do not advertise it. Use **show ip ospf** to verify the router ID selection.

Route Summarization

Keep in mind that Summary LSAs (Type 3 LSAs) do not always contain summarized routes. By default, these advertisements are not summarized.

Two types of summarization exist in OSPF—interarea that is performed on ABRs and external route summarization that is performed on routes redistributed into OSPF autonomous systems.

To configure interarea route summarization on the ABR, use the following command:

```
Router(config-router)# area area-id range address mask
```

To configure route summarization on an ASBR to summarize external routes, use the following command:

```
Router(config-router)# summary-address address mask [not-advertise] [tag tag]
```

The not-advertise optional keyword suppresses routes that match the specified prefix. The tag value can be used as a "match" value for controlling redistribution with route maps.

Default Route Advertisements in OSPF

For an OSPF router to advertise a default route into an area, the command **default-information originate** must be used. If the advertising router does not possess a default route in its routing table, you can use the **always** keyword to still generate the default route to 0.0.0.0. The complete command syntax for generating default routes is as follows:

```
Router(config-router)# default-information originate [always] [metric
  metric_value] [metric-type type-value] [route-map map-name]
```

If you do not specify a metric value, the default of 10 is used. The **metric-type** allows you to specify a Type 1 or Type 2 external route. Finally, the **route-map** option allows you to control the generation of the default route further. For example, the default route is generated only if the route map is satisfied.

Authentication

Type 1—clear text; least secure. To configure:

Step 1   Enable area authentication on all routers in the area; use this command:

```
Router(config-router)# area area_id authentication
```

Step 2   Enter the clear text password on the interface:

```
Router(config-if)# ip ospf authentication-key password
```

Type 2—MD5; most secure. To configure:

Step 1   Enable MD5 area authentication on all routers in the area:

```
Router(config-router)# area area_id authentication message-digest
```

Step 2   Set key and password on the interfaces:

```
Router(config-if)# ip ospf message-digest-key key_value md5 password
```

Changing the Cost Metric

The Cisco implementation of OSPF calculates the metric using the following formula:

cost = refbw/bandwidth

The default refbw is 100 Mbps. The bandwidth value is that which is configured on the interface using the bandwidth command. If you are using many interfaces faster than 100 Mbps, consider resetting the refbw value. You can do so on each router using the following command:

```
Router(config-router)# auto-cost reference-bandwidth refbw
```

Note that refbw is in Mbps. For example, if you wanted to ensure Gigabit Ethernet interfaces evaluate to a cost of 5, set the refbw on each router to 5,000. (Valid values are from 1 to 4,294,967).

You can also override the calculated cost value in any interface directly by using the following command:

```
Router(config-if)# ip ospf cost value
```

Values range from 1 to 65535.

Optional OSPF Interface Parameters

Additional optional interface parameters not covered elsewhere in these study sheets include the following:

- **ip ospf retransmit-interval**—Specifies the number of seconds between LSA retransmissions
- **ip ospf transmit-delay**—Sets the number of seconds required to send link-state update
- **ip ospf hello-interval**—Specifies time between Hello packets; must match on all routers in network
- **ip ospf dead-interval**—Number of seconds before router considered dead; must match on all routers in network

Administrative Distance and OSPF

Three different administrative distance values are possible for OSPF—intra-area routes, inter-area routes, and external routes. By default all are set to 110; these can be changed with the following command:

```
Router(config-router)# distance ospf {[intra-area dist1] [inter-area dist2]
  [external dist3]}
```

OSPF Passive Interface

To set a passive interface in OSPF, use the following command:

```
Router(config-router)# passive-interface interface-type interface-number
```

When used with OSPF, this command prevents the interface from sending Hello packets and therefore prevents an adjacency from forming. It also prevents the sending or receiving of routing information through the interface. The specified interface address appears as a stub network in the OSPF domain, therefore.

Configuring Route Calculation Timers

You can configure the delay between when a topology change is received and when the SPF calculation takes place. You can also configure the hold time between two consecutive SPF calculations. Use the following command:

```
Router(config-router)# timers spf spf-delay spf-holdtime
```

Changing LSA Group Pacing

Routers group LSAs and pace refreshing, checksumming, and aging functions so that the resource strain on the router is reduced. This is default behavior; it can be tweaked with the following command:

```
Router(config-router)# timers lsa-group-pacing seconds
```

Blocking LSA Flooding

You can prevent the default flooding behavior; to do so on a broadcast, nonbroadcast, and point-to-point network, use the following command:

```
Router(config-if)# ospf database-filter all out
```

On point-to-multipoint networks, use the following command:

```
Router(config-router)# neighbor ip-address database-filter all out
```

Reducing LSA Flooding

Reduces the flooding of LSAs in stable topologies by setting LSAs to "do not age"; accomplished with the following command:

```
Router(config-if)# ip ospf flood-reduction
```

Virtual Links

A virtual link is a link to the backbone through a non-backbone area. Virtual links are created between two ABRs and the area cannot be stub. The following command configures a virtual link:

```
Router(config-router)# area trainsit_area_id virtual-link router_id_of_remote
```

Virtual Links

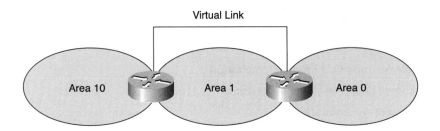

Virtual Link

Area 10   Area 1   Area 0

OSPF over On-Demand Circuits

On-demand circuit is an enhancement that allows efficient operations over dialup, ISDN, and other on-demand circuits. With this feature, periodic Hellos are suppressed, and the periodic refreshes of LSAs are not flooded over the demand circuit. These types of packets bring up the link only for the first time—or when you have a topology change that needs to be propagated.

To configure OSPF for on-demand circuits, use the following command:

```
Router(config-if)# ip ospf demand-circuit
```

If the router is part of a point-to-point topology, only one end of the demand circuit must be configured with this command, although all routers must support the feature. If the router is part of a point-to-multipoint topology, only the multipoint end must be configured with this command. Also, this feature does not work in a broadcast-based topology. Finally, the feature is not supported for use with an asynchronous interface.

Troubleshooting OSPF Route Advertisements

OSPF Neighbor Is Not Advertising Routes

- OSPF is not enabled on interface

- Advertising interface is down

- Secondary interface is in different area from primary interface

ABR Is Not Advertising Summary Route

- Area is configured as Totally Stubby Area

- ABR lacks Area 0 connectivity

- A discontiguous Area 0 exists

Neighbor Is Not Advertising External Routes

- Area is configured as stub or NSSA

- The NSSA ABR is not translating Type 7 into Type 5 LSAs

Neighbor Is Not Advertising Default Routes

- No **default-information originate** command
- No default route in the routing table
- Stub area is in use
- NSSA border router is not originating the Type 7

Troubleshooting OSPF Route Installation

OSPF Installing No Routes in Routing Table

- Network type mismatch
- IP address or subnet mask misconfiguration
- Unnumbered/numbered point-to-point configuration
- Distribute list
- Broken permanent virtual circuit (PVC) in full-mesh broadcast mode Frame network

OSPF Not Installing External Routes

- Forwarding address not known through intra-area or interarea route
- ABR not generating Type 4 LSAs

Troubleshooting Redistribution

Not Advertising External Routes

- **subnets** keyword is missing
- Distribute list

Troubleshooting Route Summarization

Router Not Summarizing Interarea Routes

- No **area range** command on ABR
- Router not summarizing external routes
- No **summary-address** command on ASBR

Troubleshooting CPUHOG Syslog Reports

CPUHOG Messages During Adjacency Establishments

- No packet-pacing code executing
- CPUHOG Messages During LSA Refresh
- No LSA group-pacing code

Troubleshooting Dial-on-Demand Routing Issues

Hello Packets Are Bringing Up the Link

- Hellos are permitted as interesting traffic

Demand Circuit Keeps Bringing Up the Link

- Link flapping
- Network type is broadcast
- PPP host route being redistributed
- One router is not demand-circuit capable

Troubleshooting SPF Calculations

SPF Running Constantly

- Flapping route
- Neighbor flapping
- Duplicate router ID

Troubleshooting Common Error Messages

"Could Not Allocate Router ID"

- No enabled interface with valid IP
- Not enough interfaces up with IP addresses for multiple OSPF processes

"%OSPF-4-BADLSATYPE: Invalid lsa: Bad LSA type" Type 6

- Neighboring router is sending MOSPF packets that are not supported on Cisco routers
- Eliminate the error with the ignore lsa mospf command

"OSPF-4-ERRRCV"

- OSPF received an invalid packet, because of a mismatched area ID, a bad checksum, or OSPF not enabled on a receiving interface

"Bad Checksum"

- Device is corrupting the packet
- Sending router's interface is bad, or a software bug exists
- Receiving router's interface is bad, or a software bug exists

General Troubleshooting Commands

show ip ospf neighbor [interface-type interface-number] [neighbor-id] [detail]—Displays OSPF-neighbor information on a per-interface basis.

show ip ospf [process-id]—Displays general information about OSPF routing processes.

show ip ospf interface [interface-type interface-number]—Displays OSPF-related interface information.

show ip ospf database—Displays lists of information related to the OSPF database for a specific router.

debug ip ospf packet—This EXEC command displays information about each Open Shortest Path First (OSPF) packet received:

```
Router# debug ip ospf packet
OSPF: rcv. v:2 t:1 l:48 rid:200.0.0.116
aid:0.0.0.0 chk:0 aut:2 keyid:1 seq:0x0
```

The possible output values are as follows:

- **v:**—Version of OSPF
- **t:**—Specifies the OSPF packet type (1: Hello, 2: DBD, 3: LSR, 4: LSU, 5: LAAck)
- **rid:**—Provides the OSPF router ID
- **aid:**—Shows the area ID
- **chk:**—Displays the checksum
- **aut:**—Provides the authentication type (0: no, 1: simple password, 2: MD5)
- **auk:**—Specifies the authentication key
- **keyed:**—Displays the MD5 key ID
- **seq:**—Provides the sequence number

BGP

BGP Introduction

Border Gateway Protocol (BGP) is an Exterior Gateway Protocol (EGP) used for routing between autonomous systems. It enables routing policies and improves security.

Exterior Gateway Protocol

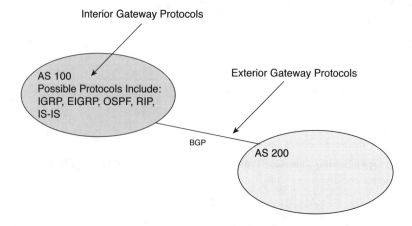

BGP is distance vector with enhancements, including the following:

- Reliable updates

- Triggered updates only

- Rich metrics (path attributes)

- Scalable to massive networks

Because of these enhancements, BGP is often described as Advanced Distance Vector. Perhaps the most technically accurate description is Path Vector.

Common uses for BGP include the following:

- Customer connected to one Internet service provider (ISP) (not always required, however)

- Customer connected to several ISPs

- Service provider networks (transit AS)

- Network cores of very large enterprise networks

Session Establishment

BGP neighbors are not discovered; they must be configured manually on both sides of the connection. Port number 179 is used. Only one session remains if both connection attempts succeed. The **show ip bgp summary** command gives an overview of the session status. Indications include Idle, Active, OpenSent, OpenConfirm, and Established. Keepalives are sent every 60 seconds. Peers can use a MD5 shared secret.

Route Processing

All routes received after the neighbor establishment are saved in memory. If more than one way to reach a destination exists, the best is selected. Use the show ip bgp command to view all of the routing information received from all neighbors.

The best route selection criteria occurs as follows in this order:

- Exclude any route with inaccessible next hop

- Prefer highest weight (local to router)

- Prefer highest local preference (global within autonomous system)

- Prefer routes that the router originated

- Prefer shortest autonomous system paths (compare length only)

- Prefer lowest origin code (IGP<EGP<Incomplete)

- Prefer lowest MED

- Prefer External paths over Internal BGP (IBGP) paths

- For IBGP paths, prefer path through closet IGP neighbor

- For External BGP (EBGP) paths, prefer the oldest path

- Prefer paths from router with lower BGP router ID

Best routes are propagated to BGP neighbors.

Best BGP routes are copied into the IP routing table based on administrative distance.

BGP process injects local routes in two different ways:

- Using the network configuration commands. This command lists networks that are candidates if they appear in the routing table.

- Using redistribution by another routing protocol.

Route Summarization

Automatic summarization is enabled by default. When you disable automatic summarization, the routes introduced locally into the BGP table are not summarized.

BGP Basic Configuration

To start BGP on your router, use the following command:

```
Router(config)# router bgp as-number
```

A public autonomous system number can be obtained from the InterNIC, or a private autonomous system number is possible in some situations (64512–65535). Only one BGP process is permitted per router.

To configure your BGP neighbors, use the following commands:

```
Router(config-router)# neighbor ip-address remote-as as-number
Router(config-router)# neighbor ip-address description neighbor description
```

The neighbor must be reachable over a directly connected subnet.

To temporarily disable a neighborship, use the following command:

```
Router(config-router)# neighbor ip-address shutdown
```

To configure MD5 authentication between neighbors, use the following command. Keep in mind the password string must match on both routers.

```
Router(config-router)# neighbor ip-address password string
```

Announcing Networks

To disable automatic summarization, use the following command:

```
Router(config-router)# no auto-summary
```

To manually define a major network use the following command:

```
Router(config-router)# network major-network-number
```

If you use this command and autosummarization is on (the default behavior), at least one of the subnets must be present in the forwarding table for the major network prefix to be advertised. If automatic summarization is disabled, an exact match is required in the forwarding table. You can use the mask keyword to specify a specific subnet with the **network** command.

If you would like to modify parameters before inserting prefixes into the BGP table, you can use a route map as follows:

```
Router(config-router)# network major-network-number route-map route-map-name
```

This option might be used for one or more of the following:

- Change the weight of a locally sourced route

- Tagging source routes with BGP communities

- Setting the local preference

- Changing the value of the MED

To advertise routes based on route redistribution, use the following command syntax:

```
Router(config)# router bgp AS
Router(config-router)# redistribute IGP
Router(config-router)# distribute-list ACL out IGP
```

One caveat here is that the routes have an origin code of unknown. This makes them seem inferior to other routes per the BGP route selection process. Notice the optional use of the distribute list syntax to suppress certain networks from being advertised in updates.

Redistribution can be configured in conjunction with a route map to reset the origin code or set other attributes:

```
Router(config)# router bgp AS
Router(config-router)# redistribute IGP route-map name
```

Classless BGP

To manually announce a classless prefix, use the following command:

```
Router(config-router)# network ip-prefix-address mask subnet-mask
```

You should also create a static route pointing to null0 to create a matching prefix in the IP forwarding table.

Aggregation in BGP

Use the following command to configure route summarization to suppress the advertising of individual networks. Remember, at least one network of the summarized space must exist in the BGP table:

```
Router(config-router)# aggregate-address address-prefix mask summary-only
```

Route Selection Using Policy Controls

AS Path Filtering with Regular Expressions

String matching—A string of characters in the regular expression matches any equivalent substring in the autonomous system path; 29 has three matches in ǀ210 291 1296 29ǀ, for example.

String matching alternatives—The "ǀ" symbol means "or."

String matching ranges and wildcards—Brackets "[]" can be used for ranges, and the "." can match any single character.

String matching delimiters—"^" matches the beginning of string; "$" matches the end of string; and "_" matches any delimiters.

String matching grouping—Parentheses can group smaller expressions into larger expressions.

String matching special characters—You can use the "\" to remove the special meaning of the character that follows.

String matching repeating operators—"*" means the expression preceding repeats zero or more times; "?" means the expression preceding repeats zero or one time; "+" the expression preceding repeats one or more times.

Here are some string matching examples:

_200_All routes going through AS 200

^200$Directly connected to AS 200

_200$Originated in AS 200

^200_.Networks behind AS 200

^[0-9]+$AS paths one AS long

^([0-9]+)(_\1)*$Networks originating in the neighbor AS

^$Networks originated in local AS

.*Matches everything

AS-path filters configured inbound on a router select those routes that are allowed.

AS-Path Filters

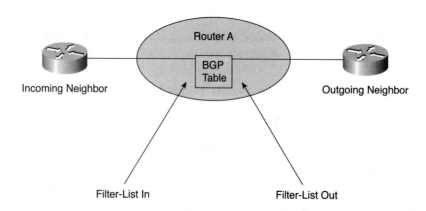

Routes that are selected enter the local BGP table when the selection is applied on the incoming routes from a neighbor. Routes that are not selected are silently dropped. Routes selected if an outbound filter is used are transmitted to the neighbor when the selection is applied. Routes that are not selected are used locally but are never sent to the neighbor.

The commands used to configure an AS-path list are relatively simple. First, configure an AS-path access list as follows:

```
Router(config)# ip as-path access-list access-list-number {permit I deny} as-
  regular-expression
```

To set up a BGP filter, use the neighbor filter-list router configuration command:

```
Router(config-router)# neighbor {ip-address I peer-group-name} filter-list
  access-list-number {in I out}
```

Monitoring the use of regular expressions is critical. To display routes matching the AS-path regular expression, use the **show ip bgp regexp** command. To display routes that conform to a specified filter list, use the **show ip bgp filter-list** command. To display a specific access list or all AS-path access lists in the router, use the **show ip as-path-access-list** command.

Prefix Lists

ISPs can use prefix lists to control the updates coming from customers.

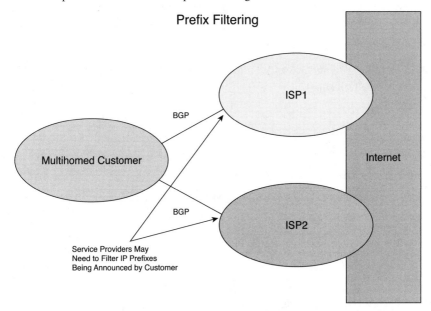

Prefix Filtering

To create an entry in a prefix list, use the ip prefix-list global configuration command:

```
Router(config)# ip prefix-list list-name [seq seq-value] deny I permit network/
  len [ge ge-value] [le le-value]
```

You can use the parameters ge and le to specify the range of the prefix length to be matched for prefixes that are more specific than **network/len**. The exact match is assumed when neither ge nor le is specified. The range is assumed to be from ge-value to 32 only if the **ge** attribute is specified. The range is assumed to be from **len** to **le-value** only if the **le** attribute is specified.

To distribute BGP neighbor information as specified in a prefix list, use the following command:

```
Router(config-router)# neighbor {ip-address | peer-group-name} prefix-list
  prefix-listname {in | out}
```

To suppress networks from being advertised in updates, use the following command:

```
Router(config-router)# distribute-list {access-list-number | name | prefix-list
  prefix-listname} out [interface-name | routing-process | autonomous-system-
  number]
```

To display information about a prefix list or prefix list entries, use the show ip prefix-list command.

Outbound Route Filtering

Outbound Route Filtering (ORF) is a prefix-based BGP feature that is enabled through the advertisement of ORF capabilities to peer routers. The advertisement of the ORF capability indicates that a BGP-speaking router can accept a prefix list from a neighbor and apply the prefix list to locally configured ORFs (if any exist). When this capability is enabled, the BGP speaker can install an inbound prefix list filter to the remote peer as an outbound filter, which reduces unwanted routing updates.

An ORF message contains the following information:

- Address Family Information (AFI) and Subsequent Address Family Information (SAFI) for which the filter should be used
- ORF type
- When to refresh (immediate or deferred refresh)
- List of ORF entries where the actual filter is defined

Commonly used ORF types are as follows:

- ORF type 1 filters based on Network Layer Reachability Information (NLRI)
- ORF type 2 filters based on standard BGP community attributes
- ORF type 3 filters based on extended BGP community attributes
- ORF type 128 filters based on Cisco proprietary implementation of prefix filtering (prefix lists)

An ORF type of NLRI-based filtering (type 1) uses the following actions:

- **ADD**—Adds a line to a prefix list filter on the remote peer
- **DELETE**—Removes a line from a filter that was previously installed on a remote peer
- **DELETE ALL**—Removes all previously installed filters on the remote peer

To advertise ORF capabilities to a peer router, use the neighbor orf prefix-list command in address family or router configuration mode:

```
Router(config-router)# neighbor {ip-address} [capability] orf prefix-list
   [receive | send | both]
```

Use the **clear ip bgp neighbor** command with the **prefix-filter** keyword to push out the existing ORF prefix list so that a new route refresh can be received from a neighbor. The neighbor uses the ORF prefix list previously negotiated.

Filtering with Route Maps

Route maps are also a power filtering tool. They can be used to accomplish the following tasks:

- Filter on IP prefixes coming from a specific autonomous system
- Filter on other BGP attributes
- Modify BGP attributes

Match clauses in the BGP route map can be based on the following:

- IP network numbers and subnet masks (prefix list or access list)
- Route originator
- Next hop
- Origin code
- Tag value attached to an Interior Gateway Protocol (IGP) route
- AS-path
- Community
- IGP route type

With a route map, the following can be set:

- Origin
- Next hop
- Weight
- Community
- Local preference
- Multi Exit Discriminator (MED)

You can apply a route map on incoming or outgoing routing information for a neighbor. The routing information must be permitted by the route map to be accepted. If the route-map has no statement explicitly permitting a route, the route is implicitly denied and dropped. The syntax required is as follows:

```
Router(config-router)# neighbor ip-address route-map name in | out
```

The **show ip bgp route-map** command displays selected routes from a BGP routing table based on the contents of a route map.

Implementing Changes in Policy

Traditional method of **clear ip bgp *** is very disruptive. Soft reconfiguration was introduced in Cisco IOS 11.2 to facilitate nondisruptive changes in BGP. When you configure **soft-reconfiguration inbound** for a neighbor, the router stores all routes received from that neighbor as an extra copy in memory. This copy is taken before any filtering is applied by the router to routes it receives. When you have completed the changes to filters and route maps that are applied on incoming information, execute the **clear ip bgp ip-address soft** in on the router in privileged EXEC mode.

When you have completed the changes to filters and route maps that are applied on the outgoing information, execute **clear ip bgp ip-address soft out** on the router in privileged EXEC mode.

Route refresh is another new feature in the Cisco implementation of BGP that is available. Routers use the route refresh feature to request a neighbor to resend all the routing information when needed. Use the **clear ip bgp *** in command to send a route refresh message to all neighbors or **clear ip bgp ip-address** in to send a route refresh message to a specific neighbor.

BGP Path Attributes

Mandatory Well-Known Attributes

Origin—Specifies the origin of the router

- IGP
- EGP
- Unknown—Route was redistributed

AS-Path—Sequence of autonomous system numbers through which the route is accessible

Next-Hop—IP address of the next hop router

Discretionary Well-Known Attributes

Local Preference—Used for consistent routing policy with an autonomous system

Atomic Aggregate—Informs neighbor autonomous system that the originating router aggregated routes

Nontransitive Attributes

Multi Exit Discriminator—Used to discriminate between multiple entry points into an autonomous system

Transitive Attributes

Aggregator—IP address and autonomous system of router that performed aggregation

Community—Used for route tagging

Influencing Route Selection Using Weights

Using Weight

You can use weight to provide local routing policy, while you can use local preference to establish autonomous system–wide routing policy.

To assign a weight to a neighbor connection, use the neighbor weight router configuration command:

```
Router(config-router)# neighbor {ip-address I peer-group-name} weight weight
```

This approach assigns weight value to all route updates from the neighbor. Higher weights are preferred.

You can also configure the router so that all incoming routes that match an AS-path filter receive the configured weight. Use the following command to do so:

```
Router(config-router)# neighbor {ip-address I peer-group-name} filter-list
  access-list-number {in I out I weight weight}
```

You can also set weight with a route map in more complex scenarios.

Using Local Preference

Local preference can be used to influence route selection within the local autonomous system; in fact, this attribute is stripped from outgoing updates via EBGP. You should decide between the use of weight or local preference. If you use local preference, all weights should be the same.

You can apply local preference in the following ways:

- Using a route map with the **set local-preference** command

- Using the **bgp default local-preference** command to change the default local preference value applied to all updates coming from external neighbors or originating locally

For verification, you can use the use the command **show ip bgp prefix** to display the locally applied value.

AS-Path Prepending

In networks where connections to multiple providers are required, it is difficult to specify a return path be used for traffic returning to the AS. One BGP mechanism you can use is AS-path prepending. AS-path prepending potentially allows the customer to influence the route selection of its service providers.

You manipulate AS-spaths by prepending autonomous system numbers to already existing AS-paths. Typically, you perform AS-path prepending on outgoing EBGP updates over the non-desired return path. Because the AS-paths sent over the nondesired link become longer than the AS-path sent over the preferred path, the nondesired link is now less likely to be used as the return path. To avoid conflicts with BGP loop prevention mechanisms, no other autonomous system number, except that of the sending AS, should be prepended to the AS-path attribute.

You can configure manual manipulation of the AS-path attribute (prepending) using a route map with the set as-path prepend command.

BGP Multi Exit Discriminator (MED)

You can apply the MED attribute on outgoing updates to a neighboring autonomous system to influence the route selection process in that autonomous system. The MED attribute is useful only when you have multiple entry points into an autonomous system.

The default value of the MED attribute is 0. A lower value of MED is more preferred. A router prefers a path with the smallest MED value but only if weight, local preference, AS-path, and origin code are equal.

MED is not a mandatory attribute; no MED attribute is attached to a route by default. The only exception is if the router is originating networks that have an exact match in the routing table (through the network command or through redistribution). In that case, the router uses the metric in the routing table as the MED attribute value.

Using the **default-metric** command in BGP configuration mode causes all redistributed networks to have the specified MED value.

You can use a route map to set MED on incoming or outgoing updates. Use the set metric command within the route map configuration mode to set the MED attribute.

You must use the command **bgp bestpath med confed** when you use MED within a confederation to influence the route selection process. A router compares MED values for those routes that originate in the confederation.

BGP Communities

A community is an attribute used to tag BGP routes. A router can apply it to any BGP route by using a route map. Other routers can then perform any action based on the tag (community) that is attached to the route.

Any BGP router can tag routes in incoming and outgoing routing updates or when doing redistribution. In addition, any BGP router can filter routes in incoming or outgoing updates or select preferred routes based on the community values. By default, communities are stripped in outgoing BGP updates.

The actual community attribute is a transitive optional attribute. The value of this attribute is a 32-bit number in the possible range of 0 to 4,294,967,200. You can tag each network in a BGP routing table with a set of communities.

The BGP standards define several filtering-oriented communities for your use:

- **no-export**—Do not advertise routes to real EBGP peers.
- **no-advertise**—Do not advertise routes to any peer.
- **local-as**—Do not advertise routes to any EBGP peers.
- **internet**—Advertise this route to the Internet community.

Because the community attribute is a transitive optional attribute, routers that do not support communities pass them along unchanged.

To define your own communities, you use a 32-bit community value that is split into two parts:

- High-order 16 bits that contain the autonomous system number of the autonomous system that defines the community meaning

- Low-order 16 bits that have local significance

You can specify a 32-bit community value as follows:

[AS-number]:[low-order-16-bits]

You use communities in well planned step-by-step fashion. Here are the steps that you should consider as well as examples of each:

Step 1   Define administrative policy goals

Example—Solve asymmetrical customer routing problems

Step 2   Design filters and path selection policy to achieve administrative goals

Example—Set local preference of customer routes to 75 for customers using the backup ISP

Step 3   Define communities to be used to achieve individual goals

Example—Community 367:20 indicates that the local preference of the route should be lowered to 75

To actually configure BGP communities, you can use the following steps:

Step 1   Configure route tagging with BGP communities

Step 2   Configure BGP community propagation

Step 3   Define BGP community access lists (community lists) to match BGP communities

Step 4   Configure route maps that match on community lists and filter routes or set other BGP attributes

Step 5   Apply route maps to incoming or outgoing updates

Route tagging with communities is always done with a route map. You can specify any number of communities; communities specified in the **set** keyword overwrite existing communities unless you specify the **additive** option.

Once you have created the route map, you can apply a route map to inbound or outbound BGP updates using the following command:

```
Router(config-router)# neighbor ip-address route-map map in | out
```

To apply a route map to redistributed routes, use the following command:

```
Router(config-router)# redistribute protocol route-map map
```

By default, communities are stripped in outgoing BGP updates; therefore, you must manually configure community propagation to BGP neighbors. You can do so using the following command:

```
Router(config-router)# neighbor ip-address send-community
```

You should keep in mind that BGP peer groups are ideal for configuring BGP community propagation toward a large number of neighbors.

You can use a standard community access list to find community attributes in routing updates. A standard community list is defined by its assigned list number. The list number uses a range from 1 to 99. Community lists are similar to standard IP access lists in these ways:

- The router evaluates the lines in the community list sequentially.

- If no line matches communities attached to a BGP route, the route is implicitly denied.

Standard community lists are different from standard IP access lists in these ways:

- The keyword internet should be used to permit any community value.

- If more values are listed in a single line, they all have to be in an update to have a match.

Here is the syntax for the creation of the standard community list:

```
Router(config)# ip community-list 1-99 permit | deny value [ value ... ]
```

To create an extended community list, use the following syntax:

```
Router(config)# ip community-list 100-199 permit | deny regexp
```

These extended community lists are like simple community lists, but they match based on regular expressions. Specifically, communities attached to a route are ordered, converted to string, and matched with regexp. You can use the .* syntax to match any community value.

Community lists are used in match conditions in route maps to match on communities attached to BGP routes.

Once you create your community lists, you can match to these lists in your route maps. A route map with community list matches a route if at least some communities attached to the route match the community list. You can use the **exact** option to ensure that all communities attached to the route have to match the community list. Remember, you can use route maps to filter routes or set other BGP attributes based on communities attached to routes.

Route Reflectors

BGP requires that all BGP peers in the same autonomous system form an IBGP session with all peers in the autonomous system. This is too difficult in many environments. Route reflectors are fully functional IBGP speakers that form IBGP sessions with other IBGP speakers, and they also perform a second function—they forward routes from other IBGP speakers to route reflector clients. The route reflector clients form IBGP sessions only with the route reflectors. The route reflectors and the clients form a cluster.

To configure route reflectors, consider these initial tasks:

- Configure the proper cluster-ID value on the route reflectors.

- Configure the route reflector with information about which IBGP neighbor sessions are reaching their clients.

- In the clients, remove all IBGP sessions to neighbors that are not a route reflector in the client cluster.

- Make sure that the IBGP neighbor is removed on both ends of the IBGP session.

The command used to configure the cluster-ID if the BGP cluster has redundant route reflectors is as follows:

```
bgp cluster-id cluster-id
```

The command used to configure the router as a BGP route reflector and configure the specified neighbor as its client is as follows:

```
neighbor ip-address route-reflector-client
```

Confederations

Confederations are another method of solving the IBGP full-mesh requirement. Confederations are smaller subautonomous systems created within the primary autonomous system to decrease the number of BGP peer connections. Five steps are used in the configuration of confederations:

Step 1   Enable BGP using the member autonomous system number

Step 2   Configure the confederation identifier using the bgp confederation identifier command

Step 3   Configure fully meshed IBGP subautonomous system neighbor relationships using the subautonomous system number as the remote auxiliary signal network (ASN) for all internal IBGP peers

Step 4   Configure other neighbors within the same parent autonomous system by specifying their subautonomous system number as the remote autonomous system number; other confederation peers from different subautonomous systems must also be identified as external confederation peers using the **bgp confederation peers** command

Step 5   Configure any EBGP neighbors as you normally would

Peer Groups

To configure one router with multiple BGP peer relationships, configurations can be quite complex. Peer groups simplify the configuration process. You make peer groups and assign neighbors with the same policies to the group. Peer group members inherit the policies assigned to the group.

To configure BGP peer groups on Cisco IOS routers, perform the following steps:

Step 1   Create a BGP peer group; use the neighbor peer-group router configuration command

Step 2   Specify parameters for the BGP peer group

Step 3   Create a BGP neighbor

Step 4   Assign a neighbor into the peer group; use the **neighbor peer-group** router configuration command

Network Backdoor Command

The **network backdoor** router configuration command causes the administrative distance assigned to the network to be forced to 200. The goal is to make Interior Gateway Protocol (IGP) learned routes preferred. A network that is marked as a backdoor is not sourced by the local router, but should be learned from external neighbors. You should be sure to verify the route is in the BGP table for the command to have the desired effect.

Configuring the BGP Maximum-Prefix Function

To control how many prefixes that a BGP router can receive from a neighbor, use the neighbor maximum-prefix router configuration command.

Route Dampening

Flapping routes create problems for BGP. An approach was created to remove the update about a flapping route until it can be guaranteed that the destination is more stable. This additional BGP scalability mechanism called route flap dampening was created to reduce route update processing requirements by suppressing unstable routes.

To enable route dampening, use the bgp dampening command.

Troubleshooting and Monitoring BGP

Important commands not included elsewhere in the BGP Study Sheets include:

- **show ip bgp neighbors ip-address**—Use the command to obtain detailed neighbor information
- **show ip bgp**—Displays all of the routes in the BGP table
- **show ip bgp ip-prefix [mask subnet-mask]**—Displays detailed information about all paths for a single prefix
- **debug ip tcp transactions**—Displays all TCP transactions
- **debug ip bgp events**—Displays significant BGP events
- **debug ip bgp keepalives**—Debugs BGP keepalive packets
- **debug ip bgp updates**—Displays all incoming or outgoing BGP updates
- **debug ip bgp updates acl**—Displays all incoming and sent updates matching an ACL
- **debug ip bgp ip-address updates [acl]**—Displays all BGP updates received from or sent to a specific neighbor

EIGRP

Enhanced Interior Gateway Routing Protocol (EIGRP) is a hybrid routing protocol—combining features of both distance vector and link-state routing protocols. Advantages include:

- VLSM support
- Rapid convergence thanks to Diffusing Update Algorithm (DUAL)

- Low CPU utilization—typically only Hellos and partial updates sent on a link

- Incremental updates

- Scalability

- Ease of configuration

- Automatic route summarization, or manual route summarization

- MD5 route authentication

EIGRP uses IP protocol 88. It uses a multicast address of 224.0.0.10 for hellos and routing updates.

EIGRP's Metric

EIGRP uses a composite metric like Interior Gateway Routing Protocol (IGRP), yet it is modified with a multiplier of 256. Bandwidth and delay are the defaults enabled. EIGRP calls the metric feasible distance. All of the possible metric values are as follows:

- **Bandwidth**—Expressed in KB; to adjust the bandwidth value assigned to an interface, use the bandwidth command.

- **Delay**—Expressed in microseconds; it can be adjusted using the delay command; when manipulating metrics, consider delay since bandwidth would effect other protocols as well.

- **Reliability**—Expressed as a number in the range of 1 to 255; 1 is a completely unreliable link.

- **Load**—Expressed as a number in the range of 1 to 255; 1 is a minimally loaded link.

- **MTU**—Maximum transmission unit; the smallest recorded MTU in the path.

The metric formula used by EIGRP is as follows:

$$\text{Metric} = [K1 * BW + ((K2 * BW)/(256 - Load)) + K3 * Delay]$$

By default, $K1 = 1, K2=0, K3=1, K4=0, K5=0$.

If you manipulate the K values on one router, you must manipulate on all.

EIGRP uses a 32-bit metric as opposed to the 24-bit metric of IGRP; the two are compatible automatically during redistribution, however.

EIGRP Packets

Hello—Establish neighbor relationships

Update—Send routing updates

Query—Ask neighbors about routing information

Reply—Respond to queries

Ack—Used to acknowledge reliable packets

The address used for Hello packets is 224.0.0.10; autonomous system numbers must match. Hellos are sent every 5 seconds on broadcast links as well as p2p serial, p2p subinterface, and multipoint circuits greater than T1. They are sent every 60 seconds on other link types. The hold time defaults to three times the Hello time. Neighborships form even if the values do not match.

EIGRP Reliability

Packets that require acknowledgement are as follows:

- Update
- Query
- Reply

Packet that do not are as follows:

- Hello
- Ack

Neighbor reset after retry limit (16) is reached. Slow neighbors are sent unicast packets instead.

Initial Route Discovery

Router discovery and route exchange happen simultaneously as follows:

Step 1   Router comes up and sends Hellos

Step 2   Reply from a neighbor includes Update

Step 3   Ack packets are sent

Step 4   Update process occurs in the opposite direction

EIGRP Discovery and Route Exchange

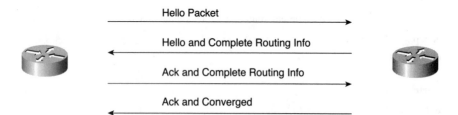

Hello Packet

Hello and Complete Routing Info

Ack and Complete Routing Info

Ack and Converged

EIGRP DUAL

Lowest cost route calculated by adding the cost between the next hop router and the destination (Advertised Distance [AD]) and the cost between the local router and the next hop. This sum is referred to as the Feasible Distance (FD).

A successor is a neighboring router that the local router has selected to forward packets to the destination. Multiple successors can exist if they have equal cost paths.

The next hop router for a backup path is called the feasible successor. To qualify as a feasible successor, a next hop router must have an AD less than the FD of the current successor route. More than one feasible successor can exist.

The feasible successor means that a new path can be selected without recalculation and is a major advantage in EIGRP for convergence.

Configuring EIGRP

To enable EIGRP, use the following command:

```
Router(config)# router eigrp autonomous-system-number
```

Then identify the networks participating with the following:

```
Router(config-router)# network network-number [wildcard-mask]
```

Using the default-network Command

Using the **default-network** command, you can configure a default route for the EIGRP process so that it propagates to other EIGRP routers within the same autonomous system. A router configured with the command considers the network listed in that command as the last-resort gateway.

Verification

A command that deserves some elaboration is the show ip eigrp topology command. The codes in the output are as follows:

Passive—This network is available and installation can occur in the routing table.

Active—This network is currently unavailable and installation cannot occur in the routing table.

Update (U)—Applies if a network is being updated (placed in an update packet); this code also applies if the router is waiting for an acknowledgment for this update packet.

Query (Q)—Applies if an outstanding query packet exists for this network other than being in the active state; also applies if the router is waiting for an acknowledgment for a query packet.

Reply (R)—Applies if the router is generating a reply for this network or is waiting for an acknowledgment for the reply packet.

Stuck in active (SIA) status—Signifies an EIGRP convergence problem for the network with which it is associated.

EIGRP Route Summarization

EIGRP performs autosummarization by default. You can enable manual summarization. Keep the following in mind regarding manual summarization:

- Summarization is configurable on a per-interface basis in any router within a network.
- When summarization is configured on an interface, the router immediately creates a route pointing to null0. This is a loop-prevention mechanism.
- When the last specific route of the summary goes away, the summary is deleted.
- The minimum metric of the specific routes is used as the metric of the summary route.

To disable autosummarization, use the **no auto-summary** command under the EIGRP router configuration mode. Use the **ip summary-address eigrp** interface command to manually create a summary route at an arbitrary network boundary within an EIGRP domain.

Unequal Cost Load Balancing

The degree to which EIGRP performs load balancing is controlled with the **variance** command.

You set the variance to a number from 1 to 128. The default is 1, which indicates equal cost load balancing. The multiplier defines the range of metric values that are accepted for load balancing by the EIGRP process.

For example, if you would like load balancing to occur between two links and one has a metric of 1000 and the other has a metric of 2000, you would need to set the variance to 2 in order to cause load balancing between the two links.

Bandwidth Utilization

By default, EIGRP uses up to 50 percent of the bandwidth of an interface or subinterface, which is set with the bandwidth parameter. This percentage can be changed on a per-interface basis by using the **ip bandwidth-percent eigrp nnn** interface configuration command. In this command, *nnn* is the percentage of the configured bandwidth that EIGRP can use. This percentage can be greater than 100. This is useful if the bandwidth is configured artificially low for routing policy reasons.

EIGRP Stub Routing

Often used in a hub and spoke topology. Only routes you specify are propagated from the stub router. The stub router responds to all queries with the message "inaccessible." A router that is configured as a stub sends a special peer information packet to all neighboring routers to report its status as a stub router. Nonstub routers do not query stub routers. The stub routing feature by itself does not prevent routes from being advertised to the stub router. You must configure the summarization or default route behavior. To configure the stub router, use the following router configuration command:

```
eigrp stub [receive-only I connected I static I summary]
```

The optional keywords with this command control which routes the router advertises to its nonstub peers.

IS-IS

Intermediate System-to-Intermediate System (IS-IS) is part of the Open System Interconnection (OSI) suite of protocols; uses Connectionless Network Service (CLNS) to provide connectionless delivery of data. The actual Layer 3 protocol is Connectionless Network Protocol (CLNP). CLNP is comparable to IP. Integrated IS-IS supports IP in addition to CLNS. IS-IS is comparable and sometimes preferred over OSPF.

You find three types of routers in IS-IS:

- **Level 1**—Learn about paths in their local area (intra-area)
- **Level 2**—Learn about paths between areas (interarea)
- **Level 1/2**—Learn about interarea and intra-area paths; equivalent to ABR in OSPF

The path of Level 2 and Level 1/2 routers is referred to as the backbone. This is more flexible than OSPF.

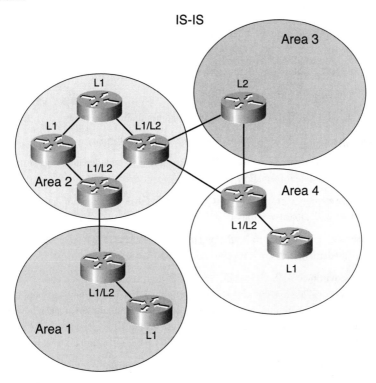

Cisco routers use a metric of 10 for all interfaces by default. Note this is essentially hop count.

IS-IS requires the use of CLNS node addresses to function properly. CLNS addresses used by routers are called network service access points (NSAPs). One part of this address is the NSAP selector byte (NSEL). An NSEL of 0 is used for routers and is called the Network Entity Title or NET. This identifies a network service. Cisco identifies the following fields in the NSAP address:

- **Area address**—1 to 13 octets; used to route between areas
- **System ID**—Fixed length of 6 octets in Cisco; IS identifier; used to route within an area
- **NSEL**—1 octet

Also, the first part of the address is called the AFI (authority and format identifier) byte. Most common setting is 49 to indicate locally administered (private). Here is an example of a typical NSAP address you might use:

    49.0001.0000.0b12.2122.00

This address breaks down as follows:

- **49**—The AFI value, and it indicates this is a privately administered device
- **0001**—The area ID
- **0000.0b12.2122**—System ID; taken from an interface (MAC address) to ensure uniqueness
- **00**—The NSEL value; it is 00 to indicate a NET (in this case, router)

IS-IS uses four types of protocol data units (PDUs):

- **Hello (ESH, ISH, IIH)**—Used to establish and maintain adjacencies
- **Link-state PDU (LSP)**—Used to distribute link-state information
- **Partial sequence number PDU (PSNP)**—Used to acknowledge and request missing pieces of link-state information
- **Complete sequence number PDU (CSNP)**—Used to describe a complete list of LSPs in the link-state database of a router

IS-IS supports broadcast mode for LANs and multipoint WANS, and it supports point-to-point for all other media; notice there is no concept of NBMA.

In broadcast environment, IS-IS uses the concept of a virtual router (pseudonode) called the Designated Intermediate System (DIS). This is roughly equivalent to the concept of the DR in OSPF, although no backup DIS exists and each router still maintains an adjacency with every other router. The DIS ensures that each router advertises only a single adjacency—the adjacency with the pseudonode. The DIS is elected based on the following criteria:

- Highest interface priority (set with the **isis priority** command)
- Highest SNPA (MAC)

IS-IS maintains a single procedure for flooding, aging, and updating LSPs. Level 1 LSPs are flooded within their local areas and Level 2 LSPs are flooded throughout the backbone. Each

IS originates its own LSP (1 for Level 1 and 1 for Level 2), and a separate database is maintained for each (Level 1 and Level 2).

The configuration steps for IS-IS include the following:

Step 1   Define areas and plan addressing (NETs) for routers.

Step 2   Enable IS-IS on the router.

Step 3   Configure the NET on the router.

Step 4   Enable IS-IS on an interface by interface basis.

Use the **router isis [tag]** global configuration mode command to enable IS-IS on the router. The tag is an optional name you can provide the IS-IS process on your router. When you enable IS-IS, Cisco makes the router a Level 1/Level 2 router by default.

Use the **net** command to configure the network entity title address. This is a router configuration command and is a requirement for IS-IS to function.

Finally, configure the interfaces that are to participate in IS-IS using the **ip router isis** interface configuration mode command. Notice no concept of the network router configuration mode command exists with IS-IS.

You should consider several optional optimization commands for IS-IS:

- **is-type {level-1 ı level-1-2 ı level-2-only}**—This command allows you to change the default Level 1/2 status of the router and save memory and bandwidth.

- **isis circuit-type {level-1 ı level-1-2 ı level-2-only}**—This command allows you to specify the type of adjacency to form over an interface; this reduces the bandwidth waste when IS-IS attempts to form adjacencies that do not exist.

- **isis metric metric {level-1 ı level-2}**—This router configuration command allows you to change the default metric of 10 that Cisco assigns to all interfaces.

- **summary-address prefix mask [level-1 ı level-2 ı level-1-2]**—This interface configuration command permits you to configure route summarization with IS-IS.

Troubleshooting IS-IS

IS-IS Adjacency Problems

- Some or all adjacencies are not establishing

    — Check for link failures

    — Verify basic configurations

    — Check for mismatched Level 1 and Level 2 interfaces

    — Check for area misconfiguration

    — Check for misconfigured subnets

    — Check for duplicate system IDs

- Adjacency in INIT state

    — Check authentication

    — Check for MTU mismatch

- Check for Hello padding consistency on both devices
- Enable debug isis adj-packets
- ES-IS adjacency formed instead of IS-IS adjacency

  - Check for this issue with the **show clns neighbors** command
  - Most likely caused by failure of IS-IS Hello processing, misconfigured authentication, or an MTU mismatch

Routing Update Problems

- Route advertisement issues—Level 1 routes

  - Check for the source LSP in the Level 1 database
  - Check for the prefix in the LSP of the source
  - Check if the LSP has expired
- Route advertisement issues—Level 2 routes

  - Check to ensure the router is connected to the Level 2 backbone
  - Check for the LSP of the source in the L2 database
- Route redistribution and Level 2-to-Level 1 route leaking problems

  - Check for the source LSP in the database
  - Check if the LSP has expired
  - Check that redistribution is configured correctly
  - Check to see if the source of the route is active
  - Check to see if the next hop is reachable in the case of a static source
  - Check to see of filtering is misconfigured
- Route-Flapping

  - Check for link in the path for flapping
  - Check for unusually high CPU utilization
  - Check the SPF log
  - Use debug isis update-packet
  - Check for LSP corruption storms

RIP v2

Classic distance vector protocol—version 2 is classless and supports VLSM, therefore. Version 2 also uses multicast packets for communication as opposed to broadcast packets. RIP version 2 supports plain text and message digest 5 (MD5) authentication.

The metric that RIP uses to rate the value of different routes is *hop count*. A directly connected network has a metric of zero; an unreachable network has a metric of 16. This small range of metrics makes RIP an unsuitable routing protocol for large networks.

Configuring RIP

Enable RIP and associate networks with the following commands:

```
Router(config)# router rip
Router(config-router)# network ip-address
```

To send unicast updates over a non-broadcast network, use the following command:

```
Router(config-router)# neighbor ip-address
```

Specifying the RIP Version

By default, RIP speaking interfaces receive RIP version 1 and version 2 packets, but send only version 1 packets. You can configure interfaces to receive and send only version 1 packets. Alternatively, you can configure the interfaces to receive and send only version 2 packets. To configure the router to send and receive packets from only one version, use the following command:

```
Router(config-router)# version {1 | 2}
```

You can override this behavior by configuring a particular interface to behave differently. To control which RIP version an interface sends, use the following commands:

```
Router(config-if)# ip rip send version 1
Router(config-if)# ip rip send version 2
Router(config-if)# ip rip send version 1 2
```

To control how packets received from an interface are processed, use the following commands:

```
Router(config-if)# ip rip receive version 1
Router(config-if)# ip rip receive version 2
Router(config-if)# ip rip receive version 1 2
```

RIP Authentication

To configure RIP authentication, use the following command:

```
Router(config-if)# ip rip authentication key-chain name-of-chain
```

Once the **key-chain** is configured, you should set the authentication mode:

```
Router(config-if)# ip rip authentication mode {text | md5}
```

RIP Route Summarization

Automatic summary addressing always summarizes to the classful address boundary, while the **ip summary-address** router configuration command summarizes addresses on a specified interface. If automatic summary addressing is enabled, automatic summarization is the default behavior for interfaces on the router not associated with dial-in clients, with or without the **ip summary-address rip** interface command present.

Route Filtering and Policy Routing

Distribute Lists

You can filter routing update traffic for any protocol by defining an access list and applying it to a specific routing protocol. You use the **distribute-list** command and link it to an access list to complete the filtering of routing update traffic.

For outbound traffic the appropriate command is as follows:

```
Router(config-router)# distribute-list {access-list-number | name} out
  [interface-name | routing-process | [autonomous-system number]]
```

For inbound traffic the appropriate command is as follows:

```
Router(config-router)# Distribute-list {access-list-number | name} in [type
  number]]
```

Using a distribute list with redistribution helps prevent route feedback. Route feedback occurs when routes originally learned from one routing protocol get redistributed back into that protocol. Route feedback can help to lead to routing loops caused by redistribution.

Route Maps

Route maps are complex access lists that allow conditions to be tested against a packet or route using the match commands. If the conditions match, actions can be taken to modify attributes of the packet or route. These actions are specified by set commands.

Several of the more common applications for route maps are as follows:

- Route filtering during redistribution
- Policy-based routing (PBR)
- Network Address Translation (NAT)
- Implementing Border Gateway Protocol (BGP) policies

To define the route map conditions and set the sequence number of route map lines, use the following command:

```
router(config)# route-map map-tag [permit | deny] [sequence-number]
```

To define the conditions to match, use the following command:

```
router(config-route-map)# match {conditions}
```

To define the actions to be taken, use the following command:

```
router(config-route-map)# set {actions}
```

Policy Routing

PBR allows you to implement policies that selectively cause packets to take different paths; this allows you to vary from the typical destination-based approach of IP. For example, you can easily configure routes to flow based on source address information. You can also mark traffic with different type of service (ToS) configurations. You implement policy-based routing through the use of route maps to implement policy.

To identify a route map to use for PBR on an interface, use the following command:

```
Router(config-if)# ip policy route-map map-tag
```

PBR must be configured before PBR fast switching can be enabled. Fast switching of PBR is disabled by default. To configure fast-switched PBR, use the ip route-cache policy command in interface configuration mode.

Redistribution

While redistribution between certain protocols has unique concerns and characteristics, the following generic steps apply to all routing protocol combinations:

Step 1   Locate the boundary router that requires configuration of redistribution

Step 2   Determine which routing protocol is the core or backbone protocol

Step 3   Determine which routing protocol is the edge or short-term protocol

Step 4   Select a method for injecting the required edge protocol routes into the core

Use the following command to redistribute routes into RIP:

```
Router(config-router)# redistribute protocol [process-id] [match route-type]
   [metric metric-value] [route-map map-tag]
```

Use the following command to redistribute routes into OSPF.

```
Router(config-router)# redistribute protocol [process-id] [metric metric-value]

 [metric-type type-value] [route-map map-tag] [subnets] [tag tag-value]
```

Use the following command to redistribute routes into EIGRP:

```
router(config-router)# redistribute protocol [process-id] [match {internal |
   external 1 | external 2}] [metric metric-value] [route-map map-tag]
```

Use the following command to redistribute routes into IS-IS:

```
router(config-router)# redistribute protocol [process-id] [level level-value]
   [metric metric-value] [metric-type type-value] [route-map map-tag]
```

Route Tagging

Various routing protocols support tag fields. This tag field provides a location where additional information about a route can be stored. This field is commonly used to identify the autonomous system from which a route was obtained when a route is learned from a different autonomous system.

Route tagging allows you to customize routing and maintain flexible policy controls.

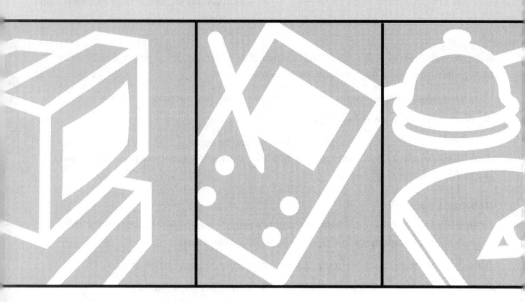

Section 5
Quality of Service

The applications coursing through the veins of your network might need varying levels of priority. Voice over IP (VoIP) traffic typically needs much higher priority than, for example, FTP traffic. Also, different applications might require different amounts of bandwidth. Fortunately, quality of service (QoS) mechanisms allow you to customize the priority and bandwidth given to your various traffic types.

The flash cards in this chapter review the need for QoS and challenge you to distinguish between the use and syntax of multiple QoS tools. Some of the approaches for you to be familiar with include marking with Differentiated Services Code Point (DSCP) values, queuing with weighted fair queuing (WFQ) and low latency queuing (LLQ), queuing on a Catalyst switch with Weighted Round Robin (WRR), performing congestion avoidance with weighted random early detection (WRED), and limiting traffic flows with committed access rate (CAR), CB-Policing, and CB-Shaping.

Question 1

List three problems that might impact latency-sensitive applications in a network without QoS enabled.

Question 2

What byte in an IPv4 packet header is used for IP Precedence or DSCP markings?

Question 3

How many levels of priority can be specified using DSCP?

Question 1 Answer

In the absence of QoS, applications might suffer from one or more of the following:

Delay (latency)—Excessive time required for a packet to traverse the network

Delay Variation (jitter)—The uneven arrival of packets, which in the case of VoIP might be interpreted by the listener as dropped voice packets

Packet Loss—Dropping packets, especially problematic for User Datagram Protocol (UDP) traffic (e.g., VoIP), which does not retransmit dropped packets

Question 2 Answer

The type of service (ToS) byte in an IPv4 packet header can be used for QoS markings at Layer 3. Specifically, the IP Precedence marking uses the 3 left-most bits in the ToS byte, while DSCP uses the 6 left-most bits in that ToS byte.

Question 3 Answer

The DSCP uses the 6 left-most bits in an IPv4 header's ToS byte. These six bits have 64 possible binary combinations. Therefore, DSCP can specify up to 64 levels of priority, in the range 0 through 63.

Question 4

Which of the following per-hop forwarding behaviors (PHBs) have the highest drop preference?

    4 AF11

    5 AF12

    6 AF22

    7 AF43

Question 5

What Layer 2 QoS marking can be used over Ethernet trunks?

Question 6

When performing QoS classification, what Cisco IOS classification feature has the ability to look into Layer 7 information?

Question 4 Answer

Of the PHBs listed, the AF12 value has the highest drop preference. The Assured Forwarding (AF) PHBs are divided into four classes. Lower classes have higher drop preferences. For example, all AF1 PHBs have a higher drop preference than any AF2 PHB. Within a class, you find three PHB values (indicated by the last digit in the PHB), where a 1 indicates a lowest drop preference, 2 indicates a medium drop preference, and 3 indicates the highest drop preference. Therefore, within the AF1 class, AF13 has a higher drop preference than AF12, which has a higher drop preference than AF11.

Question 5 Answer

Class of Service (CoS) markings can be used over IEEE 802.1Q or Inter-Switch Link (ISL) trunks. CoS uses 3 bits in an IEEE 802.1Q tag control byte or 3 bits in an ISL header. With 3 bits at its disposal, CoS values range from 0 through 7. Values 6 and 7 should not be used, because they are reserved for system and network use.

Question 6 Answer

Network-Based Application Recognition (NBAR) can perform "deep packet inspection," which involves looking beyond Layer 4 information. For example, a URL string could be recognized by NBAR, in addition to many stateful protocols that dynamically change their port numbers.

Question 7

What is the default queuing mechanism used on high-speed interfaces?

Question 8

What is the Cisco preferred queuing approach for delay-sensitive traffic, such as voice and/or video?

Question 9

Describe the operation of custom queuing.

Question 7 Answer

First-in, first-out (FIFO) is the default queuing approach used on high-speed interfaces (i.e., interfaces with speeds greater than approximately 2 Mbps). FIFO does not truly perform any QoS manipulations, such as packet reordering. Specifically, FIFO empties packets from a queue based on the order that the packets entered the queue.

Question 8 Answer

Low latency queuing (LLQ) is the Cisco preferred queuing approach for latency-sensitive traffic, because LLQ can put one or more traffic classes into a priority queue. Packets in the priority queue are serviced first, up to a specified bandwidth limit. Therefore, LLQ does not starve out lower priority packets, as priority queuing (PQ) does.

Question 9 Answer

Custom queuing is a legacy queuing approach that services up to sixteen queues in a round-robin fashion, emptying a specified number of bytes from each queue during each round-robin cycle.

Question 10

Describe the operation of IP Real Time Protocol (RTP) priority queuing.

Question 11

What type of queuing is enabled by default on slow speed interfaces (i.e., less than approximately 2 Mbps)?

Question 12

Prior to Cisco IOS Release 12.0(5)T, what formula did WFQ use to calculate a packet's sequence number, which determines when a packet is transmitted in relation to other packets?

Question 10 Answer

IP RTP priority is a legacy queuing approach for voice traffic, which places a range of UDP ports (typically port numbers 16,384 through 32,767) in a priority queue, with all other packets using WFQ.

Question 11 Answer

WFQ is enabled by default on slower speed interfaces, specifically interfaces running at or below an E1 speed. WFQ allocates a queue for each flow, for as many as 256 flows, by default. WFQ uses IP Precedence values to provide a weighting to fair queuing (FQ).

Question 12 Answer

Prior to Cisco IOS Release 12.0(5)T, WFQ used the following formula to calculate a packet's sequence number:

Sequence Number = 4096/(IP Prec. + 1)

In more recent versions of the Cisco IOS, the sequence number is:

Sequence Number = 32768/(IP Prec. + 1)

Question 13

Identify the three steps of MQC (Modular QoS CLI).

Question 14

What is the default class map behavior when multiple match statements are configured under a single class map?

Question 15

What command, issued in policy-map-class configuration mode, allocates at least 384,000 bits per second for traffic classified by the corresponding class-map?

Question 13 Answer

(1) The first step of MQC is to create class maps, with the **class-map** command, which categorizes traffic into categories.

(2) The second step of MQC creates a policy, with the **policy-map** command, which assigns policies to the class maps.

(3) The third step of MQC applies a policy map, typically to an interface, with the **service-policy** command.

Question 14 Answer

When a class map contains more than one match statement, by default, for a packet to be classified by the class map, it must meet the criteria of all of the configured match statements. This default behavior is called match-all. Optionally, a class map can be configured to "match-any," which classifies a packet under a class map if any single match criterion is met.

Question 15 Answer

In policy-map-class configuration mode, the **bandwidth 384** command allocates at least 384,000 bits per second (i.e., 384 kbps) for traffic in the corresponding class map. Note that the units of measure are in kbps, not bps. If traffic identified by the class map does not currently require 384 kbps of bandwidth, the unneeded bandwidth can be used by another application. If, however, the traffic identified by the class map needs more than 384 kbps, class-based weighted fair queuing (CBWFQ) can allow that traffic to use bandwidth assigned to another class map that is not currently needed by that other class map.

Question 16

What match command, issued in class map configuration mode, uses NBAR?

Question 17

What does 128 represent in the following command:

```
Router(config-if)#ip rsvp bandwidth 128 32
```

Question 18

Identify the command that can be used on a router to simulate the receiving and forwarding of RSVP PATH messages.

Question 16 Answer

NBAR can perform "deep packet inspection" to classify traffic all the way up to Layer 7 properties (e.g., a URL string). To tell a class map to match traffic using NBAR, use the **match protocol** command.

Question 17 Answer

In the command Router(config-if)#**ip rsvp bandwidth 128 32**, an interface is limiting the combined total bandwidth of all Resource Reservation Protocol (RSVP) reservations to no more than 128 kbps, while limiting a single reservation to 32 kbps.

Question 18 Answer

The **ip rsvp sender** command can be used to simulate that the router is receiving and forwarding PATH messages. The full syntax for the ip **rsvp sender** command is as follows:

```
ip rsvp sender session-ip-address sender-ip-address {tcp | udp | ip-
protocol} session-dport sender-sport previous-hop-ip-address previous-
hop-interface bandwidth burst-size
```

Question 19

What QoS tool does Cisco use to prevent a queue from ever filling to capacity?

Question 20

Describe the following WRED parameters: minimum threshold, maximum threshold, and mark probability denominator.

Question 21

When configuring WRED, you configure a mark probability denominator (MPD) of 4 for traffic marked with a DSCP value of 46. When the queue depth is at the maximum threshold for DSCP 46 traffic, what is the probability (in percent) that a packet marked with a DSCP value of 46 will be discarded?

Question 19 Answer

Cisco IOS can use weighted random early detection (WRED) to prevent an interface's output queue from ever filling to capacity by discarding traffic more aggressively as the queue begins to fill. Dropping decisions are made based on the traffic's priority markings.

Question 20 Answer

The minimum threshold specifies the number of packets in a queue before the queue considers discarding packets having a particular marking. The probability of discard increases until the queue depth reaches the maximum threshold. After a queue depth exceeds the maximum threshold, all other packets with a particular marking that attempt to enter the queue are discarded. However, the probability of packet discard when the queue depth equals the maximum threshold is 1/(mark probability denominator). For example, if the mark probability denominator is set to 10, then when the queue depth reaches the maximum threshold, the probability of discard for the specified marking is 1/10 (i.e., a 10 percent chance of discard).

Question 21 Answer

The probability of packet discard when the queue depth equals the maximum threshold is 1/(mark probability denominator). Therefore, if the MPD = 4, then the probability of discard is 1/4, which equals 0.25 (i.e., 25 percent).

Question 22

Identify the QoS marking that WRED references if the following command is issued:

```
Router(config-if)#random-detect
```

Question 23

What Weighted Round Robin (WRR) interface configuration mode command instructs a Catalyst switch to place traffic marked with a CoS value of 5 into queue number 4?

Question 24

Both policing and shaping tools can be used to limit bandwidth available to specific traffic. Discuss how policing and shaping differ.

Question 22 Answer

The **dscp-based** or **prec-based** option can be used with the **random-detect** command to specify the QoS markings that WRED should reference when making discard decisions. However, if neither of these parameters is used, WRED defaults to referencing IP Precedence values.

Question 23 Answer

The Switch(config-if)#**wrr-queue cos-map 4 5** command instructs a Catalyst switch to place traffic marked with a Class of Service (CoS) value of 5 into queue number 4. Once traffic with different CoS markings is placed into appropriate queues, the switch can service the queues by giving a different amount of bandwidth to each queue, based on the queue's weight. The weight of a queue can be modified with the Switch(config-if)#**wrr-queue bandwidth** command.

Question 24 Answer

Policing limits traffic rates typically by dropping excess traffic. However, shaping limits traffic rates by delaying excess traffic (i.e., buffering the excess traffic). Also, Policing can be applied either in the inbound or outbound direction on an interface, while shaping can be applied only in the outbound direction.

Question 25

Frame Relay Traffic Shaping (FRTS) is configured with a map class. Where can a Frame Relay map class be applied?

Question 26

What command configures committed access rate (CAR) for an interface?

Question 27

Identify the packets matched by the following rate-limit access list:

```
Router(config)#access-list rate-limit 1 mask 03
```

Question 25 Answer

A Frame Relay map class can be applied to an interface, subinterface, or to a data-link connection identifier (DLCI). A DLCI is a locally significant number that identifies a frame relay virtual circuit. Generic Traffic Shaping, however, can be applied to an interface or a subinterface.

Question 26 Answer

CAR uses the interface configuration mode command **rate-limit** to set a maximum rate for either an interface or for specific traffic, as specified by an access list. The **rate-limit** command also specifies a conform and exceed action for packets.

Question 27 Answer

The rate-limit access list Router(config)#**access-list rate-limit 1 mask 03** matches packets having an IP Precedence value of 0 or 1. Rate-limit access lists numbered in the range 1–99 are for IP Precedence values. Here, a wildcard mask is used to specify multiple IP Precedence values. A binary "1" in the mask indicates a "don't care bit." The wildcard mask is applied against the binary table shown the accompanying Study Sheets section.

The mask is in hexadecimal, and 03 in hex is 11 in binary. Since a "1" is a don't care bit, when applied to the binary table, IP Precedence values that have a 1 in one of the last two bit positions are matched. Referencing the table shows that IP Precedence values 0 and 1 are the only two values that have a 1 in one of the right-most bit positions.

Question 28

What policy-map-class configuration mode command specifies that traffic not exceeding a rate of 256 kbps should be transmitted and traffic that does exceed 256 kbps should be dropped?

Question 29

When performing CB-Shaping, traffic can be shaped to "average" or "peak." What formula defines the peak rate?

Question 30

What command issued from policy-map-class configuration mode configures CB-Shaping to shape traffic to an average rate of 256 kbps?

Question 28 Answer

CB-Policing is an MQC (Modular QoS CLI) approach to rate limiting. In policy-map-class configuration mode, the command **police 256000** can be issued to transmit conforming packets and drop exceeding packets. However, other conform and exceed actions can be specified optionally. Note that the units of measure are bps, not kbps.

Question 29 Answer

When shaping to peak in a CB-Shaping configuration, the peak rate can be calculated with the following formula:

Peak Rate = CIR * (1 + Be/Bc)

Note that when shaping to peak, some traffic might be dropped by the service provider, which might require the dropped packets to be retransmitted.

Question 30 Answer

CB-Shaping can specify that traffic is shaped to an average rate or to a peak rate, which attempts to exceed the CIR. To shape traffic to an average rate of 256 kbps, the following command can be used:

```
Router(config-pmap-c)#shape average 256000
```

Note that the units of measure are in bps, not kbps. Also, notice that shaping does not support conform or exceed actions, as policing does.

Question 31

How many levels of priority can be specified using IP Precedence?

Question 32

RSVP is considered to be in what category of QoS tools?

Question 33

How many queues can be used by priority queuing?

Question 31 Answer

IP Precedence uses the 3 left-most bits in an IPv4 header's ToS (Type of Service) byte. These 3 bits have 8 possible binary combinations. Therefore, IP Precedence can specify up to 8 levels of priority, in the range 0 through 7. However, Cisco recommends that values 6 and 7 never be used because they are reserved for system and network use.

Question 32 Answer

RSVP is considered to be an Integrated Services (IntServ) QoS tool. IntServ uses signaling to make requests for network resources, as opposed to the classification and marking approach used by Differentiated Services (DiffServ) tools.

Question 33 Answer

Priority queuing is a legacy queuing approach with four queues, where higher priority queues must be emptied before forwarding traffic from any lower priority queue.

Question 34

LLQ can specify bandwidth amounts for how many classes of traffic?

Question 35

List two queuing methods configured via MQC.

Question 36

Describe the characteristics of Weighted Round Robin (WRR).

Question 34 Answer

LLQ supports the configuration of bandwidth amounts (either priority or non-priority) for up to 64 classes of traffic. Only 63 of these classes can be created, because one class, the "class-default" class, is created by default.

Question 35 Answer

The Cisco MQC approach to configuring QoS tools has three steps: (1) creating class maps, (2) assigning characteristics to the classified traffic using a policy map, and (3) assigning the policy to an interface with the **service-policy** command. Two queuing methods that are configured using the MQC approach are Class-Based Weighted Fair Queuing (CB-WFQ) and Low Latency Queuing (LLQ).

Question 36 Answer

Some Cisco Catalyst switches support WRR as a queuing strategy. WRR can place traffic into different queues based on the packet's marking. Weights can be assigned to those queues to influence the bandwidth available to those queues.

Question 37

Identify two policing tools available in the Cisco IOS.

Question 38

What range of rate-limit access lists is used for matching MAC addresses?

Question 39

When configuring CB-Shaping, what is a disadvantage of shaping to "peak"?

Question 37 Answer

Current versions of the Cisco IOS support two policing tools, Committed Access Rate (CAR) and Class-Based Policing (CB-Policing). CAR is configured in interface configuration mode, while CB-Policing is configured via MQC.

Question 38 Answer

CAR can reference rate-limit access lists to identify traffic with particular IP Precedence values, MAC addresses, or Multiprotocol Label Switching (MPLS) Experimental Bit values. Following are the number ranges for each type of rate-limit access list:

IP Precedence: 1–99

MAC Address: 100–199

MPLS Experimental Bits: 200–299

Question 39 Answer

CB-Shaping supports shaping to "average" and shaping to "peak." When shaping to "average," traffic is not sent in excess of the Committed Information Rate (CIR). However, shaping to "peak" can exceed the CIR. The downside of shaping to "peak," however, is that it might result in occasional packet loss, requiring retransmission.

Question 40

When configuring CAR, what does the "continue" action indicate?

Question 41

What does the following priority queuing command specify?

```
Router(config)#priority-list 1 protocol ip high tcp www
```

Question 42

List the four queues used by priority queuing (PQ).

Question 40 Answer

When configuring Committed Access Rate (CAR), a "conform" and an "exceed" action are specified for each rate-limit command. One possible action is "continue," which indicates that the packet should be checked against the next rate-limit statement under that particular interface, instead of being immediately transmitted, as specified by the "transmit" action.

Question 41 Answer

The command Router(config)#**priority-list 1 protocol ip high tcp www** says that for priority-list 1, www traffic (i.e., TCP port 80) should be placed in the "high" queue. Note that as long as traffic is in that "high" queue, traffic from lower-priority queues is not serviced.

Question 42 Answer

Priority queuing (PQ) places packets into one of four queues. Higher priority queues must be completely emptied before traffic is forwarded from lower priority queues. The four queues used by PQ (listed from highest to lowest priority) are as follows:

1. High

2. Medium

3. Normal

4. Low

Question 43

In the following custom queuing (CQ) configuration, what percentage of bandwidth is being allocated for Telnet traffic?

```
Router(config)#queue-list 1 protocol ip 1 tcp www
Router(config)#queue-list 1 protocol ip 2 tcp telnet
Router(config)#queue-list 1 default 3
Router(config)#queue-list 1 queue 1 byte-count 1500 limit 512
Router(config)#queue-list 1 queue 2 byte-count 1500 limit 512
Router(config)#queue-list 1 queue 3 byte-count 3000 limit 512
```

Question 44

In the following custom queuing (CQ) command, what does the number 512 indicate?

```
Router(config)#queue-list 1 queue 3 byte-count 3000 limit 512
```

Question 45

Link Fragmentation and Interleaving (LFI) and compression fall under which category of QoS tools?

Question 43 Answer

In the CQ configuration, the total number of bytes serviced during each round-robin cycle is 6000 (i.e., 1500 + 1500 + 3000). Telnet traffic is placed in queue 2, and 1500 bytes are serviced from queue 2 during each round-robin cycle. Therefore, the percentage of bandwidth allocated for Telnet is 1500/6000 = 0.25 = 25 percent.

Question 44 Answer

In the command Router(config)#**queue-list 1 queue 3 byte-count 3000 limit 512**, the **512** is specifying the number of packets that can be stored in queue 3. If additional packets attempt to enter queue 3 after 512 packets are already in that queue, those newly arriving packets are discarded (i.e., "tail dropped").

Question 45 Answer

LFI and compression QoS tools make more efficient use of lower-speed WAN links. Specifically, LFI fragments large packets and interleaves smaller packets in among those fragments. Compression results in fewer bits being sent across a link, which is effectively equal to increased bandwidth. These approaches are commonly referred to as Link Efficiency Tools.

Question 46

What command configures RTP Header Compression (cRTP) on a PPP interface?

Question 47

What does the passive keyword indicate in the following command?

```
Router(config-if)#ip rtp header-compression [passive]
```

Question 48

When configuring Multilink PPP (MLP), an IP address is assigned to what type of interface?

Question 46 Answer

RTP Header Compression can be configured on an HDLC or PPP interface with the following command:

```
Router(config-if)#ip rtp header-compression [passive]
```

Question 47 Answer

When configuring RTP Header Compression, the passive keyword specifies that the interface should send compressed headers only if it has first received compressed headers.

Question 48 Answer

In an MLP configuration, physical interfaces do not have IP addresses. Instead, one or more physical interfaces are assigned to a multilink group, which points to a virtual multilink interface. The IP address is assigned to this multilink interface.

Question 49

What Multilink PPP (MLP) command associates a physical interface with interface multilink 1?

Question 50

What LFI mechanism is used in a Voice over IP over Frame Relay (VoIPovFR) environment?

Question 51

What command would you enter on a router's serial interface, configured for PPP encapsulation, to enable the AutoQoS feature to classify VoIP using NBAR?

Question 49 Answer

The following interface configuration mode command can associate one or more physical interfaces to a virtual multilink interface, which in this example is numbered 1:

```
Router(config-if)#multilink-group 1
```

Question 50 Answer

While MLP is a LFI mechanism useful for Voice over IP over PPP circuits, FRF.12 is the LFI tool of choice for a Voice over IP over Frame Relay networks.

Question 51 Answer

The syntax for configuring AutoQoS on a router interface is as follows:

```
auto qos voip [trust] [fr-atm]
```

The **trust** option tells AutoQoS to classify voice packets using based on DSCP values instead of NBAR. The fr-atm option enables the AutoQoS feature for Frame Relay-to-ATM links and is issued from DLCI configuration mode. Therefore, in this instance the interface configuration mode command that should be entered is as follows:

```
auto qos voip
```

Question 52

List at least two prerequisites for configuring AutoQoS on a router interface.

Question 53

What Catalyst 6500 Hybrid Mode command enables AutoQoS for a specific port?

Question 54

When configuring AutoQoS, under what circumstance would CDP version 2 be required on a Catalyst 6500 port?

Question 52 Answer

Following are prerequisites for configuring AutoQoS on a router interface:

CEF must be enabled.

A QoS policy must not be currently attached to the interface.

The correct bandwidth should be configured on the interface.

An IP address must be configured on an interface if its speed is less than or equal to 768 kbps.

Question 53 Answer

The command issued on a Catalyst 6500 switch operating in Hybrid Mode to enable AutoQoS for a specific port is as follows:

```
Switch#set port qos <mod/port> autoqos trust [cos | dscp]
```

Question 54 Answer

When configuring AutoQoS on a Catalyst 6500, Cisco Discovery Protocol (CDP) version 2 must be enabled for the port for the port to detect that it is connected to a Cisco IP phone.

Question 55

What type of congestion management feature does AutoQoS configure on a Cisco IOS-based Catalyst switch?

Question 55 Answer

On a router platform, the AutoQoS feature configures LLQ as the congestion management feature. However, on a Cisco IOS-based Catalyst platform, AutoQoS configures the Weighted Round Robin (WRR) congestion management mechanism.

Quality of Service (QoS) Quick Reference Sheets

Introduction

Voice, video, and data travel side-by-side over today's converged networks. Some of these traffic types (e.g., Voice over IP) need better treatment (i.e., higher priority) than other types of traffic (e.g., FTP). Fortunately, Cisco offers a suite of QoS tools for providing special treatment for special traffic.

In the absence of QoS, traffic might suffer from one or more of the following symptoms:

- **Delay (latency)**—Excessive time required for a packet to traverse the network

- **Delay Variation (jitter)**—The uneven arrival of packets, which in the case of Voice over IP can be interpreted by the listener as dropped voice packets

- **Packet Loss**—Dropping packets, especially problematic for User Datagram Protocol (UDP) traffic (e.g., Voice over IP), which does not retransmit dropped packets

You have two categories of QoS tools, Integrated Services (IntServ) and Differentiated Services (DiffServ). Integrated Services provides QoS by guaranteeing treatment to a particular traffic flow. A commonly used IntServ tool is RSVP (Resource Reservation Protocol).

As the name suggests, Differentiated Services differentiates (i.e., classifies) between different types of traffic and provides different levels of service based on those distinctions. Instead of forcing every network device to classify traffic, DiffServ can mark packets with a particular priority marking that can be referenced by other network devices.

ToS and IP Precedence

Packet marking can be accomplished by altering bits in an IPv4 header's type of service (ToS) byte. Two common markings that use the ToS byte are IP Precedence and DSCP.

IP Precedence is an older approach than DSCP and uses the three left-most bits in the ToS byte. With three bits to use, IP Precedence values can range from 0–7. Cisco recommends that IP Precedence values 6 and 7 never be used, because they are reserved for network use.

Cisco IOS accepts either an IP Precedence number or its equivalent name, as shown in the following table:

IP Precedence Value	Name
0	routine
1	priority
2	immediate
3	flash
4	flash-override
5	critical
6	internet
7	network

DSCP

DSCP uses the 6 left-most bits in an IPv4 header's ToS (Type of Service) byte. With six bits at its disposal, DSCP has up to 64 DSCP values (0–63) assigned to various classes of traffic. With so many values to select from, to maintain relative levels of priority among routers, the IETF recommends selected DSCP values for use. These values, called Per-Hop Behaviors (PHBs), determine how packets are treated at each hop along the path from the source to the destination.

Layer 3 packet markings

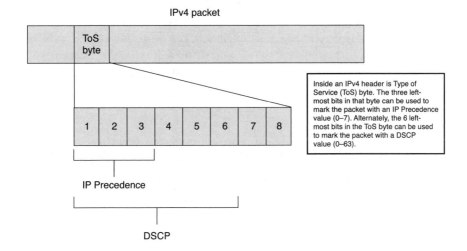

IPv4 packet

When configuring a router to mark or recognize a DSCP value, the number itself can be used. However, a more convenient method is to use the name of specific DSCP values. Assured Forwarding (AF) PHBs are typically used to identify different levels of priority for data applications. For latency-sensitive applications, however, the Expedited Forwarded (EF) PHB can be used. A listing of commonly used PHB names and their corresponding DSCP values is shown in the following table:

class = Prec = Top 3 bits

drop pref high

PHBs	Low Drop Preference	Medium Drop Preference	High Drop Preference
Class 1	AF11 (10)	AF12 (12)	AF13 (14)
Class 2	AF21 (18)	AF22 (20)	AF23 (22)
Class 3	AF31 (26)	AF32 (28)	AF33 (30)
Class 4	AF41 (34)	AF42 (36)	AF43 (38)
	EF (46)		

low

NB drop pref decreases w 1st digit but increases w. 2nd digit. of AF

Notice that the Assured Forwarding PHBs are grouped into four classes. Examining these DSCP values in binary reveals the three left-most bits of all the Class 1 AF PHBs are 001 (i.e., a decimal value of 1); the three left-most bits of all the Class 2 AF PHBs are 010 (i.e., a decimal value of 2); the three left-most bits of all the Class 3 AF PHBs are 011 (i.e., a decimal value of 3); and the three left-most bits of all the Class 4 AF PHBs are 100 (i.e., a decimal value of 4). Since IP Precedence examines these three left-most bits, all Class 1 DSCP values would be interpreted by an IP Precedence-aware router as an IP Precedence value of 1. The same applies to the Class 2, 3, and 4 PHB values.

In a similar fashion, the three left-most bits of the EF PHB are 101 (i.e., a decimal value of 5). Therefore, the EF PHB would be interpreted by an IP Precedence–aware router as an IP Precedence of 5, the highest IP Precedence value that we should assign.

CoS

While an IP header's ToS byte can be used for Layer 3 markings, a class of service (CoS) marking can be used for Layer 2 markings. Specifically, CoS markings are applied to frames crossing an IEEE 802.1Q or an Inter-Switch Link (ISL) trunk. Regardless of the trunk type, CoS markings use three bits. So, like IP Precedence, CoS values range from 0–7, and again, values 6 and 7 are reserved.

NBAR

Cisco offers multiple approaches to identify packets to mark. For example, packets could be classified and marked if they match a particular access list or if they came into a router on a particular interface. However, one of the most powerful Cisco IOS tools for performing packet classification is Network-Based Application Recognition (NBAR). NBAR has the ability to look beyond Layer 4 information, all the way up to the Application Layer, where NBAR can recognize such packet attributes as character strings in a URL.

Queuing Techniques

Just marking a packet does not change its operation, unless QoS tools are enabled that can reference that marking. Fortunately, multiple QoS tools can make forwarding or dropping decisions based on these markings. Queuing techniques are often referred to as congestion management tools.

Queuing tools decide how packets are emptied from an interface's output queue. Several queuing tools are available in the IOS:

- **First-In, First-Out (FIFO)**—The default queuing mechanism on high-speed interfaces (i.e., greater than 2.048 Mbps), which does not reorder packets

- **Weighted Fair Queuing (WFQ)**—The default queuing mechanism on low-speed interfaces, which makes forwarding decisions based on a packet's size and priority marking

- **Low Latency Queuing (LLQ)**—The preferred queuing method for voice and video traffic, where traffic can be classified in up to 64 different classes, with different amounts of bandwidth given to each class, and includes the ability to give priority treatment to one or more classes

- **Priority Queuing**—A legacy queuing approach with four queues, where higher priority queues must be emptied before forwarding traffic from any lower priority queues

- **Custom Queuing**—A legacy queuing approach that services up to 16 queues in a round-robin fashion, emptying a specified number of bytes from each queue during each round-robin cycle

- **Class-Based Weighted Fair Queuing (CBWFQ)**—Very similar to LLQ, with the exception of having no priority queuing mechanism

- **IP RTP Priority**—A legacy queuing approach for voice traffic, which placed a range of User Datagram Protocol (UDP) ports in a priority queue, with all other packets treated with WFQ

Weighted fair queuing (WFQ) is enabled by default on slow speed interfaces (i.e., 2.048 Mbps and slower). WFQ allocates a queue for each flow, for as many as 256 flows by default. WFQ uses IP Precedence values to provide a weighting to fair queuing (FQ). When emptying the queues, FQ, sometimes called "flow-based queuing," does "byte-by-byte" scheduling. Specifically, FQ looks one byte deep into each queue to determine if an entire packet can be sent. FQ then looks another byte deep into the queue to determine if an entire packet can be sent. As a result, smaller traffic flows and smaller packet sizes have priority over bandwidth hungry flows with large packets.

In the following example, three flows simultaneously arrive at a queue. Flow A has three packets, which are 128 bytes each. Flow B has a single 96-byte packet. Flow C has a single 70-byte packet. After 70 byte-by-byte rounds, FQ can transmit the packet from flow C. After an additional 26 rounds, FQ can transmit the packet from flow B. After an additional 32 rounds, FQ can transmit the first packet from flow A. Another 128 rounds are required to send the second packet from flow A. Finally, after a grand total of 384 rounds, the third packet from flow A is transmitted.

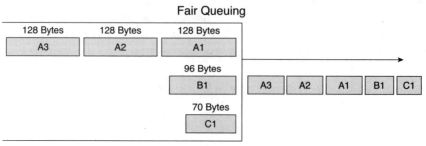

Output Queue

With WFQ, a packet's IP Precedence influences the order in which it is emptied from a queue. Consider the previous scenario with the addition of IP Precedence markings. In this scenario, flow A's packets are marked with an IP Precedence of 5, while flow B and flow C have default IP Precedence markings of 0. The order of packet servicing with WFQ is based on "sequence numbers," where packets with the lowest sequence numbers are emptied first.

The sequence number is the "weight" of the packet multiplied by the number of byte-by-byte rounds that must be completed to service the packet (i.e., just as in the FQ example). The Cisco IOS calculates a packet's weight differently depending on the IOS version. Prior to Cisco IOS Release 12.0(5)T, the formula for weight was WEIGHT = 4096/(IP Prec. + 1). In more recent versions of the Cisco IOS, the formula for weight is WEIGHT = 32768/(IP Prec. + 1). Using the pre-Cisco IOS Release 12.0(5)T formula, the sequence numbers are as follows:

A1 = 4096 / (5 + 1) * 128 = 87,381

A2 = 4096 / (5 + 1) * 128 + 87381 = 174,762

A3 = 4096 / (5 + 1) * 128 + 174762 = 262,144

B1 = 4096 / (0 + 1) * 96 = 393,216

C1 = 4096 / (0 + 1) * 70 = 286,720

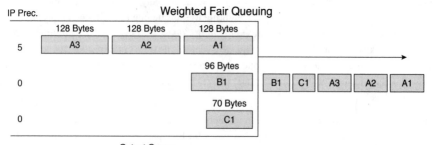

Output Queue

Sequence Number* = 4096/(IP Prec. + 1)

* In IOS 12.0(5)T and later, the Sequence Number = 32768/(IP Prec. + 1).

Therefore, after the weighting is applied, WFQ empties packets from the queue in the following order: A1 – A2 – A3 – C1 – B1. With only FQ, packets are emptied from the queue in the following order: C1 – B1 – A1 – A2 – A3.

Custom queuing (CQ) enhances some of the characteristics of WFQ by allowing the administrator to specify which traffic goes into a particular queue. Also, a "weight" can be assigned to each of the queues, which specifies how many bytes are emptied from a queue during each round-robin servicing of the queues. Consider the following custom queuing example:

```
Router(config)#queue-list 1 protocol ip 1 tcp www
Router(config)#queue-list 1 protocol ip 2 tcp telnet
Router(config)#queue-list 1 default 3
Router(config)#queue-list 1 queue 1 byte-count 1500 limit 512
Router(config)#queue-list 1 queue 2 byte-count 1500 limit 512
Router(config)#queue-list 1 queue 3 byte-count 3000 limit 512
!
Router(config)#interface serial 0/1
Router(config-if)#bandwidth 128
Router(config-if)#custom-queue-list 1
```

In the preceding example, a queue-list (numbered 1) is defined. The queue-list specifies that World Wide Web traffic goes in queue 1. Telnet traffic goes in queue 2, and other traffic (i.e., default traffic) goes in queue 3. Custom queuing (CQ) services these queues in a round-robin fashion. As CQ empties the queues, the number of bytes emptied from each queue is influenced with the **byte count** option seen in the example. The number packets that can be placed in a particular queue can also be specified with the **limit** option. In the preceding example, each queue can accommodate 512 packets. Finally, the queue-list is applied to interface Serial 0/1.

In the preceding example, 1,500 bytes are emptied from queue 1 and from queue 2 during each round-robin cycle, while 3,000 bytes are emptied from queue 3 during each round-robin cycle. Therefore, a bandwidth percentage for each traffic type can be calculated as follows:

> Total Number of Bytes Serviced During Each Round-Robin Cycle = 1500 + 1500 + 3000 = 6000
>
> Percentage of Bandwidth for World Wide Web Traffic = 1500/6000 = .25 = 25 Percent
>
> Percentage of Bandwidth for Telnet Traffic = 1500/6000 = .25 = 25 Percent
>
> Percentage of Bandwidth for Default Traffic = 3000/6000 = .5 = 50 Percent

CQ does, however, have a "deficit" issue. Specifically, when CQ is emptying bytes from a queue, it cannot send a partial packet. Consider a situation where two packets are in queue 1, a 1,499-byte packet and a 1,500-byte packet. Queue 1 is configured to forward 1,500 bytes per round. After the 1,499 byte packet is transmitted, the 1,500-byte level has not yet been reached. CQ, therefore, sends the following packet. Since CQ cannot send a partial packet, it sends the entire 1,500-byte packet. As a result, even though queue 1 was configured to send only 1,500 bytes per round, in this example, 2,999 bytes were forwarded.

On the Cisco 12000 Series of routers, this deficit issue is overcome with MDRR (Modified Deficit Round Robin). MDRR keeps track of the extra bytes sent, and adjusts how many bytes can be sent in subsequent rounds. MDRR can operate in either of two modes:

- **Strict priority**—Defines a priority queue that must be completely empty before any other traffic is sent.

- **Alternate priority**—Is a "low latency queue," which alternates with each of the other queues, so that traffic is not "starved out." For example, consider queues 1, 2, and 3, where queue 1 is a low latency queue. With alternate priority mode, the queues would be serviced as follows: 1, 2, 1, 3, 1.

Also, with DRR queuing, the number of bytes transmitted in one round is defined as MTU + (Weight – 1) * 512. This number of bytes is transmitted from a queue, or until the queue is empty. If more than this number of bytes is sent, to finish servicing a packet that had already started to be serviced, the DRR remembers this deficit, and in the next round, the deficit is subtracted from the number of bytes to service from the queue.

Priority queuing (PQ) can give "strict" priority to latency-sensitive application (e.g., e-commerce applications). PQ gives priority to specific packets by placing those packets in a "high" priority queue. Other packets are placed in a "medium," "normal," or "low" queue. However, if any packets are in the high queue, none of the packets in lower priority queues are sent. Similarly, when packets are in the "medium" queue, no packets are sent from the "normal" or "low" queues. While this approach does accomplish the goal of giving priority to specific traffic, it can lead to protocol starvation. Consider the following PQ example:

```
Router(config)#priority-list 1 protocol ip high tcp www
Router(config)#priority-list 1 protocol ip medium tcp telnet
Router(config)#priority-list 1 default low
!
Router(config)#interface serial 0/1
Router(config-if)#priority-group 1
```

In the preceding example, a priority-list (numbered 1) is created. The priority-list specifies that World Wide Web traffic goes in the "high" queue. Telnet traffic goes in the "medium" queue, while all other traffic (i.e., default traffic) goes in the "low" queue.

The priority-list is then applied to interface Serial 0/1. The potential for protocol starvation exists, because if at any time you have World Wide Web packets in the "high" queue, none of the packets from lower priority queues are forwarded, until all of the World Wide Web packets have been forwarded.

IP Real Time Protocol (RTP) priority combines some of the best aspects of PQ and WFQ. Specifically, IP RTP priority allows a range of UDP ports to be placed in a priority queue, while all other packets are treated with WFQ. Therefore, voice over IP packets, which use UDP ports, can be assigned to the priority queue. Fortunately, to prevent protocols starvation, a bandwidth limit is set for the priority queue. IP RTP priority is configured using the following interface configuration mode command:

```
Router(config-if)#ip rtp priority starting-udp-port port-number-range bandwidth
```

Note that the **port-number-range** is not the last port number in the range. Rather, it is the number of ports in the range. For example, the following command specifies that 64 kbps of bandwidth should be made available for packets using UDP ports in the range 16384–32767:

```
Router(config-if)#ip rtp priority 16384 16383 64
```

Notice that the sum of the **starting-udp-port** and the **port-number-range** equals the last UDP port number in the range (i.e., 16384 + 16383 = 32767). The main drawback of IP RTP priority is its inability to place TCP ports in the priority queue. As an example, H.323 call setup uses TCP ports. These call setup packets, however, cannot be placed in a priority queue, using IP RTP priority.

Fancy Queuing

With modern versions of the Cisco IOS, Cisco recommends CBWFQ or LLQ approaches to queuing. Both methods are configured using MQC, the Modular QoS (quality of service) CLI (command-line interface).

The first step of MQC is to create class maps, which categorize traffic types. The following command enters class-map configuration mode:

```
Router(config)#class-map [match-any | match-all] class-name
```

Once in class-map configuration mode, multiple match statements can be used to match traffic, and all traffic meeting the criteria specified by the **match** command is categorized under the class map. If multiple match statements are specified, by default, all match statements must be met before a packet is classified by the class map. However, by using the **match-any** option, if any individual match condition is met, then the packet is classified by the class map.

After the class maps are defined, the first step of MQC is complete. The second step is to create a policy map to assign characteristics (e.g., marking) to the classified traffic.

To enter policy map configuration mode, issue the command:

```
Router(config)#policy-map policy-name
```

From policy map configuration mode, enter policy-map-class configuration mode with this command:

```
Router(config-pmap)#class class-name
```

From policy-map-class configuration mode, QoS policies can be assigned to traffic classified by the class map. Finally, in the third step, the policy map is applied to an interface, Frame Relay map class, or Asynchronous Transfer Mode (ATM) virtual circuit with this command:

```
Router(config-if)#service-policy {input | output} policy-map-name
```

Here is an LLQ example that illustrates the MQC approach:

```
Router(config)#class-map SURFING
Router(config-cmap)#match protocol http
Router(config-cmap)#exit
Router(config)#class-map VOICE
Router(config-cmap)#match protocol rtp
Router(config-cmap)#exit
Router(config)#policy-map CCIESTUDY
Router(config-pmap)#class SURFING
Router(config-pmap-c)#bandwidth 128
Router(config-pmap-c)#exit
Router(config-pmap)#class-map VOICE
Router(config-pmap-c)#priority 256
Router(config-pmap-c)#exit
Router(config-pmap)#exit
Router(config)#interface serial 0/1
Router(config-if)#service-policy output CCIESTUDY
```

In the preceding example, NBAR is being used to recognize HTTP traffic, and that traffic is placed in the SURFING class. Note that NBAR is invoked with the Router(config-cmap)# **match protocol** command. Voice packets are placed in the VOICE class. The CCIESTUDY policy map gives 128 kbps of bandwidth to the HTTP traffic, while giving 256 kbps of priority bandwidth to voice traffic. The policy map is then applied outbound to interface Serial 0/1.

Integrated Services

The IntServ model uses signaling to allow an application to reserve bandwidth for the duration of the application. RSVP is the primary QoS signaling protocol. One of the main characteristics of signaling to consider is that signaling is performed end-to-end. Specifically, each router along the path from the source to the destination must agree to the reservation request.

In the following RSVP example, the interface is limiting the combined total of all RSVP reservations to no more than 128 kbps, while limiting a single reservation to 32 kbps:

```
Router(config-if)#ip rsvp bandwidth 128 32
```

When RSVP sets up a reservation, it uses PATH messages downstream from the requestor. If all RSVP routers are willing to establish the reservation, then RESV messages are sent back towards the requestor. The **ip rsvp sender** command can be used to simulate that the router is receiving and forwarding PATH messages. The full syntax for the **ip rsvp sender** command is as follows:

```
ip rsvp sender session-ip-address sender-ip-address {tcp | udp | ip-protocol}
  session-dport sender-sport previous-hop-ip-address previous-hop-interface
  bandwidth burst-size
```

Weighted RED

The purpose of weighted random early detect (WRED) is to prevent an interface's output queue from filling to capacity, because if a queue is completely full, all newly arriving packets are discarded. Some of those packets might be high priority, and some might be low priority.

However, if the queue is full, no room exists for any packet. WRED is referred to as a congestion avoidance QoS tool.

With a congestion avoidance tool, drop thresholds are defined for various markings (e.g., DSCP markings). Therefore, as a queue begins to fill, lower priority packets are dropped more aggressively than higher priority packets, thus preventing the queue from ever filling to capacity. The Cisco congestion avoidance tool of choice is WRED.

WRED can be configured in interface configuration mode. However, an MQC approach is also supported. Three parameters that can be configured for each IP Precedence value or DSCP value include the minimum threshold, maximum threshold, and mark probability denominator. The minimum threshold specifies the number of packets in a queue before the queue considers discarding packets having a particular marking. The probability of discard increases until the queue depth reaches the maximum threshold. After a queue depth exceeds the maximum threshold, all other packets with a particular marking that attempt to enter the queue are discarded. However, the probability of packet discard when the queue depth equals the maximum threshold is 1 / (mark probability denominator). For example, if the mark probability denominator were set to 10, then when the queue depth reached the maximum threshold, the probability of discard for the specified marking would be 1 / 10 (i.e., a 10 percent chance of discard).

Weighted Random Early Detection (WRED)

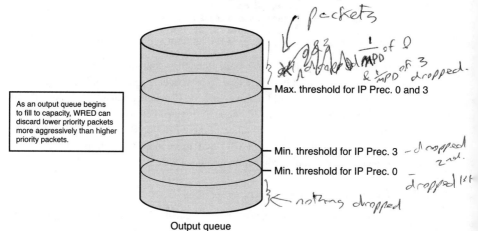

As an output queue begins to fill to capacity, WRED can discard lower priority packets more aggressively than higher priority packets.

Max. threshold for IP Prec. 0 and 3

Min. threshold for IP Prec. 3

Min. threshold for IP Prec. 0

Output queue

When configuring WRED, the Cisco IOS automatically assigns default values to these parameters. However, these parameters can be altered, and the marking WRED pays attention to (i.e., IP Precedence or DSCP) can be specified. Following is the syntax to enable WRED in interface configuration mode:

```
Router(config-if)#random-detect [dscp-based ¦ prec-based]
```

If neither **dscp-based** nor **prec-based** is specified, WRED defaults to **prec-based**. Following is the syntax to specify WRED parameters for both IP Precedence values and DSCP values:

```
Router(config-if)#random-detect precedence precedence_value minimum-threshold
 maximum-threshold mark-probability-denominator
```

```
Router(config-if)#random-detect dscp dscp_value minimum-threshold maximum-
 threshold mark-probability-denominator
```

To specify WRED parameters for a specific class of traffic, using the MQC approach, the exact commands shown preceding can be entered in policy-map-class configuration mode.

To reinforce this syntax, consider the example that follows, where the goal is to configure WRED on interface Ethernet 0/0. After the output queue depth reaches 25 packets, the possibility is introduced that a DSCP value of AF13 be discarded. Packets marked with a DSCP value of AF12 should not be discarded until the queue depth reaches 30 packets, and finally, packets marked with a DSCP value of AF11 should not have any chance of discard until the queue depth reaches 35 packets. If the queue depth exceeds 100 packets, there should be a 100 25 percent chance of discard for these three DSCP values. However, when the queue depth is exactly 100 packets, the percent chance of discard for these various packet types should be 25 percent.

```
Router(config)#interface ethernet 0/0
Router(config-if)#random-detect dscp-based
Router(config-if)#random-detect dscp af13 25 100 4    — in packets.
Router(config-if)#random-detect dscp af12 30 100 4    — min thresh, max, mpd
Router(config-if)#random-detect dscp af11 35 100 4
```

or: Router(config pmap-c)#

Examine the solution, and notice that the mark probability denominator is 4. This value was chosen to meet the requirement that there be a 25 percent change of discard when the queue depth equals the maximum threshold (i.e., 1 / 4 = .25). Also, notice that a DSCP value of AF13 is dropped before a DSCP value of AF12, which is dropped before a DSCP value of AF11. This approach is consistent with the definition of these Per-Hop Behaviors (PHBs), because the last digit in the Assured Forwarding (AF) DSCP name indicates its drop preference. For example, a value of AF13 would drop before a value of AF12.

WRR/Queue Scheduling

Some Cisco Catalyst switches also support their own queuing method, called Weighted Round Robin (WRR). For example, a Catalyst 2950 switch has four queues, and WRR can be configured to place frames with specific CoS markings into certain queues (e.g., CoS values 0 and 1 are placed in Queue 1).

Weights can be assigned to the queues, influencing how much bandwidth the various markings receive. The queues are then serviced in a round robin fashion. On some platforms, one of the switch's queues can be designated as an "expedite" queue, which gives priority treatment to frames in that queue. Specifically, the expedite queue must be empty before any additional queues are serviced. This behavior can lead to protocol starvation.

Following is an example of a WRR configuration:

```
Switch(config)#interface gig 0/5
Switch(config-if)#wrr-queue bandwidth 1 2 3 4
Switch(config-if)#wrr-queue cos-map 4 5
```

In the preceding example, the **wrr-queue** command is assigning the weights 1, 2, 3, and 4 to the switch's four queues. The first queue, with a weight of 1, for example, gets only one-third the bandwidth given to the third queue, which has a weight of 3. The **wrr-queue cos-map** command is instructing frames marked with a CoS of 5 to enter the fourth queue.

Shaping Versus Policing/CAR

While some of the congestion management techniques can guarantee bandwidth amounts, you might want to limit bandwidth usage in some situations. For example, you might need to prevent oversubscription of a link. Two categories of traffic conditioning exist:

- **Policing**—Limits traffic rates, with excess traffic being dropped
- **Shaping**—Limits traffic rates, with excess traffic being delayed (i.e., buffered)

As seen in the preceding, shaping buffers excess traffic, while policing drops excess traffic. These characteristics suggest that policing is more appropriate on high-speed interfaces, while shaping is more appropriate on low-speed interfaces.

For policing and shaping tools to limit bandwidth, they don't transmit all of the time. Specifically, they send a certain number of bits or bytes at line rate, and then they stop sending until a specific timing interval (e.g., 1/8th of a second) is reached. Once the timing interval is reached, the interface again sends a specific amount of traffic at line rate; it stops; and it waits for the next timing interval. This process repeats over and over, allowing an interface to send an average bandwidth that might be below the physical speed of the interface.

Both policing and shaping configurations can specify a committed information rate (CIR), committed burst (Bc), and excess burst (Be).

The CIR is the average number of bits sent during one second. The Bc indicates how many bits or bytes can be sent at line rate during a timing interval. The Be allows more than Bc bits or bytes to be sent during a timing interval if some bits or bytes were unused during a previous timing interval.

While policing and shaping can be configured using the MQC method previously described, legacy methods include committed access rate (CAR) for policing, Generic Traffic Shaping (GTS) for shaping, and Frame Relay Traffic Shaping (FRTS) for shaping. GTS can be applied to an interface or a subinterface, while FRTS can be applied to an interface, subinterface, or a Frame Relay DLCI. Other queuing methods, such as PQ, CQ, or WFQ, can be applied to traffic after GTS shaped it. However, GTS uses WFQ in its shaping queue.

CAR is configured in interface configuration mode with the following command:

```
Router(config-if)#rate-limit {input | output} cir bc be conform-action action
  exceed action action
```

The **conform-action** specifies how the router treats the packet if it conforms to the CIR, and the **exceed action** specifies how the router treats the packet if it exceeds the CIR. Examples of these actions include the following:

- **transmit**—Forwards the packet
- **continue**—Checks the next rate-limit statement
- **drop**—Discards the packet

In the following CAR configuration, an interface is limiting incoming traffic to 128 kbps. Packets conforming to that rate limit are transmitted, and packets exceeding that rate limit are dropped.

```
Router(config-if)#rate-limit input 128000 1500 500 conform-action transmit
  exceed-action drop
```

CAR's **rate-limit** command can also apply to specific traffic through the use of an access list.

```
Router(config-if)#rate-limit {input | output} [access-group [rate-limit]
  access_list_number cir bc be conform-action action exceed-action action
```

Consider the following access list–based CAR example:

Committed Access Rate (CAR)

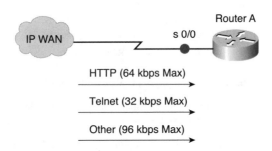

```
RouterA(config)#access-list 101 permit tcp any any eq www
RouterA(config)#access-list 102 permit tcp any any eq 23
RouterA(config)#interface serial 0/0
RouterA(config-if)#rate-limit input access-group 101 64000 1500 1500 conform-
  action transmit exceed-action drop
RouterA(config-if)#rate-limit input access-group 102 32000 1500 1500 conform-
  action transmit exceed-action drop
RouterA(config-if)#rate-limit input 96000 1500 1500 conform-action transmit
  exceed-action drop
```

The goal of the preceding example is to limit incoming web traffic to 64 kbps, Telnet traffic to 32 kbps, and all other traffic to 96 kbps on interface Serial 0/0. If any of these traffic categories exceed the defined bandwidth limits, the excess packets should be dropped, and all traffic conforming to the bandwidth limits should be transmitted.

CAR is not limited to just standard and extended IP access lists. Rate-limit access lists are also supported, and these access lists can match MAC addresses, MPLS experimental bits, and IP Precedence values. The numbering for these rate-limit access lists is as follows:

IP Precedence—1–99

MAC Address—100–199

Multiprotocol Label Switching (MPLS) Exp Bits—200–299

Use the following command to configure a rate-limit access list:

access-list rate-limit *acl* {*precedence* | *mac-address* | *exp-bit_value* | **mask** *mask*}

The following example limits traffic sourced from MAC address 00a0.1234.5678 to 1 Mbps:

```
Router(config-if)#rate-limit input access-group rate-limit 101 1000000 2048 2048
  conform-action transmit exceed-action drop
Router(config-if)#exit
Router(config)#access-list rate-limit 101 00a0.1234.5678
```

A wildcard mask can also be used to specify multiple IP Precedence or MPLS experimental bit values. As with traditional IP access list wildcard masks, a binary "1" in the mask indicates a "don't care bit." The wildcard mask is applied against the following binary table:

0—00000001

1—00000010

2—00000100

3—00001000

4—00010000

5—00100000

6—01000000

7—10000000

Therefore, the command **access-list rate-limit 1 mask 03** would match packets with an IP Precedence value of 0 or 1. The mask is in hexadecimal, and 03 in hex is 11 in binary. Since a "1" is a don't care bit, when applied to the previous table, IP Precedence values that have a 1 in one of the last two bit positions are matched. Referencing the table shows that IP Precedence values 0 and 1 are the only two values that have a 1 in one of the right-most bit positions.

A more modern approach to policing is Class-Based Policing (CB-Policing), which uses the previously described MQC process. The goal of the following CB-Policing example is to limit outgoing web traffic to 100 kbps and Telnet traffic to 50 kbps on interface Ethernet 0/0.

CB-Policing

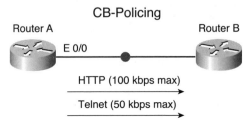

```
RouterA(config)#class-map WEB
RouterA(config-cmap)#match protocol http
RouterA(config-cmap)#exit
RouterA(config)#class-map TELNET
RouterA(config-cmap)#match protocol telnet
RouterA(config-cmap)#exit
RouterA(config)#policy-map POLICING_EXAMPLE
RouterA(config-pmap)#class WEB
RouterA(config-pmap-c)#police 100000
RouterA(config-pmap-c)#exit
RouterA(config-pmap)#class-map TELNET
RouterA(config-pmap-c)#police 50000
RouterA(config-pmap-c)#exit
RouterA(config-pmap-c)#exit
RouterA(config-pmap)#exit
RouterA(config)#interface ethernet 0/0
RouterA(config-if)#service-policy output POLICING_EXAMPLE
```

Shaping can also be configured using this MQC approach. When configuring CB-Shaping, traffic can either be shaped to "average" or shaped to "peak." If **shape average** is specified, traffic is sent at the CIR, with bursting of Be bits per timing interval allowed. If **shape peak** is specified, the router attempts to forward traffic at the peak rate: Peak Rate = CIR * (1 + Be/Bc). The shaping to peak method can result in occasional packet loss, requiring retransmission.

In the following CB-Shaping example, CBWFQ is combined with CB-Shaping to specify that HTTP traffic can have at least 128 kbps but no more than 256 kbps, as the packets exit the Serial 0/0 interface. Note that the units of measure for the CIR are in bps.

CB-Shaping and CB-WFQ

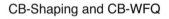

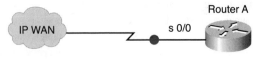

```
RouterA(config)#class-map HTTP
RouterA(config-cmap)#match protocol http
RouterA(config-cmap)#exit
RouterA(config)#policy-map WEB
RouterA(config-pmap)#class HTTP
RouterA(config-pmap-c)#shape average 256000
RouterA(config-pmap-c)#bandwidth 128
RouterA(config-pmap-c)#exit
RouterA(config-pmap)#exit
RouterA(config)#interface serial 0/0
RouterA(config-if)#service-policy output WEB
```

Link Efficiency Tools

As a final category of QoS tools, consider how to make the most of the often limited bandwidth on wide-area network (WAN) links. Data could be compressed before it is sent, or large payloads could be fragmented, so that smaller payloads could be interleaved in among those fragments to prevent excessive serialization delay (the time it takes for packets to exit an interface). This approach is referred to as Link Fragmentation and Interleaving (LFI). The category of tools under which compression and LFI fall is called, "Link Efficiency Tools." First, consider header compression.

One way to preserve bandwidth on the WAN is to compress the TCP and/or UDP headers. However, this "compression" does not actually run any sort of compression algorithm. Rather, header compression leverages the fact that most of the information in a packet's header does not change during the session. For example, the source and destination IP addresses usually remain the same during the session. Likewise, the source and destination TCP/UDP port numbers do not typically vary during the session. Therefore, information that does not change during the session is cached in the routers at each end of a link. A much slimmed down header containing things such as the Session Context ID (CID), which identifies the particular flow that the packet is associated with, and perhaps a checksum is sent as a compressed header. The routers at each end of the link combine the compressed header with the cached header to generate a standard header, which is applied to a packet before sending the packet to the destination.

Following is the syntax to configure TCP header compression in interface configuration mode for both PPP or High-Level Data Link Control (HDLC) links and Frame Relay circuits:

Router(config-if)#**ip tcp header-compression [passive]**—Enables TCP header compression on a PPP or HDLC interface

Router(config-if)#**frame-relay ip tcp header-compression [passive]**—Enables TCP header compression on a Frame Relay interface

Voice is carried by the Real Time Protocol (RTP), which is encapsulated inside UDP. When combined, the IP, UDP, and RTP headers on voice packets total approximately 40 bytes in size. However, after enabling RTP Header Compression (cRTP), the header size is reduced to approximately 2–4 bytes, thus permitting more voice calls on a WAN link. Following is the syntax to configure RTP header compression in interface configuration mode for PPP, HDLC, or Frame Relay circuits.

Router(config-if)#**ip rtp header-compression [passive]**—Enables RTP header compression on a PPP or HDLC interface

Router(config-if)#**frame-relay ip rtp header-compression [passive]**—Enables RTP header compression on a Frame Relay interface

Notice the optional **passive** keyword in the preceding commands. When the **passive** keyword is specified, these interfaces send compressed headers only if they receive compressed headers.

In the following configuration example, routers R1 and R2 are interconnected using their Serial 0/0 interfaces. The goal is to configure RTP Header Compression (cRTP) between the routers:

RTP Header Compression

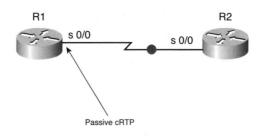

```
R1(config)#interface serial 0/0
R1(config-if)#ip rtp header-compression passive

R2(config)#interface serial 0/0
R2(config-if)#ip rtp header-compression
```

Note that only one side of the link uses the **passive** keyword. If both sides are set to be passive, RTP Header Compression does not occur because neither side of the link ever sends compressed headers.

To reduce the latency experienced by a large packet exiting an interface (i.e., serialization delay), Multilink PPP (MLP) can be used in a PPP environment, and FRF.12 can be used in a Voice over IP over Frame Relay environment. First, consider MLP.

Multilink PPP, by default, fragments traffic. This characteristic can be leveraged for QoS purposes, and MLP can be run even over a single link. The MLP configuration is performed under a virtual multilink interface, and then one or more physical interfaces can be assigned to the multilink group. The physical interface does not have an IP address assigned. Rather, the virtual multilink interface has an IP address assigned. For QoS purposes, a single interface is typically assigned as the sole member of the multilink group. Following is the syntax to configure MLP:

Router(config)#**interface multilink** [*multilink_interface_number*]—Creates a virtual multilink interface

Router(config-if)#**ip address** *ip_address subnet_mask*—Assigns an IP address to the virtual multilink interface

Router(config-if)#**ppp multilink**—Configures fragmentation on the multilink interface

Router(config-if)#**ppp multilink interleave**—Shuffles the fragments

Router(config-if)#**ppp fragment-delay** [*serialization_delay*]—Specifies how long it takes for a fragment to exit the interface

Router(config-if)#**encapsulation ppp**—Enables PPP encapsulation on the physical interface

Router(config-if)#**no ip address**—Removes the IP address from the physical interface

Router(config-if)#**multilink-group** [*multilink_group_number*]—Associates the physical interface with the multilink group

In the following example, the goal is to configure MLP on routers R1 and R2 so that they have a serialization delay of 10 ms on their Serial 0/0 interfaces.

Multilink PPP

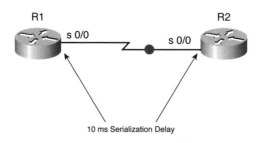

```
R1(config)#interface multilink 1
R1(config-if)#ip address 10.1.1.1 255.255.255.0
R1(config-if)#ppp multilink
R1(config-if)#ppp multilink interleave
R1(config-if)#ppp fragment-delay 10
R1(config-if)#exit
R1(config)#interface serial 0/0
R1(config-if)#encapsulation ppp
R1(config-if)#no ip address
R1(config-if)#multilink-group 1

R2(config)#interface multilink 1
R2(config-if)#ip address 10.1.1.2 255.255.255.0
R2(config-if)#ppp multilink
R2(config-if)#ppp multilink interleave
R2(config-if)#ppp fragment-delay 10
R2(config-if)#exit
R2(config)#interface serial 0/0
R2(config-if)#encapsulation ppp
R2(config-if)#no ip address
R2(config-if)#multilink-group 1
```

LFI can also be performed on a Frame Relay link using FRF.12. The configuration for FRF.12 is based on a Frame Relay Traffic Shaping configuration. Only one additional command is given, in map-class configuration mode, to enable FRF.12. The syntax for that command is as follows:

Router(config-map-class)#**frame-relay fragment** *fragment-size* — Specifies the size of the fragments

As a rule of thumb, the packet size should be set to the line speed divided by 800. For example, if the line speed is 64 kbps, the fragment size can be calculated as follows:

Fragment Size = 64,000 / 800 = 80 bytes

This rule of thumb specifies a fragment size (80 bytes) that creates a serialization delay of 10 ms.

The following example shows an FRF.12 configuration to create a serialization delay of 10 ms on a link that is clocked at a rate of 64 kbps. Since FRF.12 is configured as a part of Frame Relay traffic shaping, CIR and Bc values are also specified.

FRF.12

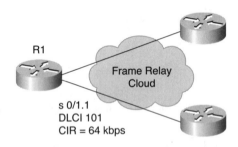

```
R1(config)#map-class frame-relay FRF12-EXAMPLE
R1(config-map-class)#frame-relay cir 64000
R1(config-map-class)#frame-relay bc 640
R1(config-map-class)#frame-relay fragment 80
R1(config-map-class)#exit
R1(config)#interface serial 0/1
R1(config-if)#frame-relay traffic-shaping
R1(config-if)#interface serial 0/1.1 point-to-point
R1(config-subif)#frame-relay interface-dlci 101
R1(config-fr-dlci)#class FRF12-EXAMPLE
```

AutoQoS

Optimizing a QoS configuration for Voice over IP (VoIP) can be a daunting task. Fortunately, Cisco added a feature called "AutoQoS" to many of its router and switch platforms to automatically generate router-based or switch-based VoIP QoS configurations.

The following router platforms support AutoQoS:

- 1700 Series
- 2600 Series

- 3600 Series

- 3700 Series

- 7200 Series

Cisco also supports the AutoQoS feature on the following Catalyst switch series:

- 2950 (EI)

- 3550

- 4500

- 6500

On a router platform, the following command enables AutoQoS from either interface configuration mode or from DLCI configuration mode (for a Frame Relay circuit):

```
Router(config-if)#auto qos voip [trust] [fr-atm]
```

The **trust** option indicates that Auto QoS should classify voice traffic based on DSCP markings, instead of using NBAR. The **fr-atm** option enables AutoQoS feature for Frame Relay–to–ATM links and is issued from DLCI configuration mode.

Before enabling AutoQoS on a router interface, consider these prerequisites:

- CEF must be enabled.

- A QoS policy must not be currently attached to the interface.

- The correct bandwidth should be configured on the interface.

- An IP address must be configured on an interface if its speed is less than 768 kbps.

Note that the interface's bandwidth determines which AutoQoS features are enabled. If an interface's bandwidth is less than 768 kbps, it is considered a low-speed interface. On a low-speed interface, AutoQoS configures Multilink PPP (MLP), which requires an IP address on the physical interface. AutoQoS takes that IP address from the physical interface and uses it for the virtual multilink interface it creates.

To verify that AutoQoS is configured for a router interface, you can use the following command:

```
Router#show auto qos voip [interface interface-identifier]
```

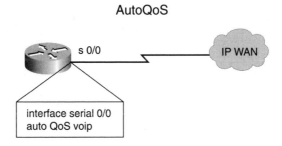

AutoQoS

The Catalyst 6500 running in Hybrid Mode (i.e., using the CatOS for switch functions) also supports AutoQoS. To enable AutoQoS on a Hybrid Mode Catalyst 6500 you must first enable AutoQoS globally and then for a specific port. Following are the required commands:

> Switch#**set qos autoqos**—Globally enables AutoQoS

> Switch#**set port qos** <*mod/port*> **autoqos trust [cos | dscp]**—Enables AutoQoS for a specific port

Note that the Catalyst 6500 can trust either CoS or DSCP values for its queuing decision. If the port is trusting DSCP markings, you can add the following command, which recognizes that the port is connected to a Cisco IP Phone or a Cisco SoftPhone, which is software that runs on a PC:

```
Switch#set port qos <mod/port> autoqos voip
 [ciscosoftphone | ciscoipphone]
```

The port must have CDP (Cisco Discovery Protocol) version 2 enabled to recognize an attached Cisco IP Phone. Although they do not recognize a Cisco SoftPhone, AutoQoS can be configured on Catalyst 2950 (EI) and 3550 switches, and their AutoQoS feature does recognize a Cisco IP Phone. To configure AutoQoS on these platforms, issue the following commands from interface configuration mode:

> Switch(config-if)#**auto qos voip trust**—Configures the interface to trust CoS markings for classifying VoIP traffic

> Switch(config-if)#**auto qos voip cisco-phone**—Detects the presence of a Cisco IP Phone, using CDP

To troubleshoot and verify AutoQoS on a Catalyst switch, the following commands can be used:

> Switch#**show auto qos [interface** *interface-identifier*]—Displays the configuration applied by AutoQoS

> Switch#**show mls qos interface [**interface-identifier*]—Displays interface-level QoS statistics

This section has broadly addressed the features enabled by AutoQoS. The specific features are shown in the following table:

QoS Mechanism	Router Feature	Switch Feature
Classification	NBAR and DSCP	Port Trust States
Marking	CB-Marking	CoS to DSCP Remarking
Congestion Management	LLQ	WRR
Shaping	CB-Shaping or FRTS	
Link Efficiency	Header Compression and LFI	

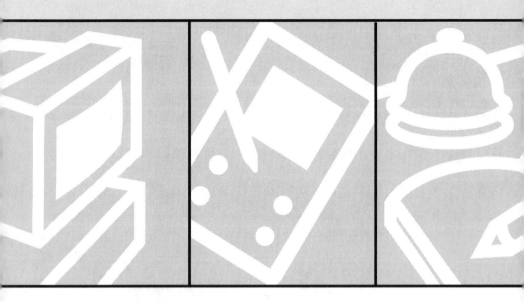

Section 6
WAN

Wide-area networking technologies are more heavily used and more important than ever as networks have become more and more far-reaching and more and more mission-critical traffic has hit the data network.

This section ensures that CCIE—Routing/Switching candidates are familiar with such key WAN technologies as Frame Relay, Integrated Services Digital Network (ISDN), and Asynchronous Transfer Mode (ATM).

Question 1

Which series of International Telecommunications Union (ITU) standards deals with ISDN concepts, terminology, and general methods?

Question 2

What are the number of channels in ISDN BRI, what type of channels are they, and what is the capacity of each?

Question 3

What are the number of channels in ISDN PRI, what type of channels are they, and what is the capacity of each?

Question 1 Answer

The I Series of standards deals with ISDN concepts, terminology, and general methods.

Question 2 Answer

Basic Rate Interface (BRI) ISDN features one 16 kbps D channel and two 64 kbps B channels.

Question 3 Answer

Primary Rate Interface (PRI) features one 64 kbps D channel and twenty-three 64 kbps B channels; in Europe features 30 B channels.

Question 4

What is the ISDN standard term for a device that possesses a native ISDN interface (ISDN-ready)?

Question 5

What is the ISDN standard term for a device that does not possess a native ISDN interface and that requires a terminal adapter (TA) for the ISDN signal?

Question 6

What is the ISDN standard term for a device that converts the BRI signals into a form used by the ISDN digital line; it is also the boundary between the carrier's ISDN network and the customer premises equipment (CPE)?

Question 4 Answer

Terminal equipment type 1 (TE1) indicates a device that possesses a native ISDN interface (ISDN-ready).

Question 5 Answer

Terminal equipment type 2 (TE2) indicates a device that does not possess a native ISDN interface and that requires a terminal adapter (TA) for the ISDN signal.

Question 6 Answer

Network Termination 1 (NT1) indicates a device that converts the BRI signals into a form used by the ISDN digital line; it is also the boundary between the carrier's ISDN network and the CPE.

Question 7

What is the ISDN standard term for a device that aggregates and switches all ISDN lines at the customer location—often this is incorporated into a private branch exchange (PBX)?

Question 8

What is the ISDN standard reference point used to describe the connection between a TE2 and the TA?

Question 9

What is the ISDN standard reference point used to describe the connection from the end user CPE and the NT2?

Question 7 Answer

Network Termination 2 (NT2) indicates a device that aggregates and switches all ISDN lines at the customer location; often this is incorporated into a PBX.

Question 8 Answer

The R reference point describes the connection between a TE2 and the TA.

Question 9 Answer

The S reference point describes the connection from the end user CPE and the NT2.

Question 10

What is the ISDN standard reference point used to describe the connection between the NT2 and NT1?

Question 11

What is the ISDN standard reference point used to describe the connection between the NT1 and the carrier's ISDN network?

Question 12

What does the U indicate on an ISDN interface for a Cisco router?

Question 10 Answer

The T reference point describes the connection between the NT2 and NT1.

Question 11 Answer

The U reference point describes the connection between the NT1 and the carrier's ISDN network.

Question 12 Answer

A U interface has a built-in NT1.

Question 13

In what modes can you configure the ISDN switch type on a Cisco router?

Question 14

You are configuring dial-on-demand routing (DDR) on your router and want to configure the amount of time the link stays up after interesting traffic has stopped flowing. What command enables you to do this?

Question 15

What configuration component is often required when two service profile identifiers (SPIDs) are configured and you want to receive incoming calls on the second B channel?

Question 13 Answer

The ISDN switch type can be configured in global configuration mode and interface configuration mode.

Question 14 Answer

You can use the **dialer idle-timeout** interface configuration command to specify how long the link stays up after interesting traffic has stopped flowing.

Question 15 Answer

If you configure two SPIDs on your router, you might also need to configure a local directory number (LDN). This follows the SPID entry in the **isdn spid1** and **spid2** commands. It is required only when two SPIDs are configured and you want to receive incoming calls on the second B channel.

Question 16

What command do you use to bind a dialer-list to a particular interface to specify interesting traffic?

Question 17

You want to configure your DDR environment so that you have a quicker disconnect when contention waiting for the line exists. What command enables you to configure this?

Question 18

What dialer map command allows Routing Information Protocol (RIP) version 1 routing updates to pass over an ISDN circuit?

Question 16 Answer

You use the **dialer-group** command to apply a dialer-list to an interface.

Question 17 Answer

When you have contention, the **dialer fast-idle** command enables you to configure the disconnect time in this situation.

Question 18 Answer

If broadcast/multicast updates need to pass over an ISDN circuit, be sure to include the **broadcast** keyword.

Question 19

How do you map a physical interface to a dialer pool when configuring dialer profiles?

Question 20

What command do you use inside a dialer interface to specify the name of the router to be called?

Question 21

What does the value of 30 indicate in the following command:

```
Router(config-if)# backup delay 10 30
```

Question 19 Answer

Map the logical interface to a physical interface(s) using the **dialer pool** command. On the physical interface, use the **dialer pool-member** command.

Question 20 Answer

Configure the name of the remote router to be called using the **dialer remote-name** command.

Question 21 Answer

In this case, the backup interface enables 10 seconds after it notices the primary link has failed. It disconnects 30 seconds after the primary link becomes operational.

Question 22

Of the backup interface, dialer watch, and floating static route methods, which does not require interesting traffic?

Question 23

What ISDN troubleshooting command presents summary information for Layers 1 through 3?

Question 24

You need to verify the dialer map statements that are created on your Cisco router. What command can you use to do this?

Question 22 Answer

The dialer watch method does not require interesting traffic.

Question 23 Answer

Use the **show isdn status** command to verify Layers 1 through 3.

Question 24 Answer

You can verify the dialer map statements with the **show dialer map** command.

Question 25

What does User-Network Interface (UNI) describe in Frame Relay?

Question 26

What does Network-to-Network Interface (NNI) describe in Frame Relay?

Question 27

What are the two ranges of data-link connection identifiers (DLCIs) that are reserved?

Question 25 Answer

The connection between customer (DTE) and service provider (DCE) is known as UNI.

Question 26 Answer

The NNI describes how different Frame Relay provider networks interconnect. Providers often use ATM in the cloud to carry the Frame Relay data.

Question 27 Answer

DLCIs 0–15 and 1008–1023 are reserved.

Question 28

What does an Local Management Interface (LMI) status indication of Inactive indicate for a permanent virtual circuit (PVC)?

Question 29

What is the command that you use to enable Frame Relay on an interface that is to communicate with a non-Cisco Frame Relay router?

Question 30

What is the command to disable Inverse Address Resolution Protocol (IARP) on a Frame Relay interface?

Question 28 Answer

Inactive indicates that the local connection is functioning but the remote connection is not.

Question 29 Answer

```
Router(config-if)# encapsulation frame-relay ietf
```

Question 30 Answer

```
Router(config-if)# no frame-relay inverse-arp
```

Question 31

What is the correct syntax to configure a static mapping in a Frame Relay environment?

Question 32

What are the two options available for the creation of a Frame Relay subinterface?

Question 33

Split horizon issues can be resolved through the use of which type of Frame Relay subinterface?

Question 31 Answer

```
Router(config-if)# frame-relay map protocol protocol-address dlci
   [broadcast] [ietf | cisco]
```

Question 32 Answer

A Frame Relay subinterface can be configured as point-to-point or multipoint.

Question 33 Answer

Point-to-point subinterfaces resolve split horizon issues; multipoint interfaces are not guaranteed to do so.

Question 34

Name an advantage to the use of multipoint subinterfaces in Frame Relay?

Question 35

Where do you configure a network layer address in a Frame Relay subinterface configuration?

Question 36

What command must you use to properly configure DLCIs in point-to-point Frame Relay subinterface configurations?

Question 34 Answer

Multipoint interfaces allow the conservation of subnet addresses.

Question 35 Answer

You configure the network layer address on the subinterface; network layer addressing should be removed from the major interface.

Question 36 Answer

```
Router(config-subif)# frame-relay interface-dlci dlci-number
```

Question 37

You want to convert one of your point-to-point subinterfaces to a multipoint configuration. What must you do after you have made the appropriate configuration commands?

Question 38

What is the CIR value in Frame Relay terminology?

Question 39

What is the BECN value in Frame Relay terminology?

Question 37 Answer

You must reboot the router.

Question 38 Answer

Committed information rate (CIR) is the rate in bps at which the Frame Switch agrees to transfer data; usually averaged over a time period called committed rate measurement interval (T_c).

Question 39 Answer

Backward Explicit Congestion Notification (BECN) is a bit that can be set to indicate congestion on the switch; Cisco IOS Software Release 11.2 IOS and higher allows a router to respond to this bit setting.

Question 40

What Frame Relay traffic has the DE bit set?

Question 41

You are configuring Frame Relay traffic shaping, and you want to define the average and peak rates on the virtual circuit (VC) associated with the map class. What command do you use?

Question 42

You are configuring Frame Relay traffic shaping, and want to specify that the router should dynamically fluctuate the rate based on BECNs. What command do you use to configure this?

Question 40 Answer

The discard eligibility (DE) indicator is set on the oversubscribed traffic.

Question 41 Answer

```
Router(config-map-class)# frame-relay traffic-rate average [peak]
```

Question 42 Answer

```
Router(config-map-class)# frame-relay adaptive-shaping
```

Question 43

What command do you need to clear the dynamically created DLCI mappings in Frame Relay?

Question 44

What two mechanisms are used to identify an ATM connection?

Question 45

What command do you use to create a PVC on the ATM interface?

Question 43 Answer

Use the **clear frame-relay-inarp** command to clear dynamically created mappings.

Question 44 Answer

ATM connections are identified with a virtual path identifier (VPI) and virtual channel identifier (VCI).

Question 45 Answer

To create a PVC on the ATM interface, use the following command:

```
Router(config-if)# pvc [name] vpi/vci [ilmi | qsaal | smds]
```

Question 46

What command do you use to map a Layer 3 protocol address to the PVC in ATM?

Question 47

What is ATM adaptation Layer 1 used for and is the data sent compressed or uncompressed?

Question 48

What is ATM adaptation Layer 2 used for, and is the data sent compressed or uncompressed?

Question 46 Answer

To map a Layer 3 protocol address to the PVC, use the following command:

```
Router(config-if-atm-vc)# protocol protocol protocol-address
  [[no]broadcast]
```

Question 47 Answer

ATM adaptation Layer 1 is used for voice and video applications; data is sent uncompressed.

Question 48 Answer

ATM adaptation Layer 2 is used for voice and video applications; data is sent compressed.

Question 49

What is ATM adaptation Layer 3-4 typically used for?

Question 50

What is the ATM adaptation Layer 5 used for primarily and does it support connection-oriented or connectionless data?

Question 51

What ATM encapsulation option dedicates the specified circuit to a single protocol?

Question 49 Answer

ATM adaptation Layer 3-4 can be used for Switched Multimegabit Data Service (SMDS).

Question 50 Answer

ATM adaptation Layer 5 is the primary AAL for data and supports both connection-oriented and connectionless data.

Question 51 Answer

Use the **aal5mux** encapsulation option to dedicate the specified circuit to a single protocol.

Question 52

What ATM encapsulation option multiplexes two or more protocols over the same virtual circuit?

Question 53

What are the five standard service categories that ATM uses to provide differing bandwidth, loss, and latency?

Question 54

What is the Cisco extension service category?

Question 52 Answer

Use the **aal5snap** encapsulation option to multiplex two or more protocols over the same virtual circuit.

Question 53 Answer

Constant bit rate (CBR)

Variable bit rate real time (VBR RT)

Variable bit rate non-real time (VBR NRT)

Available bit rate (ABR)

Unspecified bit rate (UBR)

Question 54 Answer

UBR+

Question 55

What is the keyword that is required in the ppp authentication pap command that configures authentication one-way?

Question 56

What two configuration commands are needed on each router to configure two-way Password Authentication Protocol (PAP) authentication?

Question 57

You are configuring two-way Challenge Handshake Authentication Protocol (CHAP) authentication, and you want to send a username that is different from the router host name. What commands are required for this?

Question 55 Answer

The **callin** keyword in the **ppp authentication** command is the key to the authentication being one-way.

Question 56 Answer

Use the **ppp authentication pap** command and also the **ppp pap sent-username** command on each router.

Question 57 Answer

If you want your router to send a username other than its host name, you can configure this using the following commands:

```
Router(config-if)# ppp chap hostname MyNewName
Router(config-if)# ppp chap password MyNewPassword
```

Question 58

You are configuring the load that triggers multilink behavior. Explain the format and meaning of the load value?

Question 59

What command enables you to control how quickly channels are added to a multilink PPP bundle?

Question 60

What command allows a router to function as a callback server by accepting callback requests from a client?

Question 58 Answer

The load argument represents a utilization percentage; it is a number between 1 and 255, where 255 is 100 percent.

Question 59 Answer

The following command enables you to increase the frequency of interface load calculations:

```
Router(config-if)# load-interval value-in-seconds
```

Question 60 Answer

```
Router(config-if)# ppp callback accept
```

Question 61

What command configures a dialer map class for PPP callback?

Question 62

What PPP callback–related command forces key security functions including disconnecting calls that are not properly configured for callback and disconnecting any unauthenticated dial-in users?

Question 61 Answer

```
Router(config-map-class)# dialer callback-server [username]
```

Question 62 Answer

```
Router(config-if)# dialer callback-secure
```

WAN
Quick Reference Sheets

Overview

Digital connectivity from the core of the provider delivered to the home or office customer. Still used today as a backup technology. The International Telecommunications Union (ITU) still coordinates the Integrated Services Digital Network (ISDN) movement; topic areas include:

- **E-series**—Telephone network standards

- **I-series**—ISDN concepts, terminology, and general methods

- **Q-series**—Encompass switching and signaling; Q.921 describes the ISDN data-link process of Link Access Procedure on the D channel (LAPD); this is an encapsulation option for the D channel; Q.931 specifies Layer 3 functions

Cisco supports two interface types:

- **Basic Rate Interface (BRI)**—One 16 kbps D channel and two 64 kbps B channels

- **Primary Rate Interface (PRI)**—One 64 kbps D channel and twenty-three 64 kbps B channels; in Europe there are thirty B channels

Standard terminology describes the ISDN customer premises equipment (CPE) options:

- **TE1 (Terminal Equipment Type 1)**—Indicates a device that possesses a native ISDN interface (ISDN-ready)

- **TE2 (Terminal Equipment Type 2)**—A device that does not possess a native ISDN interface and that requires a terminal adapter (TA) for the ISDN signal

- **NT1 (Network Termination 1)**—A device that converts the BRI signals into a form used by the ISDN digital line; the boundary between the carrier's ISDN network and the CPE

- **NT2 (Network Termination 2)**—A device that aggregates and switches all ISDN lines at the customer location; often this is incorporated into a PBX

- **TA (Terminal Adapter)** —A device that allows a TE2 to connect properly to the ISDN network

Standard reference points describe the areas between the various CPE options:

- **R**—Connection between a TE2 and the TA

- **S**—Connection from the end user CPE and the NT2

- **T**—Connection between the NT2 and NT1

- **U**—Connection between the NT1 and the carrier's ISDN network

Cisco routers use the reference points to describe their interfaces. For example, an S/T interface on the Cisco router indicates an external NT1 is required. A U interface has a built-in NT1.

While PPP and High-Level Data Link Control (HDLC) can be used for encapsulation over ISDN, PPP is typically used for its multilink and authentication options.

Basic ISDN Configuration

You must configure the ISDN switch type in use on the router, and typically you must configure service profile identifiers (SPIDs) for each B channel. The SPID allows the terminal to be identified and is typically a phone number followed by additional digits.

You can configure the switch type in global configuration mode on the router, or you can specify it for an interface. Interface configurations override global configurations.

Use the **isdn switch-type** command to set the switch type and the interface configuration mode **isdn spid[1-2]** command to set the SPIDs.

Configuring Dial-On-Demand Routing (DDR)

You define "interesting" traffic that brings up the link. You can use the **dialer idle-timeout** interface configuration command to specify how long the link stays up after interesting traffic has stopped flowing.

Typical configuration tasks include the following:

Step 1   Configure the switch type and the SPIDs—for example:

```
Router(config)# interface BRI0
Router(config-if)# isdn switch-type basic-5ess
Router(config-ig)# isdn spid1 80055512121111
Router(config-ig)# isdn spid2 80055512201111
```

If you configure two SPIDs on your router, you might need to also configure an LDN (local directory number). This follows the SPID entry in the **isdn spid1** and **spid2** commands. It is required only when two SPIDs are configured, and you want to receive incoming calls on the second B channel.

Step 2   Specify interesting traffic. This is accomplished with a dialer-list. The syntax is as follows:

```
Router(config)# dialer-list dialer-group protocol protocol-
  name [permit | deny | list] access-list number
```

Once you create the dialer-list, you can assign it to an interface (physical or logical) using the **dialer-group** command. Make sure the dialer-group number you use in the dialer-list statement matches the number you use in the **dialer-group** command. Remember also, while the interesting traffic you define dictates what traffic brings up the connection, once the connection is active, any traffic can flow across it by default.

Step 3   Configure dialer information. You can specify the idle time before the line is disconnected using the following command:

```
Router(config-if)# dialer idle-timeout seconds [inbound |
  either]
```

By default, this command applies to inbound and outbound calls, but notice that you can manipulate this default setting. Only packets that match the dialer group reset the idle timer.

The preceding command functions when no contention for the line exists. When contention exists, the **dialer fast-idle** command is used. The command syntax follows:

```
Router(config-if)# dialer fast-idle seconds
```

Using a Dialer String

If you use the **dialer-string** interface configuration command, the router can call only the single destination for all outgoing calls. If you have multiple possible destinations and you want to make a call to a specific location based on a Layer 3 address, use the **dialer-map** command. For even more sophistication, you can move beyond these "legacy DDR" approaches and use logical dialer interfaces.

Here is an example of a dialer string configuration:

```
Router(config-if)# dialer string 8005551212
```

Using a Dialer Map

Dialer maps allow you to associate called numbers for IP addresses. Here is an example:

```
Router(config-if)# dialer map ip 172.16.10.10 name RouterB 8005551212
```

If routing updates are to pass across the link, you must include the **broadcast** keyword.

Dynamic IP Addressing

When using the popular PPP over ISDN, you can configure the client to receive its IP address dynamically. Here is an example of the configuration (notice that only directly relevant commands are shown):

Dynamic Addressing Server—R4

```
R4(config)# ip local pool default 10.20.0.10 10.20.0.50
R4(config)# ip address-pool local
R4(config)# interface bri 0/0
R4(config-if)# peer default ip address pool
```

Dynamic Addressing Client

```
R1(config)# interface bri 0/0
R1(config-if)# ip address negotiated
```

Using Dialer Interfaces

A dialer interface is a logical structure created to contain the configuration options. The dialer interface is bound to a physical interface when a connection is made. Dialer pools define which logical interfaces can associate with which physical interfaces.

To use a dialer interface approach follow these steps:

Step 1   Remove all of the legacy DDR commands from the physical interface.

Step 2   Configure the logical interface using the **interface dialer** command.

Step 3   Configure the name of the remote router to be called using the **dialer remote-name** command.

Step 4   Map the logical interface to a physical interface(s) using the **dialer pool** command. On the physical interface, use the **dialer pool-member** command.

Step 5   Define the interesting traffic; be sure to associate the definition with the logical interface. Also, provide a dialer string on the logical interface.

Step 6   Configure any other optional parameters on the dialer interface.

Here is an example of the configuration of a dialer interface; note this example stresses only the commands relevant for our discussion here:

```
Router(config)# dialer-list 1 protocol ip permit
Router(config)# interface BRI0
Router(config-if)# dialer pool-member 10
Router(config-if)# interface Dialer1
Router(config-if)# ip address 10.10.0.1 255.255.0.0
Router(config-if)# encapsulation ppp
Router(config-if)# dialer remote-name Central
Router(config-if)# dialer string 8005551212
Router(config-if)# dialer pool 10
Router(config-if)# dialer-group 1
```

NOTE Certain configuration commands must be configured on both the logical and physical interfaces! For example:

```
encapsulation ppp
ppp authentication chap
```

Using ISDN as a Backup

Floating Static Routes

One simple option is the use of a floating static route. Floating static routes were defined in the General Networking Theory section under administrative distance. They are static routes with an artificially high administrative distance, making them employed only when the dynamically implemented route fails.

Backup Interface

A backup interface stays idle until certain conditions are met, and then it activates. Here is a sample configuration, using the BRI interface to back up a serial interface:

```
Router(config)# interface serial 0/0
Router(config-if)# backup interface bri 0/0
Router(config-if)# backup delay 10 30
```

In this case, the backup interface enables 10 seconds after it notices the primary link has failed. It disconnects 30 seconds after the primary link becomes operational.

You can also use the **backup load** command to configure the backup interface to come up when a certain load is on the primary link.

Dialer Watch

The dialer watch approach has an interface monitor a specific route or set of routes. The commands required for this configuration are simple:

```
Router(config-if)# dialer watch-group group-number
Router(config)# dialer watch-list group-number ip ip-address address-mask
```

Notice that the **dialer watch-group** command binds a watch list to an interface. The watch list specifies the routes to watch.

This table compares the methods of backup for an interface:

Backup Interface	Floating Static Route	Dialer Watch
Requires the primary interface to fail	Uses static route with higher administrative distance	Watches routes and employs backup if route is missing
Encapsulation could be a factor in success	Encapsulation independent	Encapsulation independent
Does not consider end-to-end connectivity	Based on the existence of a route	Based on the existence of a route
Requires interesting traffic	Requires interesting traffic	Does not require interesting traffic
Not dependent on a routing protocol	Dependent on a routing protocol's convergence time	Dependent on a routing protocol's convergence time
Routing protocol independent	All routing protocols supported	EIGRP/OSPF only
Limited to one router/one interface	One router	Supports multiple router scenarios
Can be used for bandwidth on demand	Bandwidth on demand is not possible	Bandwidth on demand is not possible

ISDN Troubleshooting

Use the **show isdn status** command to verify Layers 1 through 3.

Use **debug isdn q931** for further troubleshooting at Layer 3.

Use the **show isdn active** command to display information about the current call.

For verification of DDR, use the **show dialer** command.

For verification of dialer map statements, use the **show dialer map** command.

Frame Relay

Frame Relay Operation

Connection between customer (data terminal equipment—DTE) and service provider (data communications equipment—DCE) is known as User-Network Interface (UNI). Frame Relay always runs here. The Network-to-Network Interface (NNI) is used to describe how different Frame Relay provider networks interconnect. Providers often use Asynchronous Transfer Mode (ATM) in the cloud to carry the Frame Relay data.

Frame Relay multiplexes many virtual circuits (VCs) over a single physical transmission link. It uses data-link connection identifiers (DLCIs) on each DTE to identify the different circuits. The DLCI is typically only locally significant between the DTE and the frame switch. Some providers allow the customers to choose the DLCI. DLCIs 0–15 and 1008–1023 are reserved. The specific range of DLCIs available is dependent upon the Local Management Interface (LMI) type in use. DLCIs must be mapped to a remote IP address to direct traffic over the correct VC. Cisco routers support dynamic (Inverse Address Resolution Protocol — ARP) and manual mappings of DLCIs to remote IP addresses.

Frame Relay

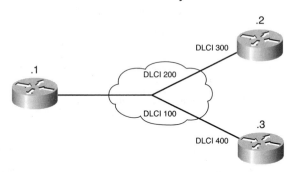

172.16.23.0/24

LMI provides signaling and status updates between the DTE and DCE. It also provides the DTE with its DLCI. The LMI can be autosensed on Cisco IOS Release 11.2 or higher. One of three types is used—Cisco, American National Standards Institute (ANSI), Q.933. Possible LMI status indications include the following:

- **Active**—Connection is active and the routers can exchange data

- **Inactive**—Local connection is functioning but the remote connection is not

- **Deleted**—No LMI received from switch, DLCI removed from switch, or no service from DTE to DCE

NBMA network capability allows customer to communicate with any remote site provided the provider has established a VC. A hub and spoke is often used because of the per-VC charge that typically exists. Permanent virtual circuit (PVC) or switched virtual circuit (SVC) can be used—typically PVC.

Configuring Basic Frame Relay

To set the encapsulation to Frame Relay, use the following command:

```
Router(config-if)# encapsulation frame-relay [cisco I ietf]
```

If you must specify the LMI type, use this command:

```
Router(config-if)# frame-relay lmi-type {ansi I cisco I q933a}
```

For dynamic address mapping (IARP), no further configuration is required. If IARP has been disabled on an interface, you can enable it with the following command:

```
Router(config-if)# frame-relay inverse-arp
```

To configure a static mapping, use the following command:

```
Router(config-if)# frame-relay map protocol protocol-address dlci [broadcast]
[ietf | cisco]
```
The keywords indicate the following:

- **protocol-address**—Specifies the destination protocol address

- **dlci**—The DLCI number needed to connect to the remote protocol address

- **broadcast**—Specifies that broadcasts/multicasts should be forwarded; often used to ensure routing protocol traffic should be sent across the PVC

- **ietf/cisco**—Used to specify the Frame Relay encapsulation type

Subinterfaces

Subinterfaces can solve split horizon issues that arise with distance vector protocols and hub and spoke topologies. Subinterfaces might be configured as point-to-point or multipoint. Split horizon can still be an issue in the multipoint environment. Multipoint does offer an advantage in that a single subnet is needed as opposed to multiple subnet addresses. The steps for a Frame Relay subinterface configuration include the following:

Step 1   Remove any network layer addressing assigned at the physical interface level.

Step 2   Configure Frame Relay encapsulation at the physical interface level.

Step 3   Create the subinterface using the following command:

```
Router(config)# interface serial number.subinterface-number
{multipoint | point-to-point}
```

Step 4   Step 4—Assign the subinterface a network address; you can use the **ip unnumbered** command.

Step 5   Step 5—If you configured a point-to-point subinterface—or if your are multipoint and using IARP—you must configure the local DLCI using the following command:

```
Router(config-subif)# frame-relay interface-dlci dlci-number
```

NOTE   You cannot assign a subinterface to point-to-point communications and then reassign to multipoint without rebooting the router. To work around this, just select a new subinterface number.

Frame Relay Example

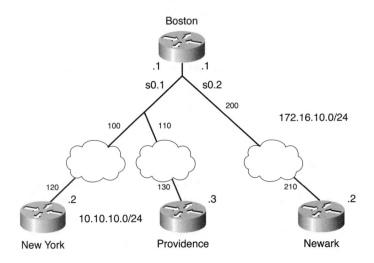

Here is an example:

```
Boston(config)# interface serial 0
Boston(config-if)# encapsulation frame-relay
Boston(config-if)# no ip address
Boston(config-if)# no shutdown
Boston(config-if)# interface serial 0.1 multipoint
Boston(config-if)# ip address 10.10.10.1 255.255.255.0
Boston(config-if)# frame-relay map ip 10.10.10.2 100 broadcast
Boston(config-if)# frame-relay map ip 10.10.10.3 110 broadcast
Boston(config-if)# interface serial 0.2 point-to-point
Boston(config-if)# ip address 172.16.10.1 255.255.255.0
Boston(config-if)# frame-relay interface-dlci 200

New York(config)# interface serial 0
New York(config-if)# encapsulation frame-relay
New York(config-if)# ip address 10.10.10.2 255.255.255.0
New York(config-if)# frame-relay map ip 10.10.10.1 120 broadcast
New York(config-if)# frame-relay map ip 10.10.10.3 120 broadcast
New York(config-if)# no shutdown

Providence(config)# interface serial 0
Providence(config-if)# encapsulation frame-relay
Providence(config-if)# ip address 10.10.10.3 255.255.255.0
Providence(config-if)# frame-relay map ip 10.10.10.1 130 broadcast
Providence(config-if)# frame-relay map ip 10.10.10.2 130 broadcast
Providence(config-if)# no shutdown
```

```
Newark(config)# interface serial 0
Newark(config-if)# encapsulation frame-relay
Newark(config-if)# ip address 172.16.10.2 255.255.255.0
Newark(config-if)# frame-relay interface-dlci 210
Newark(config-if)# no shutdown
```

Frame Relay Traffic Shaping

Flow Terminology

Local Access Rate—Clock speed of the connection to the Frame Relay cloud; rate at which data flows into or out of the network

Committed Information Rate (CIR)—Rate in bps at which the Frame switch agrees to transfer data; usually averaged over time called committed rate measurement interval (T_c)

Oversubscription—The sum of all the CIRs of the VCs coming into the device exceeds the access line speed

Committed Burst (Bc)—Maximum data in bits that the Frame switch agrees to transfer during any T_c; CIR/Tc = Bc

Excess Burst (Be)—Maximum number of bits the Frame switch attempts to transfer beyond the CIR for the first time interval only

Forward Explicit Congestion Notification (FECN)—Frame switch sets this bit to indicate congestion is being experienced

Backward Explicit Congestion Notification (BECN)—Another bit that can be set to indicate congestion on the switch; Cisco IOS Release 11.2 and higher allows a router to respond to this bit setting

Discard Eligibility (DE) indicator—The DE bit is set on the oversubscribed traffic

Frame Relay Traffic shaping is often used when a speed mismatch exists between sites or you notice that Frame Relay connections are occasionally congested.

Configuring traffic shaping involves the following steps:

Step 1   Specify a map class with the following command:

```
Router(config)# map-class frame-relay map-class-name
```

Step 2   Configure the options for traffic shaping; The following options are available:

• Define the average and peak rates on the VC associated with the map class; use the following command:

```
Router(config-map-class)# frame-relay traffic-rate average
    [peak]
```

- Specify the router dynamically fluctuates the rate based on BECNs; use the following command:

  ```
  Router(config-map-class)# frame-relay adaptive-shaping
  ```

- Specify a queuing strategy for the virtual circuit; see the QoS Study Sheets section for possible configurations.

Step 3   Map the map class to virtual circuits on the interface; use the following command:

```
Router(config-if)# frame-relay class map-class-name
```

Step 4   Enable traffic shaping with the following command:

```
Router(config-if)# frame-relay traffic-shaping
```

Verifying Frame Relay

show interface—Encapsulation verification

show frame-relay pvc—Status and traffic statistics; BECN and FECN data

show frame-relay map—View DLCI mappings

show frame-relay lmi—LMI traffic statistics

debug frame-relay lmi—Displays LMI information

clear frame-relay-inarp—Clears dynamically created mappings

show traffic-shape—Displays the current traffic shaping configuration

show traffic-shape statistics—Displays the current traffic shaping statistics

debug frame-relay lmi—Displays information on the LMI packet exchange

debug frame-relay packet—See packet level of Frame Relay activities

ATM

Overview

ATM is an ITU-T standard for cell relay where routers convey information for multiple service types including voice, video, or data. ATM can use PVCs, SVCs, and connectionless service. ATM connections are identified with a virtual path identifier (VPI) and virtual channel identifier (VCI).

Configuring PVCs

Required tasks:

- Creating a PVC
- Mapping a protocol address to a PVC

Optional tasks include:

- Configuring the ATM adaptation layer (AAL) and encapsulation type
- Configuring PVC traffic parameters
- Configuring PVC discovery
- Enabling Inverse Address Resolution Protocol (ARP)
- Configuring a PVC to pass broadcast traffic (routing protocols)
- Assigning a VC class to a PVC

To create a PVC on the ATM interface, use the following command:

```
Router(config-if)# pvc [name] vpi/vci [ilmi | qsaal | smds]
```

The keywords indicate the following:

- **name**—Optional name to easily identify the PVC and later enter ATM-VC configuration mode
- **ilmi**—This keyword creates the ILMI PVC on VCI 16; this is needed if you want to configure SVCs
- **qsaal**—Signaling PVC with VCI 5 needed in SVC
- **smds**—Allows PVC to handle Switched Multimegabit Data Service (SMDS) over ATM

NOTE When you create PVC, it is assigned a VCD (Virtual Circuit Descriptor).

To map a Layer 3 protocol address to the PVC, use the following command:

```
Router(config-if-atm-vc)# protocol protocol protocol-address [[no]broadcast]
```

The **broadcast** keyword allows you to run routing protocols across the PVC.

Here is a sample configuration showing these required steps and ease of configuration thanks to the **name** keyword:

ATM PVC Example Topology

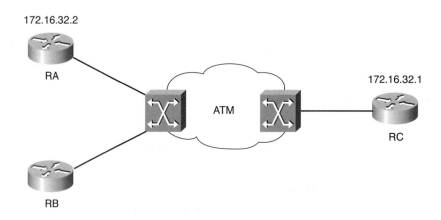

172.16.32.2

RA

ATM

172.16.32.1

RC

RB

```
RC# configure terminal
RC(config)# interface atm 1/0
RC(config-if)# pvc MYATMPVC 12/41
RC(config-if-atm-vc)# end
RC#
RC# configure terminal
RC(config)# interface atm 1/0
RC(config-if)# pvc MYATMPVC
RC(config-if-atm-vc)# protocol ip 172.16.32.2 broadcast
```

You can verify the PVC you created with the **show atm pvc** command, and you can verify the proper protocol mapping with the **show atm map** command. If you create an ATM PVC as we did above, you have created an unspecified bit rate (UBR) PVC with a peak rate that is the full capacity of the interface. The PVC also features the Subnetwork Access Protocol (SNAP) encapsulation type.

Routing Over ATM

Routing protocol traffic can be ensured to pass over the PVC on a per-destination basis using the ATM mapping statement. You can also globally enable routing protocols over the PVC using the **broadcast** command with the protocol statement in virtual circuit configuration mode.

Configuring the AAL and Encapsulation

ATM Adaptation Layer 1—Used for voice and video applications; data is sent uncompressed

ATM Adaptation Layer 2—Used for voice and video applications; data is sent compressed

ATM Adaptation Layer 3–4—Can be used for SMDS

ATM Adaptation Layer 5—This is the primary AAL for data and supports both connection-oriented and connectionless data

Use the **aal5mux** encapsulation option to dedicate the specified circuit to a single protocol; use the **aal5snap** encapsulation option to multiplex two or more protocols over the same virtual circuit. Use the **encapsulation** command in interface-ATM-VC configuration mode.

The options for the command include the following:

- **aal5ciscoppp**
- **aal5mux**
- **aal5nlpid**
- **aal5snap**
- **ciscoppp**
- **nlpid**
- **snap**

When you specify **mux** as the encapsulation, you must follow the keyword with a protocol keyword.

Service Categories

ATM uses five standard service categories to provide differing bandwidth, loss, and latency. There is also a Cisco extension category:

- Constant Bit Rate (CBR)
- Variable Bit Rate Real-Time (VBR-RT)
- Variable Bit Rate Non Real-Time (VBR-NRT)
- Available Bit Rate (ABR)
- Unspecified Bit Rate (UBR)
- UBR+

You can specify only one category per VC connection. To configure these parameters, use one of the following parameters in (config-if-atm-vc) mode:

> **abr: output-pcr output-mcr**
>
> **vbr-rt: peak-rate average-rate burst**
>
> **vbr-nrt: output-pcr output-scr output-mbs**
>
> **ubr: output-pcr**

PPP

PAP

PAP One-Way

One-way authentication indicates you want a calling router (the client) to be authenticated only by a called router (the server). Here is the simple configuration:

Client Router

```
Client(config)# interface bri 0/0
Client(config-if)# encapsulation ppp
Client(config-if)# ppp authentication pap callin
Client(config-if)# ppp pap sent-username Client password matchingpass
```

Notice the use of the **callin** keyword in the **ppp authentication** command. This is the key to the authentication being one-way. This causes the client to not ask the server to provide its credentials for authentication.

Here is the configuration of the "server":

```
Server(config)# username Client password matchingpass
Server(config)# interface bri 0/0
Server(config-if)# encapsulation ppp
Server(config-if)# ppp authentication pap
```

You see nothing fancy here at all; you just need to make sure you have the appropriate username and password in the database on this router that authenticates the calling "client."

PAP Two-Way

This configuration is simple—use the **ppp authentication pap** command and also the **ppp pap sent-username** command on each router.

CHAP

CHAP One-Way

Note the similarity to the PAP one-way configuration.

Client Router

```
Client(config)# username Server password matchingpass
Client(config)# interface bri 0/0
Client(config-if)# encapsulation ppp
Client(config-if)# ip address 10.10.0.1 255.255.0.0
Client(config-if)# ppp authentication chap callin
Client(config-if)# dialer map ip 10.10.0.2 name Server broadcast 5551212
```

Notice the use of the **callin** keyword in the **ppp authentication** command. This is the key to the authentication being one-way. This causes the client to not ask the server to provide its credentials for authentication. Also, notice you have no need for the **sent-username** command.

Here is the configuration of the "server":

```
Server(config)# username Client password matchingpass
Server(config)# interface bri 0/0
Server(config-if)# ip address 10.10.0.2
Server(config-if)# encapsulation ppp
Server(config-if)# ppp authentication chap
Server(config-if)# dialer map ip 10.10.0.1 name Client broadcast 5551220
```

CHAP Two-Way

This configuration follows the one-way configuration; simply no need for the **callin** keyword exists, however.

Configuring CHAP Using a Unique Hostname

If you want your router to send a username other than its hostname, you can configure this using the following commands:

```
Router(config-if)# ppp chap hostname MyNewName
Router(config-if)# ppp chap password MyNewPassword
```

Multilink

To activate an interface for Multilink PPP (MPPP) operation, use the following command:

```
Router(config-if)# ppp multilink
```

To set the point at which additional B channels are added to a MPPP bundle, use the following command:

```
Router(config-if)# dialer load-threshold load [inbound | outbound | either]
```

The key to this command is the *load* argument. This argument represents a utilization percentage; it is a number between 1 and 255, where 255 is 100 percent. The **outbound/inbound/both** options allow you to specify which traffic should be considered in this calculation.

You can also control how quickly MPPP channels are added to the bundle. The following command allows you to increase the frequency of interface load calculations:

```
Router(config-if)# load-interval value-in-seconds
```

You can also manipulate the delay MPPP uses before adding another link with the following command:

```
Router(config-if)# ppp timeout multilink link add 3 value-in-seconds
```

PPP Callback

PPP callback allows a router to request that a peer router call back. This is easiest to think of in terms of a client/server relationship. The client wants the server system to callback. The configuration command needed on the client is as follows:

```
Router(config-if)# ppp callback request
```

The commands required on the server include the following:

```
Router(config-if)# ppp callback accept
```

The preceding command configures the server to accept callback requests.

```
Router(config-if)# dialer map protocol next-hop-address name hostname class
  classname dial-string
```

The preceding command maps the next hop address to the host name and phone number, using the name of the map class established for PPP callback on this interface.

```
Router(config-map-class)# map-class dialer classname
```

This command configures a dialer map class for PPP callback.

```
Router(config-map-class)# dialer callback-server [username]
```

This command configures a dialer map class as a callback server.

Here is a sample configuration of a callback server:

```
interface bri 0
ip address 10.20.20.7 255.255.255.0
encapsulation ppp
dialer map ip 10.20.20.8 name boston class dial1
 81012345678901
dialer-group 1
ppp callback accept
ppp authentication chap
!
map-class dialer dial1
dialer callback-server username
```

Optional commands that can be used with callback include the following:

```
Router(config-if)# dialer callback-secure
```

This command forces key security functions including disconnecting calls that are not properly configured for callback and disconnecting any unauthenticated dial-in users.

```
Router(config-if)# dialer enable-timeout seconds
```

This allows you to modify how long the server waits to call back.

```
Router(config-if)# dialer hold-queue number
```

This allows you to configure the number of interesting outgoing packets a client queues while waiting for a callback from the server.

Caller Identification

Caller ID screening allows the call from the client to the server to be accepted or rejected based on the caller ID message in the ISDN setup message. Caller ID screening also allows the server to initiate a callback to the calling client.

For legacy DDR, use the following command:

```
Router(config-if)# isdn caller remote-number callback
```

For a dialer profile, use the following:

```
Router(config-if)#
```

Section 7
IP Multicast

IP multicast technologies allow a source to send traffic to a large number of receivers very efficiently. Examples of IP multicast applications include a company's CEO sending a corporate-wide video to thousands of receivers or a Cisco CallManager sending music on hold to multiple IP phones.

The flash cards in this chapter review IP multicast addressing and protocols. Also, these flash cards examine the syntax used to configure IP multicast protocols, such as PIM Sparse Mode.

Question 1

Why is weighted random early detect (WRED) not effective for IP multicast?

Question 2

Describe the potential benefit of multicast versus unicast or broadcast.

Question 3

What protocol is used by IP multicast receivers to request membership in an IP multicast group?

Question 1 Answer

IP multicast sends packet via User Datagram Protocol (UDP) (i.e., best effort). WRED causes TCP flows to enter TCP Slow Start and is therefore ineffective for the UDP packets used by IP multicast.

Question 2 Answer

A video feed being sent to multiple users in an organization could consume a tremendous amount of bandwidth if the video were unicast to each receiver. A broadcast sends the packets to devices that might not want the packets. Fortunately, multicast can send a single copy of each packet from the source to only those devices wanting to receive the packet.

Question 3 Answer

IP multicast receivers use the Internet Group Management Protocol (IGMP) to request membership in a multicast group. This "IGMP join report" message is sent to a receiver's next hop router. After the router adds an interface to its OIL (Outgoing Interface List), the router periodically sends "IGMP Query" messages out of that interface to determine if any receivers still exist off that interface.

Question 4

By default, how often does an IP multicast-enabled router send IGMP queries out of an interface attached to receivers?

Question 5

List two enhancements of IGMP Version 2 over IGMP Version 1.

Question 6

What happens to an IGMPv2 report message that is sent by an IGMPv2 receiver to an IGMPv1 router?

Question 4 Answer

To determine if any IP multicast receivers exist off a router interface, by default, an IP multicast-enabled router sends an IGMP query message every 60 seconds. After two queries have been sent out of an interface without a response, the router prunes the interface from its OIL.

Question 5 Answer

IGMP Version 2 sends group-specific queries and supports the sending of "leave" messages to inform the router that a receiver is leaving the multicast group.

Question 6 Answer

An IGMPv1 router interprets an IGMPv2 report message as invalid, and it is ignored. Therefore, an IGMPv2 host must send IGMPv1 reports to an IGMPv1 router.

Question 7

When multiple IP multicast-enabled routers exist on a broadcast segment, such as an Ethernet segment, only one router should be responsible for sending queries to the segment. What determines which router on a segment becomes the "querier"?

Question 8

Describe the characteristics of the Cisco Group Management Protocol (CGMP).

Question 9

Describe the purpose and operation of IGMP snooping.

Question 7 Answer

An IGMP-designated querier on a broadcast segment is the router with the lowest unicast IP address. Therefore, only one router on a broadcast segment has the responsibility of sending IGMP queries every 60 seconds.

Question 8 Answer

The Cisco Group Management Protocol (CGMP) is a Cisco-proprietary protocol, typically found on lower-end switches, that lets the router send two MAC addresses to the switch when the router receives an IGMP report from a joining device. One of those MAC addresses is the Unicast Source Address (USA), which is the MAC address of the device desiring to join the group. The switch already knows, from its CAM table, to which interface that MAC addresses attached. The other MAC address is the Group Destination Address (GDA), which is the MAC address of the multicast group. Therefore, when a switch receives a frame destined for a particular multicast MAC address, the switch knows to which interface or interfaces the frame should be forwarded.

Question 9 Answer

IGMP snooping is a method of training a switch which of its interfaces are connected to multicast receivers. However, IGMP snooping acts independently of router operations. Therefore, IGMP snooping is even compatible with non-Cisco routers.

The switch enabled for IGMP snooping eavesdrops in on the IGMP messages being exchanged between receivers and a router. By watching those IGMP packets, the switch can determine which of its interfaces are connected to receivers for particular multicast groups.

Question 10

What range of IP addresses is reserved for IP multicast addresses?

Question 11

What range of IP multicast addresses is used for Source Specific Multicast (SSM)?

Question 12

What range of IP multicast addresses is designated for Limited Scope Addresses?

Question 10 Answer

IP multicast uses Class D IP addresses, which are in the range 224.0.0.0 through 239.255.255.255.

Question 11 Answer

Source Specific Multicast (SSM) uses the address range 232.0.0.0–232.255.255.255. SSM allows a receiver to specify that it wants to receive content for a multicast group from a specific source. As a result, servers with different content can simultaneously transmit to the same multicast group address.

Question 12 Answer

The IP multicast address space 239.0.0.0—239.255.255.255 is reserved for Limited Scope Addresses. These addresses are used for internal multicast applications (i.e., traffic that doesn't leave an autonomous system), much like the 10.x.x.x/8 address space is a "private" address space.

Question 13

Identify the IP multicast address that addresses all multicast hosts.

Question 14

Given an AS number of 65000, calculate the corresponding IP multicast address space, using GLOP addressing.

Question 15

Given a multicast IP address of 224.1.10.10, calculate the corresponding multicast MAC address.

Question 13 Answer

The IP multicast address 224.0.0.1 addresses all IP multicast hosts, while 224.0.0.2 addresses all IP multicast routers.

Question 14 Answer

GLOP addresses provide a globally unique multicast address range, based on AS numbers. As an example, if a company had an AS number of 65000, then its globally unique range of multicast IP addresses would be 233.253.232.0–233.253.232.255. The AS number is used to calculate the second and third octets in this address range. First, convert the AS number to hexadecimal (i.e., 65000 in decimal equals FD-E8 in hexadecimal). FD in hexadecimal equals 253 in decimal, and E8 in hexadecimal equals 232 in decimal. The first octet of a GLOP address is always 233.

Question 15 Answer

1. First, convert the last three octets to binary.
0000.0001.0000.1010.0000.1010
2. If the left-most bit isn't already 0, it should be changed to a 0, because the 25th bit of a multicast MAC address is always 0.
0000.0001.0000.1010.0000.1010
3. Convert each nibble (i.e., 4-bit section) into its hexadecimal equivalent.
01-0a-0a
4. Prepend 01-00-5e to the calculated address to produce the multicast MAC address.
These steps yield a multicast MAC address of 01-00-5e-01-0a-0a.

Question 16

Describe the purpose and operation of RPF check.

Question 17

Discuss the characteristics of a Source Distribution Tree.

Question 18

Describe the concept of a Shared Distribution Tree.

Question 16 Answer

Reverse Path Forwarding (RPF) check is used to combat the issue of receiving duplicate packets in an IP multicast network. Cisco routers use the RPF check mechanism to determine if a multicast packet is entering a router on the appropriate interface. An RPF check examines the source address of an incoming packet and checks it against the router's unicast routing table to see what interface should be used to get back to the source network. If the incoming multicast packet is using that interface, then the RPF check passes, and the packet is forwarded. If the multicast packet is coming in on a different interface, then the RPF check fails, and the packet is discarded.

Question 17 Answer

A Source Distribution Tree creates a loop-free path from each IP multicast source router to the last hop router (i.e., the router attached to the receiver). If multiple sources contain the same content, multiple trees are created, one from each source router to the last hop router. As a result, routers have increased memory utilization. However, the Source Distribution Tree does create an optimal path between each source router and the last hop router.

Question 18 Answer

A Shared Distribution Tree uses the concept of a rendezvous point (RP). Source routers (i.e., the routers attached to the source) create a Source Distribution Tree to the RP. The RP then forwards the multicast traffic down a Shared Tree to all of the last hop routers (i.e., the routers attached to receivers). Since the last hop routers do not have a multicast routing entry for each server, because they are using a wildcard entry to represent all sources for a multicast group, less memory overhead exists on the routers. However, a Shared Distribution Tree might suffer from a suboptimal path, since IP multicast packets flow through the RP.

Question 19

What command enables IP multicast routing on a router?

Question 20

After a last hop router has formed a source path tree with the first hop router, in a Protocol Independent Multicast-Sparse Mode (PIM-SM) configuration, it no longer needs to receive IP multicast traffic from an RP. What message does the last hop router then send to the RP?

Question 21

What interface configuration mode syntax is used to configure PIM?

Question 19 Answer

The global configuration mode command **ip multicast-routing** enables IP multicast routing on a router. After enabling IP multicast routing globally, individual interfaces can be configured to support IP multicast using a command such as **ip pim sparse-mode**.

Question 20 Answer

Since the last hop router no longer needs multicast traffic from the RP, because it is receiving the multicast traffic directly from the first hop router, it sends an (S,G) RP-bit prune message to the RP, requesting the RP to stop sending multicast traffic for that particular multicast group.

Question 21 Answer

The interface configuration mode command to configure PIM is as follows:

ip pim {dense-mode | sparse-mode | sparse-dense-mode}

Note that **sparse-dense-mode** is recommended for use in an Auto RP environment, because the interface will operate in **dense-mode** long enough to learn the location of an RP. After an RP is learned, the interface then operates in **sparse-mode**.

Question 22

Describe Shortest Path Tree (SPT) switchover.

Question 23

What command displays a router's IP multicast routing table?

Question 24

On a router with one or more interfaces running in PIM-SM, what global command defines the IP address of a Rendezvous Point (RP)?

Question 22 Answer

In a PIM-SM environment, the process of cutting over from the path via the RP to the direct path is called Shortest Path Tree (SPT) switchover.

Question 23 Answer

The command **show ip mroute** displays a router's IP multicast routing table. Included in the command's output are (S, G) and/or (*, G) entries, a router's IIF (Incoming Interface List), and OIL (Outgoing Interface List).

Question 24 Answer

The command **ip pim rp-address ip-address** globally defines the IP address of an RP. Statically configuring an RP, however, has scalability limitations. To overcome these limitations, you can use Auto RP or Bootstrap Router (BSR) to automatically configure a router with the RP's IP address.

Question 25

In an Auto RP configuration, what address is used by candidate RPs to inform a mapping agent of their candidacy?

Question 26

In an Auto RP configuration, what address is used by a mapping agent to inform other IP multicast routers in the topology of the address of an RP?

Question 27

In an Auto RP configuration, on what router(s) is the command ip pim send-rp-announce issued?

Question 25 Answer

In an Auto RP configuration, candidate RPs multicast their candidacy to a mapping agent using IP multicast address 224.0.1.39. The mapping agent then advertises RP information to other IP multicast-enabled routers in the topology.

Question 26 Answer

After a mapping agent learns the location of one or more candidate RPs, the mapping agent advertises an RP's IP address to other IP multicast routers in the topology using IP multicast address 224.0.1.40.

Question 27 Answer

The command **ip pim send-rp-announce** is used on routers willing to serve as an RP. These routers are called candidate RPs.

Question 28

In an Auto RP configuration, on what router is the command ip pim send-rp-discovery issued?

Question 29

In a BSR configuration, what command should be issued on routers willing to serve as an RP?

Question 30

In a PIMv2 BSR configuration, what command is issued on routers willing to serve as the bootstrap router?

Question 28 Answer

The command **ip pim send-rp-discovery** is issued on a mapping agent. The mapping agent advertises the location of an RP to other IP multicast-enabled routers in the topology using IP multicast address 224.0.1.40.

Question 29 Answer

In a PIMv2 BSR configuration, routers can be configured to potentially serve as an RP with the global configuration mode command **ip pim rp-candidate interface ttl group-list acl**.

Question 30 Answer

In a PIMv2 BSR configuration, a mapping agent uses PIMv2 messages to advertise the location of an RP to IP multicast–enabled routers in the topology. The command issued on routers willing to serve as the bootstrap router (i.e., the BSR) is **ip pim bsr-candidate interface hash-mask-length [priority]**.

Question 31

What version of PIM is required to support the BSR feature?

Question 32

What type of IP multicast addressing uses an organization's Border Gateway Protocol (BGP) AS number to provide a range of globally unique IP multicast addresses?

Question 33

IP multicast route entries can have "(S, G) entries." What do the S and G represent in these entries?

Question 31 Answer

The Bootstrap Router (BSR) feature is a standards-based method for making the IP address of an RP known to other multicast routers in the topology. PIM Version 2 is required to support BSR.

Question 32 Answer

GLOP addressing uses an AS number to create a globally unique range of IP multicast addresses. Specifically, the AS number is used to calculate the second and third octets of the IP multicast address, and the GLOP standard specifies that the first octet in the IP multicast address is 233.

Question 33 Answer

With an (S, G) entry in an IP multicast routing table, the S refers to the unicast source address, and the G refers to the multicast group address. For example, an entry of (192.168.1.1, 224.1.1.1) refers to IP multicast traffic flowing from a source with an address of 192.168.1.1 to a group address of 224.1.1.1.

Question 34

What range of IP multicast addresses are considered Globally Scoped addresses?

Question 35

What number is in the first octet of an IP multicast GLOP address?

Question 36

In hexadecimal, what is the first half of multicast MAC address?

Question 34 Answer

IP multicast Globally Scoped addresses are in the range 224.0.1.0 through 238.255.255.255. Note, however, that other designated address ranges (i.e., Source Specific Multicast and GLOP addressing) exist within the Globally Scoped range.

Question 35 Answer

The first octet in a GLOP address is always 233. The second and third octets are calculated based on a BGP AS number.

Question 36 Answer

The first half (i.e., the first 24 bits) of a MAC address, in hexadecimal is 01-00-5e.

Question 37

What is the value of the 25th bit in a multicast MAC address?

Question 38

Where do the last 23 bits in a multicast MAC address come from?

Question 39

In an Auto RP environment, what is the role of a mapping agent?

Question 37 Answer

When constructing a multicast MAC address, the first 24 bits, in hexadecimal, are 01-00-5e. The next bit, the 25th bit, is always 0.

Question 38 Answer

The last 23 bits of an IP multicast address come directly from the last 23 bits in the corresponding IP address. Since the entire IP address isn't represented in MAC address, you have the potential for overlap, where multiple IP multicast addresses map to the same MAC address.

Question 39 Answer

In an Auto RP environment, routers willing to serve as a RP announce their candidacy to a mapping agent. The mapping agent then advertises the IP address of an RP to other IP multicast–enabled routers in the topology.

Question 40

What type of IP multicast distribution tree uses (*, G) entries?

Question 41

What is the purpose of GMRP?

Question 42

Describe the purpose of RGMP?

Question 40 Answer

Shared Distribution Trees leverage (*, G) IP multicast route entries to minimize memory usage on routers in the topology. Specifically, the * is a wildcard indicating any source. Therefore, multiple sources could be sending to a multicast group G, and all of those sources could be represented with a single (*, G) entry.

Question 41 Answer

The GARP Multicast Registration Protocol (GMRP) allows a receiver (e.g., a PC that wants to participate in a multicast session) to inform its upstream switch that the receiver wants to receive traffic for a specific multicast group.

Question 42 Answer

Just because a router is enabled for IP multicast does not mean that it wants to receive traffic for every IP multicast group. Fortunately, a Cisco-proprietary protocol called RGMP (Router-port Group Management Protocol) allows a router to inform its upstream switch that the router wants to receive traffic only for specific IP multicast groups.

Question 43

List at least two approaches for constraining IP multicast frames to switch ports that are connected to receivers, or downstream routers that need to receive specific multicast frames.

Question 44

What is the best command to use for identifying the IGMP querier on a multiaccess network?

Question 45

Identify the purpose of the show ip igmp group command.

Question 43 Answer

By definition, when a switch receives a multicast frame, it forwards that frame out of all its other ports, because the destination MAC address is a multicast MAC address and is not in the switch's MAC address table. Fortunately, several approaches are available for constraining these multicast frames on switches, including the following:

CGMP

IGMP Snooping

GMRP

RGMP

Question 44 Answer

The command **show ip igmp interface [interface-id]** identifies the IP address of an IGMP querier on a multiaccess network segment. By default, this designated querier is the router on that segment with the lowest unicast IP address.

Question 45 Answer

The **show ip igmp group** command displays the IP multicast groups that a router is aware of. Additionally, this command displays which interfaces are participating in these IP multicast groups.

Question 46

To what address does an IGMPv1 router send an IGMP Query message?

Question 47

What type of distribution tree is used by PIM-DM?

Question 48

If you have two routers that can forward traffic from a multicast source onto the same Ethernet segment, by default, what determines which router is the PIM forwarder?

Question 46 Answer

IGMPv1 does not support group-specific queries. Therefore, an IGMPv1 router sends IGMP Query messages to 224.0.0.1, which addresses all IP multicast hosts.

Question 47 Answer

PIM-Dense Mode (PIM-DM) uses a Source Distribution Tree, while PIM-Sparse Mode (PIM-SM) is based on a Shared Distribution Tree.

Question 48 Answer

By default, the PIM forwarder is elected based on the highest unicast IP address on the routers. A PIM forwarder should not be confused with an IGMP querier, which is elected based on the lowest unicast IP address on the routers.

Question 49

What PIM-DM message is used in the election of a PIM forwarder?

Question 50

If a router has been pruned off a PIM-DM distribution tree, what type of packet can that router send to rejoin the tree?

Question 49 Answer

PIM-DM uses assert messages to elect PIM forwarders. By default, the highest IP address on these routers determines the PIM forwarder. However, this behavior can be influenced by specifying a metric, which overrides this default behavior.

Question 50 Answer

In a PIM-DM environment, a router that has been previously pruned from the distribution tree can rejoin the tree by sending a Graft packet to its upstream router.

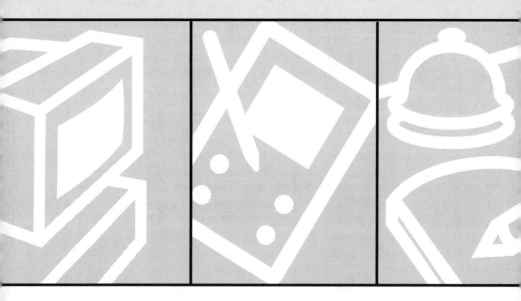

IP Multicasting
Quick Reference Sheets

Introduction

Consider a video stream that needs to be sent to multiple recipients in a company. One approach is to unicast the traffic. The source server sends a copy of every packet to every receiver. Obviously, this approach has serious scalability limitations.

An alternate approach is to broadcast the video stream, so that the source server has to send each packet only once. However, everyone in the network receives the packet in that scenario even if they do not want it.

IP multicast technologies provide the best of both worlds. With IP multicast, the source server sends only one copy of each packet, and packets are sent only to intended recipients.

Specifically, receivers join a multicast group, denoted by a Class D IP address (i.e., in the range 224.0.0.0 through 239.255.255.255). The source sends traffic to the Class D address, and through switch and router protocols, packets are forwarded only to intended stations. These multicast packets are sent via User Datagram Protocol (UDP) (i.e., best effort). Therefore, congestion avoidance mechanisms such as weighted random early detect (WRED), which causes TCP flows to go into TCP slow start, are not effective for multicast. When doing a multicast design, also be aware of the potential for duplicate packets being received and the potential for packets arriving out of order.

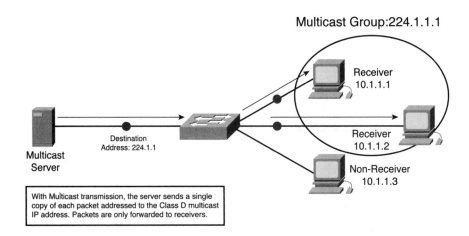

Multicast Group:224.1.1.1

With Multicast transmission, the server sends a single copy of each packet addressed to the Class D multicast IP address. Packets are only forwarded to receivers.

IGMP/CGMP

The protocol used between clients (e.g., PCs) and routers to let routers know which of their interfaces have multicast receivers attached is IGMP (Internet Group Management Protocol). There are three versions of IGMP. However, only two versions are in wide-scale deployment:

- **IGMP Version 1**—When a PC wants to join a multicast group, it sends an IGMP Report message to the router, letting the router know it wants to receive traffic for a specific group. Every 60 seconds, by default, the router sends an IGMP Query message to determine if the PC still wants to belong to the group. There can be up to a 3-minute delay before the time the router realizes that the receiver left the group. The destination address of this router query is 224.0.0.1, which addresses all IP multicast hosts.

- **IGMP Version 2**—Similar to IGMP Version 1, except that IGMP Version 2 can send queries to a specific group, and a "Leave" message is supported. Specifically, a receiver can proactively send a Leave message when it no longer wants to participate in a multicast group, allowing the router to prune its interface earlier.

IGMP Version 1 and Version 2 hosts and routers do have some interoperability. When an IGMPv2 hosts sends an IGMPv2 report to an IGMPv1 router, the IGMP message type appears to be invalid, and it is ignored. Therefore, an IGMPv2 host must send IGMPv1 reports to an IGMPv1 router.

In an environment with an IGMPv2 router and a mixture of IGMPv1 and IGMPv2 receivers, the Version 1 receivers respond normally to IGMPv1 or IGMPv2 queries. However, the Version 2 router must ignore any Leave message while IGMP receivers are present, because if the router processed the IGMPv2 Leave message, it would send a group-specific query, which would not be correctly interpreted by an IGMPv1 receiver.

IGMPv2 Router with v1 and v2 Receivers

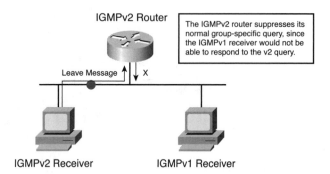

IGMPv2 Router

The IGMPv2 router suppresses its normal group-specific query, since the IGMPv1 receiver would not be able to respond to the v2 query.

Leave Message ↑↓ X

IGMPv2 Receiver   IGMPv1 Receiver

As mentioned earlier, multicast routers can periodically send queries out of an interface to determine if any multicast receivers still exists off that interface. However, you might have a situation where more than one multicast router exists on a broadcast media segment (e.g., Ethernet). Therefore, one router must be designated as the "querier" for that segment. This IGMP designated querier is the router that has the lowest unicast IP address.

To determine which router on a multiaccess network is the querier, issue the following command:

```
Router#show ip igmp interface [interface-id]
```

The output from the preceding command identifies the IP address of the IGMP querier. Additionally, the following command displays the IP multicast groups that a router is aware of:

```
Router#show ip igmp group
```

When a Layer 2 switch receives a multicast frame on an interface, by default, the switch floods the frame out all other interfaces. To prevent this behavior, the switch needs awareness of what interfaces are connected to receivers for specific multicast groups. Approaches for training the switch include the following:

- **CGMP (Cisco Group Management Protocol)**—A Cisco-proprietary approach used on lower-end switches that allows a Cisco router to inform a Cisco switch which of its interfaces are connected to multicast receivers for specific multicast groups

- **IGMP Snooping**—Used on higher-end switches; allows a switch to autonomously determine which interfaces are connected to receivers for specific multicast groups by eavesdropping on the IGMP traffic being exchanged between clients and routers

- **GMRP (GARP Multicast Registration Protocol)**—A standards-based approach for letting a receiver proactively inform its upstream switch that the receiver wants to belong to a specific multicast group

- **RGMP (Router-Port Group Management Protocol)**—A proprietary approach that allows a switch to send IP multicast packets to only multicast-enabled routers that want to receive traffic for specific IP multicast groups

Addressing

In a multicast network, the source sends multicast packets with a Class D destination address. The 224.0.0.0 through 239.255.255.255 address range is the Class D address range, because the first 4 bits in the first octet of a Class D address are 1110.

Some ranges of addresses in the Class D address space are dedicated for special purposes:

224.0.0.0–224.0.0.255—Reserved link local addresses

224.0.1.0–238.255.255.255—Globally scoped addresses

232.0.0.0–232.255.255.255—Source specific multicast addresses

233.0.0.0–233.255.255.255—GLOP addresses

239.0.0.0–239.255.255.255—Limited scope addresses

- **Reserved link local addresses**—Are used, for example, by many network protocols. Open Shortest Path First (OSPF) uses 224.0.0.5 and 224.0.0.6. RIPv2 uses 224.0.0.9, and Enhanced Interior Gateway Routing Protocol (EIGRP) uses 224.0.0.10. Other "well-known" addresses in this range include 224.0.0.1, which addresses all multicast hosts, and 224.0.0.2, which addresses all multicast routers.

- **Globally scoped addresses**—Are used for general-purpose multicast applications, and they have the ability to extend beyond the local autonomous system.

- **Source specific multicast (SSM) addresses**—Are used in conjunction with IGMPv3, to allow a multicast receiver request, not only for membership in a group, but also to request specific sources to receive traffic from. Therefore, in an SSM environment, multiple sources with different content can all be sending to the same multicast destination address.

- **GLOP addresses**—Provide a globally unique multicast address range, based on AS numbers. As an example, if a company had an AS number of 65000, its globally unique range of multicast IP addresses would be 233.253.232.0–233.253.232.255. The AS number is used to calculate the second and third octets in this address range. First, convert the AS number to hexadecimal (i.e., 65000 in decimal equals FD-E8 in hexadecimal). FD in hexadecimal equals 253 in decimal, and E8 in hexadecimal equals 232 in decimal. The first octet of a GLOP address is always 233.

- **Limited scope addresses**—Are used for internal multicast applications (i.e., traffic that doesn't leave the AS), much like the 10.x.x.x/8 address space is a "private" address space.

In addition to Layer 3 addresses, multicast applications must also have Layer 2 addresses (i.e., MAC addresses). Fortunately, these Layer 2 addresses can be constructed directly from the Layer 3 multicast addresses. A MAC address is a 48-bit address, and the first half (i.e., 24 bits) of a multicast MAC address (in hex) is 01-00-5e. The 25th bit is always 0. The last 23 bits in the multicast MAC address come directly from the last 23 bits of the multicast IP address. Consider the following examples:

- Given a multicast IP address of 224.1.10.10, calculate the corresponding multicast MAC address:

  — First, convert the last three octets to binary:

  0000.0001.0000.1010.0000.1010

  — If the leftmost bit isn't already 0, it should be changed to a 0, because the 25th bit of a multicast MAC address is always 0:

  0000.0001.0000.1010.0000.1010

  — Convert each nibble (i.e., 4-bit section) into its hexadecimal equivalent:

  01-0a-0a

  — Prepend 01-00-5e to the calculated address to produce the multicast MAC address:

  01-00-5e-01-0a-0a

- Given a multicast IP address of 224.129.10.10, calculate the corresponding multicast MAC address.

  — First, convert the last three octets to binary:

  1000.0001.0000.1010.0000.1010

  — If the leftmost bit isn't already 0, it should be changed to a 0, because the 25th bit of a multicast MAC address is always 0:

  0000.0001.0000.1010.0000.1010

  — Convert each nibble (i.e., 4-bit section) into its hexadecimal equivalent:

  01-0a-0a

  — Prepend 01-00-5e to the calculated address to produce the multicast MAC address:

  01-00-5e-01-0a-0a

Notice that both Layer 3 IP addresses translated into the same Layer 2 MAC address. This overlap permits 32 Layer 3 multicast addresses to map to the same Layer 2 multicast MAC address. So, care must be taken when selecting Layer 3 multicast addresses to avoid this overlap.

Distribution Trees

To combat the issue of receiving duplicate packets, Cisco routers perform a Reverse Path Forwarding (RPF) check to determine if a multicast packet is entering a router on the correct interface. An RPF check examines the source address of an incoming packet and checks it against the router's unicast routing table to see what interface should be used to get back to the source network. If the incoming multicast packet is using that interface, the RPF check passes, and the packet is forwarded. If the multicast packet is coming in a different interface, the RPF check fails, and the packet is discarded.

Reverse Path Forwarding (RPF) Check

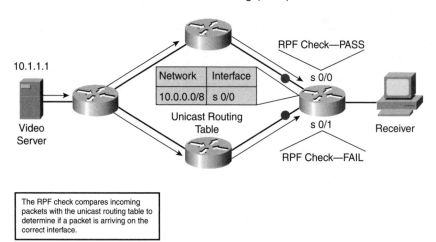

The RPF check compares incoming packets with the unicast routing table to determine if a packet is arriving on the correct interface.

Only members of a multicast group receive packets destined for that group. However, the sender does not need to be a member of the group.

Multicast traffic flows from a source to a destination over a "distribution tree," which is a loop-free path. The two types of distribution trees are as follows:

- **Source distribution tree**—A source distribution tree creates an optimal path between each source router and each last hop router (i.e., a router connected to a receiver) at the expense of increased memory usage. Source distributions trees place (S, G) states in a router's multicast routing table to indicate the address of the source (S) and the address of the group (G).

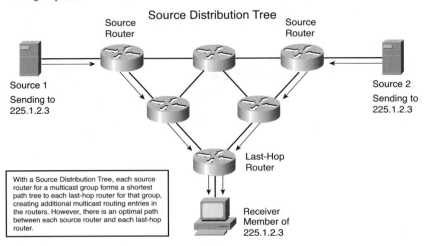

Source Distribution Tree

Source Router

Source Router

Source 1
Sending to
225.1.2.3

Source 2
Sending to
225.1.2.3

Last-Hop Router

With a Source Distribution Tree, each source router for a multicast group forms a shortest path tree to each last-hop router for that group, creating additional multicast routing entries in the routers. However, there is an optimal path between each source router and each last-hop router.

Receiver
Member of
225.1.2.3

- **Shared distribution tree**—A shared distribution tree creates a tree from a central "rendezvous point" (RP) router to all last hop routers, with source distribution trees being created from all sources to the rendezvous point, at the expense of increased delay. Shared distribution trees place (*, G) states in a router's multicast routing table to indicate that any device could be the source (i.e., using the wildcard [*] character) for the group (G). This (*, G) state is created in routers along the shared tree from the RP to the last hop routers. Since each source for a group does not require its own (S, G), the memory requirement is less for a shared tree compared to a source tree.

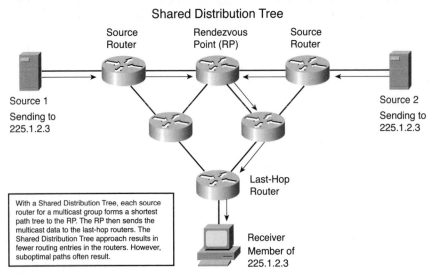

Shared Distribution Tree

Source Router

Rendezvous Point (RP)

Source Router

Source 1
Sending to
225.1.2.3

Source 2
Sending to
225.1.2.3

Last-Hop Router

With a Shared Distribution Tree, each source router for a multicast group forms a shortest path tree to the RP. The RP then sends the multicast data to the last-hop routers. The Shared Distribution Tree approach results in fewer routing entries in the routers. However, suboptimal paths often result.

Receiver
Member of
225.1.2.3

PIM-DM Mechanics

Cisco routers use the Protocol Independent Multicast (PIM) protocol to construct IP multicast distribution trees. PIM's protocol independence suggests that it can run over an IP network, regardless of the underlying unicast routing protocol, such as OSPF or EIGRP. The two varieties of PIM are PIM-Dense Mode (PIM-DM) and PIM-Sparse Mode (PIM-SM). PIM-DM uses a source distribution tree, while PIM-SM uses a shared distribution tree.

A router is globally enabled for multicast routing with the following global configuration mode command:

```
Router(config)#ip multicast-routing
```

Once IP multicast is globally enabled, individual interfaces need to be configured for PIM support. To configure an interface to participate in an IP multicast network using PIM, issue the following interface configuration mode command:

```
Router(config-if)#ip pim {dense-mode | sparse-mode | sparse-dense-mode}
```

Cisco recommends **sparse-dense-mode**, which uses Dense Mode to automatically learn the location of an RP, after which the interface runs in Sparse Mode. First, consider the formation of a PIM-Dense Mode distribution tree:

Step 1   A multicast source comes up and begins flooding multicast traffic throughout the network.

Step 2   If more than one router is forwarding over a common broadcast medium (e.g., an Ethernet link), "Assert" messages are used to determine the PIM forwarder. The router with the better metric, or (by default) the highest IP address, wins the election.

Step 3   Some routers might not have multicast receivers for the group whose traffic is currently being flooded. Those routers send a "Prune" message to their upstream router, requesting that their branch of the distribution tree be pruned off. However, if another router is on the same broadcast medium as the router that sent the prune, and if that other router does have IP multicast receivers attached, the Prune message is ignored. The reason that the Prune message is ignored is because the router that is attached to IP multicast receivers sends a "Join Override" message.

Step 4   If a receiver comes up on a router that was previously pruned from the tree, that router can rejoin the tree by sending a "Graft" packet.

A major consideration for PIM-DM, however, is that this "flood-and-prune" behavior repeats every three minutes. Therefore, PIM-DM does not scale well. A better alternative is PIM-Sparse Mode (PIM-SM).

PIM-SM Mechanics

Next, consider the formation of a PIM-Sparse Mode distribution tree:

Step 1　A receiver sends an IGMP Report message to its router indicating that it wants to participate in a particular multicast group. The receiver's router (i.e., the "last hop router") sends a Join message to the RP, creating (*, G) state along a shared tree between the RP and the last hop router.

Step 2　A source comes up and creates a source tree between its router (i.e., "the first hop router") and the RP. (S, G) state is created in routers along this path. However, before the source tree is completely established, the source sends its multicast packets to the RP encapsulated inside of unicast Register messages.

Step 3　After the RP receives the first multicast packet over the source tree, it sends a Register Stop message to the source, telling the source to stop sending the multicast traffic inside of Register messages. Two trees now exist: (1) a source tree from the first hop router to the RP and (2) a shared tree from the RP to the last hop router. However, this might not be the optimal path.

Step 4　The last hop router observes from where the multicast traffic is arriving, and the last hop router sends a Join message directly to the first hop router to form an optimal path (i.e., a source path tree) between the source and the receiver.

Step 5　Because the last hop router no longer needs multicast traffic from the RP, because it is receiving the multicast traffic directly from the first hop router, it sends an (S, G) RP-bit prune message to the RP, requesting the RP to stop sending multicast traffic.

Step 6　With the shared tree to the last hop router pruned, the RP no longer needs to receive multicast traffic from the first hop router. So, the RP sends an (S, G) Prune message to the first hop router. At this point, traffic flows in an optimal path from the first hop router to the last hop router. The process of cutting over from the path via the RP to the direct path is called Shortest Path Tree (SPT) Switchover.

Comparing PIM-DM versus PIM-SM suggests that PIM-SM offers the benefits of PIM-DM (i.e., optimal pathing) without PIM-DM's flood-and-prune behavior.

A distribution tree's topology can be determined by examining the multicast routing table of multicast routers in the topology. The **show ip mroute** command displays a router's multicast routing table, as shown in the following:

```
Router#show ip mroute
IP Multicast Routing Table
Flags: D - Dense, S - Sparse, B - Bidir Group,
 s - SSM Group, C - Connected, L - Local,
 P - Pruned, R - RP-bit set, F - Register flag,
```

```
T - SPT-bit set, J - Join SPT,
M - MSDP created entry,
X - Proxy Join Timer Running,
A - Candidate for MSDP Advertisement,
U - URD,
I - Received Source Specific Host Report,
Z - Multicast Tunnel,
Y - Joined MDT-data group,
y - Sending to MDT-data group
Timers: Uptime/Expires
Interface state: Interface, Next-Hop or VCD,
   State/Mode

(*, 224.0.100.4), 02:37:12, RP is 192.168.47.14,
   flags: S
   Incoming interface: Serial0, RPF neighbor
   10.4.53.4
   Outgoing interface list:
      Ethernet1, Forward/Sparse, 02:37:12/0:03:42
      Ethernet2, Forward/Sparse, 02:52:12/0:01:23

(192.168.46.0/24, 224.0.100.4), 02:37:12,
   flags: RT
   Incoming interface: Ethernet1, RPF neighbor
   10.4.53.4
   Outgoing interface list:
      Ethernet2, Forward/Sparse, 02:44:21/0:01:47
```

Notice the highlighted (*, G) and (S, G) entries. Other valuable information contained in the mroute table includes the IIF (Incoming Interface List), which shows on which interface traffic is entering the router, and the OIL (Outgoing Interface List), which shows the router interfaces over which the multicast traffic is being forwarded.

Rendezvous Points

In a PIM-SM network, one or more routers need to be designated as rendezvous points (RPs). Non-RPs can be configured to point to a statically defined RP with the global configuration mode command **ip pim** *rp-address ip-address*. However, in larger topologies, Cisco recommends that RPs be automatically configured.

Cisco routers support two methods for automatically configuring an RP, Auto-RP and BSR. Auto-RP is a Cisco-developed solution. Routers willing to serve as an RP are called "candidate RPs," and they make their candidacy known to other routers called "mapping agents" using the multicast address 224.0.1.39. A mapping agent then makes the location of an RP known to other multicast routers in the network using the multicast address 224.0.1.40. By default, the mapping agent advertises the candidate RP with the highest IP address.

The global configuration command **ip pim send-rp-announce** *interface* **scope** *ttl* [**group-list** *acl*] is issued on candidate RPs. To identify a router as a mapping agent, use the global configuration mode command **ip pim send-rp-discovery scope** *ttl*.

While Auto-RP is a Cisco approach, PIMv2 added a standards-based approach to make the location of RPs known throughout the multicast network. Specifically, PIMv2, which uses protocol number 103, supports a feature called Bootstrap Router (BSR), which performs a similar function to Auto-RP. Routers that are candidates to become the RP can be configured with the global configuration mode command **ip pim rp-candidate** *interface ttl* **group-list** *acl*. Routers that are candidates to become the bootstrap router (similar to an Auto-RP mapping agent) can be configured with the global configuration mode command **ip pim bsr-candidate** *interface hash-mask-length* [**priority**]. Since BSR leverages PIM messages, reserved multicast group addresses (e.g., 224.0.1.40 used by Auto-RP) are not required for RP advertisement.

Section 8
Security

As more and more mission critical data is introduced to the network, security becomes more important than ever.

While a CCIE track is dedicated to the area of security in today's networks, it is important that you have a fundamental understanding of key security principles including general security of the device and LAN-based security mechanisms. This section ensures that you achieve just that.

Question 1

What is the meaning of the none keyword in the following command:

```
aaa authentication login mylist group tacacs+ enable none
```

Question 2

If a switch's configuration features the aaa new-model command with no authentication lists configured, what is a possible result?

Question 3

When is it appropriate to use the login command in line configuration mode?

Question 1 Answer

The **none** keyword ensures the user is allowed access if the previous authentication methods return an ERROR.

Question 2 Answer

Administrators that Telnet to the device are prompted for a username and password from the local database when no username or passwords exist there.

Question 3 Answer

Use the **login** command to enable password checking on a line (for example, virtual terminal lines [VTY]). You cannot use the **login** command on a line when authentication, authorization, and accounting (AAA)/TACACS+ is in use. You use the **login authentication** command instead.

Question 4

What specific privilege level does the router assign when a user logs in using the enable password?

Question 5

You are considering the implementation of the Cisco AAA. In addition to the use of authentication and authorization, you are also considering calling upon accounting. What is the Cisco recommendation to minimize accounting records when using the aaa accounting global configuration command?

Question 6

What is the transport protocol used by RADIUS?

Question 4 Answer

Level 15 is the level of access permitted by the enable password. Level 1 is normal EXEC mode user privileges.

Question 5 Answer

For minimal accounting, you can include the **stop-only** keyword to send a "stop" record accounting notice at the end of the requested user process. If you require more detail, you can include the **start-stop** keyword, so that RADIUS or TACACS+ sends a "start" accounting notice at the beginning of the requested process and a "stop" accounting notice at the end of the process.

Question 6 Answer

RADIUS relies upon User Datagram Protocol (UDP), whereas TACACS+ relies upon TCP.

Question 7

What are the possible number ranges for a standard IP access list?

Question 8

What are the possible number ranges for an extended IP access list?

Question 9

What are the possible number ranges for an Ethernet type code access list?

Question 7 Answer

1–99, 1300–1999

Question 8 Answer

100–199, 2000–2699

Question 9 Answer

200–299

Question 10

What are the possible number ranges for an Ethernet address access list?

Question 11

How many access lists are you typically permitted on a Cisco device?

Question 12

What is located at the end of every access list?

Question 10 Answer

700–799

Question 11 Answer

You are permitted one access list per protocol, per interface, per direction.

Question 12 Answer

The implicit deny all statement.

Question 13

What is the default interval over which access list usage related syslog messages are collected and then displayed?

Question 14

What effect (if any) does logging access lists have on Cisco Express Forwarding (CEF)?

Question 15

What is the correct syntax to create a named extended IP access list in the Cisco IOS?

Question 13 Answer

The default time interval is 5 minutes.

Question 14 Answer

Logging access list usage does not permit CEF to function on the traffic.

Question 15 Answer

Router(config)# **ip access-list extended name**

Question 16

You have noticed the fragment keyword in several access list statements you have observed. What is the impact of this keyword?

Question 17

What command do you use to enable the Turbo ACL feature?

Question 18

What are the two steps involved with created a time-based access list in the Cisco IOS?

Question 16 Answer

If the **fragment** keyword is specified in an access list entry, that particular access list entry applies only to noninitial fragments of packets; the fragment is either permitted or denied accordingly.

Question 17 Answer

```
Router(config)# access-list compiled
```

Question 18 Answer

First you need to define the time range in global configuration mode; then you need to reference this time range in the access control list.

Question 19

What is the command required to assign an access control list to a line on your Cisco router?

Question 20

What are the three types of secure MAC addresses that can be used in port security on a LAN switch?

Question 21

What port security violation mode drops packets with unknown source addresses until you remove a sufficient number of secure MAC addresses or increase the number of maximum allowable addresses? This mode also provides you with notification.

Question 19 Answer

```
Router(config-line)# access-class access-list-number {in ¦ out}
```

Question 20 Answer

You can configure these types of secure MAC addresses:

Static secure MAC addresses

Dynamic secure MAC addresses

Sticky secure MAC addresses

Question 21 Answer

The restrict mode drops packets with unknown source addresses until you remove a sufficient number of secure MAC addresses or increase the number of maximum allowable addresses; this mode also provides you with notification.

Question 22

You have configured the BPDU Guard feature on the PortFast-enabled ports of a Catalyst switch. What state is the port placed in when a bridge protocol data unit (BPDU) arrives on the port?

Question 23

What command would you use to prevent a switch from taking over as the Spanning Tree Protocol (STP) root of the network?

Question 24

What 802.1X authentication port state should you use when you want the port to begin in an unauthorized state and check for authorization when a client attempts to access the port?

Question 22 Answer

The port is placed in an error-disable state.

Question 23 Answer

Use the command **spanning-tree guard root** in interface configuration mode to enable this feature.

Question 24 Answer

Auto

Question 25

Between RADIUS and TACACS+, which is a standards-based security protocol?

Question 25 Answer

RADIUS is a standards-based security protocol, while a TACACS+ is a Cisco protocol.

Security
Quick Reference Sheets

Access Lists

Many types of access lists are available in Cisco IOS for many different protocols. Here is a complete list:

Protocol	Range
IP	1–99, 1300–1999
Extended IP	100–199, 2000–2699
Ethernet type code	200–299
Ethernet address	700–799
Transparent bridging (protocol type)	200–299
Transparent bridging (vendor code)	700–799
Extended transparent bridging	1100–1199
DECnet and extended DECnet	300–399
Xerox Network Systems (XNS)	400–499
Extended XNS	500–599
AppleTalk	600–699
Source-route bridging (protocol type)	200–299
Source-route bridging (vendor code)	700–799
IPX	800–899
Extended IPX	900–999

Protocol	Range
IPX SAP	1000–1099
Standard Virtual Integrated Network Service (VINES)	1–100
Extended VINES	101–200
Simple VINES	201–300

You are permitted one access list per protocol, per interface, per direction.

Access Controls Lists

One access list per protocol, per direction, per interface

fa 0/0

Server

Inbound access list filters traffic before entering the router; an outbound access list filters traffic before it exits the router

At the end of every access list is an implied "deny all traffic" access control entry (ACE). Therefore, if a packet does not match any of your criteria statements, the packet is blocked.

Remember that the order of access list statements is important! For example, if you create a criteria statement that explicitly permits all traffic, no statements added later are ever checked.

When you are editing an access list and need to reorder entries, you should first delete the old list with the **no access-list** command. If you do not first delete the previous version of the access list, when you copy or type commands on your router, you append additional access control list statements to the end of the existing access list.

The following access lists are supported for IP:

- Standard access lists for filtering based on source address

- Extended access lists for filtering on source or destination address or port numbers

- Dynamic extended IP access lists that grant access per user to a specific source or destination host basis through a user authentication process

- Reflexive access lists that allow IP packets to be filtered based on session information

To create a standard access list, use the following syntax:

```
Router(config)# access-list access-list-number {deny I permit} source [source-
    wildcard] [log]
```

The Cisco IOS software can provide logging messages about packets permitted or denied by a standard IP access list. The first packet that triggers the access list causes an immediate logging message, and subsequent packets are collected over 5-minute intervals before they are displayed or logged. You can use the **ip access-list log-update** command to set the number of packets that cause the system to generate a log message. If you enable Cisco Express Forwarding (CEF) and then create an access list that uses the log keyword, the packets that match the access list are not CEF switched.

To create an extended access list, use the following command:

```
Router(config)# access-list access-list-number {deny | permit} protocol source
   source-wildcard destination destination-wildcard [precedence precedence]
   [tos tos] [established] [log | log-input] [time-range time-range-name]
   [fragments]
```

You can identify IP access lists with a name rather than a number. To create a standard access list, use the following command:

```
Router(config)# ip access-list standard name
```

To create an extended access list, use the following command:

```
Router(config)# ip access-list extended name
```

You can specify whether or not the system examines noninitial IP fragments of packets when applying an IP extended access list. Before this option was added, nonfragmented packets and the initial fragment of a packet were processed by IP extended access lists, but noninitial fragments were permitted by default. The IP Extended Access Lists with Fragment Control feature allows more granularity of control over noninitial packets.

The optional **fragments** keyword is available with four IP access list commands (**access-list** [IP extended], **deny** [IP], **dynamic**, and **permit** [IP]). By specifying the **fragments** keyword in an access list entry, that particular access list entry applies only to noninitial fragments of packets; the fragment is either permitted or denied accordingly.

The Turbo Access Control Lists (Turbo ACL) feature processes access lists more expediently than conventional access lists.

To enable the Turbo ACL feature, use the following command:

```
Router(config)# access-list compiled
```

Use the **show access-list compiled** EXEC command to verify that the Turbo ACL feature has been successfully configured on your router.

You can implement access lists based on the time of day and week using the **time-range** global configuration command. To do so, first define the name and times of the day and week of the time range and then reference the time range by name in an access list to apply restrictions to the access list.

To restrict access to a vty and the addresses in an access list, use the following command:

```
Router(config-line)# access-class access-list-number {in | out}
```

To restrict access to an interface, use the following command:

```
Router(config-if)# ip access-group {access-list-number | access-list-name} {in | out}
```

LAN Security

Switch Port Security

You can use the port security feature to restrict input to an interface by limiting and identifying MAC addresses of the stations allowed to access the port.

You can configure these types of secure MAC addresses:

- **Static secure MAC addresses**—Manually configured by using the **switchport port-security mac-address** MAC address interface configuration command

- **Dynamic secure MAC addresses**—Dynamically learned, stored only in the address table and removed when the switch restarts

- **Sticky secure MAC addresses**—Dynamically learned or manually configured, stored in the address table, and added to the running configuration; these addresses can be saved in the configuration file

To enable sticky learning, enter the **switchport port-security mac-address sticky** interface configuration command.

You can configure the interface for one of three violation modes, based on the action to be taken if a violation occurs:

- **Protect**—Packets with unknown source addresses are dropped until you remove a sufficient number of secure MAC addresses or increase the number of maximum allowable addresses.

- **Restrict**—Packets with unknown source addresses are dropped until you remove a sufficient number of secure MAC addresses or increase the number of maximum allowable addresses; you are notified.

- **Shutdown**—Port security violation causes the interface to immediately become error-disabled and turns off the port LED; it also sends an Simple Network Management Protocol (SNMP) trap, logs a syslog message, and increments the violation counter.

The following commands are used to enable and configure port security:

```
Switch(config-if)# switchport port-security
Switch(config-if)# switchport port-security maximum value [vlan [vlan-list]]
Switch(config-if)# switchport port-security violation {protect | restrict | shutdown}
Switch(config-if)# switchport port-security mac-address mac-address [vlan vlan-id]
Switch(config-if)# switchport port-security mac-address sticky
```

You can use port security aging to set the aging time for static and dynamic secure addresses on a port. Two types of aging are supported per port:

- **Absolute**—The secure addresses on the port are deleted after the specified aging time.

- **Inactivity**—The secure addresses on the port are deleted only if the secure addresses are inactive for the specified aging time.

```
Switch(config-if)# switchport port-security aging {static | time time | type
{absolute | inactivity}}
```

BPDU Guard

The BPDU Guard feature can be globally enabled on the switch or can be enabled per interface.

At the global level, you can enable BPDU Guard on PortFast-enabled ports by using the **spanning-tree portfast bpduguard default** global configuration command. Spanning tree shuts down ports that are in a PortFast-operational state. In a valid configuration, PortFast-enabled ports do not receive BPDUs. Receiving a BPDU on a PortFast-enabled port signals an invalid configuration, such as the connection of an unauthorized device, and the BPDU guard feature puts the port in the error-disabled state.

At the interface level, you can enable BPDU Guard on any port by using the **spanning-tree bpduguard enable** interface configuration command without also enabling the PortFast feature. When the port receives a BPDU, it is put in the error-disabled state.

Root Guard

Your LAN topology can be changed dramatically if a switch is introduced that takes over as the root. You can avoid this situation by enabling Root Guard on key switch interfaces. If BPDUs show up on the interface that would cause a recalculation, Root Guard places the interface in the root-inconsistent (blocked) state to prevent the remote switch from becoming the root switch or being in the path to the root.

Use the command **spanning-tree guard root** in interface configuration mode to enable this feature.

802.1X Port-Based Authentication

The Institute of Electrical and Electronic Engineer (IEEE) 802.1X standard defines a client-server–based access control and authentication protocol that restricts unauthorized clients from connecting to a LAN through publicly accessible ports. The authentication server authenticates each client connected to a switch port before making available any services offered by the switch or the LAN.

802.1X Port-Based Authentication

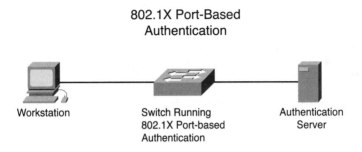

| Workstation | Switch Running 802.1X Port-based Authentication | Authentication Server |

You control the port authorization state by using the **dot1x port-control** interface configuration command and these keywords:

- **force-authorized**—Disables 802.1X authentication and causes the port to transition to the authorized state without any authentication exchange required

- **force-unauthorized**—Causes the port to remain in the unauthorized state, ignoring all attempts by the client to authenticate

- **auto**—Enables 802.1X authentication and causes the port to begin in the unauthorized state

The 802.1X port-based authentication is supported in two topologies:

- Point-to-point
- Wireless LAN

Use the following commands to enable 802.1X authentication:

```
Switch(config)# aaa new-model
Switch(config)# aaa authentication dot1x {default} method1 [method2...]
Switch(config)# dot1x system-auth-control
Switch(config-if)# dot1x port-control auto
```

Device Security/Access

Remember—you will find no substitute for physical security of your Cisco devices. Not only can the devices be easily stolen, but access to the console port allows for passwords to be reset and security into the network to be breached. After ensuring your devices are physically secured, you should place passwords on the various operating modes of your device.

It is very simple to set local passwords and security on your router or switch in order to help protect the operating modes and line access.

Use the following syntax to protect access to the console port with a local password:

```
CiscoDevice(config)# line console 0
CiscoDevice(config-line)# login
CiscoDevice(config-line)# password cisco
```

Notice that the preceding command **login** permits the use of local password checking on the line. You can use the **no login** command to disable password checking.

The sample syntax is used to protect the Telnet lines with a local password as follows:

```
CiscoDevice(config)# line vty 0 4
CiscoDevice(config-line)# login
CiscoDevice(config-line)# password cisco
```

NOTE   The preceding passwords are stored in the configuration in plain text. To ensure that they are encrypted—along with all other plain text passwords that might exist—use the **service password-encryption** command.

For enacting local security, you have the ability to configure 16 different privilege levels, numbered 0 through 15. To configure a privilege level for users and associate commands with that privilege level, use the **privilege** command in global configuration mode. For example, to set the use of the configure command to level 14, use the following command:

```
privilege exec level 14 configure
```

To protect access to privileged mode, you can use the **enable password** global configuration command. You can specify a privilege level if you are using various levels in your local security model. If no level is specified, the default level 15 is assumed. This privilege level provides full access to the privileged mode commands by default.

For additional protection, you should use the **enable secret** command to set an encrypted privileged mode password. Again, you can use the level argument to assign the password to a particular privilege level.

It is a best practice to set both versions of the privileged mode password (**enable password** and **enable secret**), but you should set them to different values. If you attempt to set the passwords the same, you get a warning, but the password is still accepted. After you set a password using the **enable secret** command, a password set using the **enable password** command works only if the enable secret is disabled or an older version of Cisco IOS software is being used, such as when running an older rxboot image.

Also part of the local security model is the **username** command. The **username** command provides username and/or password authentication for login purposes only. Add a username entry for each remote system that the local router communicates with and requires authentication from (for example, Challenge Handshake Authentication Protocol [CHAP] used with PPP). The remote device must have a username entry for the local router. This entry must have the same password as the local router's entry for that remote device. You can also use this command for defining usernames that get special treatment. For example, you can use this command to define a "guest" username that does not require a password, but connects the user to a general-purpose information service.

AAA

You can also ensure security in the network through the use of AAA—authentication, authorization, and accounting.

Authentication

Authentication can be accomplished using usernames and passwords configured locally on the switch; one or more RADIUS servers; one or more TACACS+ servers.

You can and should configure multiple authentication sources. For example, if your TACACS+ servers are unavailable (an ERROR is returned when access fails), you should have authentication seamlessly failover to some other method—perhaps the local username and password database on the device.

TACACS+

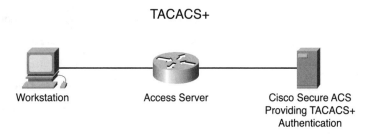

| Workstation | Access Server | Cisco Secure ACS Providing TACACS+ Authentication |

To configure authentication on a router or switch, perform the following:

Step 1 Enable AAA on the device using the **aaa new-model** command. This command permits the use of modern security protocols such as TACACS+, RADIUS, and Kerberos.

Step 2 Define the source of authentication. For example, you can use the **tacacs-server host** command to define the TACACS+ servers you are using for authentication. You can then use the **aaa group server tacacs+** command to group these servers.

Step 3 Define a list of authentication methods to try using the **aaa authentication login** command. If you specify TACACS+ servers first and you get no response from them (an ERROR is returned), the next listed method is tried.

Step 4 Apply a method list to router or switch line using the **login authentication** command.

Authorization

Once authenticated, a user is placed in user EXEC mode by default. Configure authorization with the following steps:

Step 1 Configure the RADIUS or TACACS+ servers that contain the authorization database. These are typically already defined for you using Step 1 from the configuration of authentication.

Step 2 Define a method list of authorization methods that are to be tried in sequence using the **aaa authorization** command. In this command, you not only specify the authorization sources (for example, a group of TACACS+ servers), but you also specify the function or service needing authorization. This is done with one of the following keywords:

- **commands**—The authorization server must return permissions to use any command at any level.

- **config-commands**—The server must return permission to use a configuration command.

- **configuration**—The server must return permission to enter configuration mode.

- **exec**—The server must return permission for the user to run an EXEC session.

- **network**—The server must return permission to use network-related servies.

- **reverse-access**—The server must return permission for a reverse Telnet session.

Step 3 Finally, apply the authorization method list to a specific line on the device using the **authorization** command.

Accounting

The RADIUS and TACACS+ servers can also collect usage information for auditing or even billing purposes.

Step 1 Define the accounting servers; typically this is completed in Step 1 of the authentication process.

Step 2 Define a method list providing a sequence of accounting methods using the command **aaa accounting**. In this command you specify functions that trigger accounting, for example:

- **system**—Major events such as reload

- **exec**—User authentication into an Exec session

- **commands**—Information about any executed commands

You can also specify that certain types of accounting records be sent:

- **start-stop**—Events are recorded when they start and stop
- **stop-only**—Events are recorded when they stop
- **none**—No events are recorded

Step 3   Apply the accounting method to a line on the device using the **accounting** command.

RADIUS Versus TACACS

Be aware of the differences between these two security protocols, as outlined here:

	RADIUS	TACACS+
Transport Protocol	User Datagram Protocol (UDP)	TCP
Encryption	Encrypts only the password	Encrypts entire body
AAA	Combines authentication and authorization	Separates AAA functions
Standards-based	Industry standard	Cisco proprietary

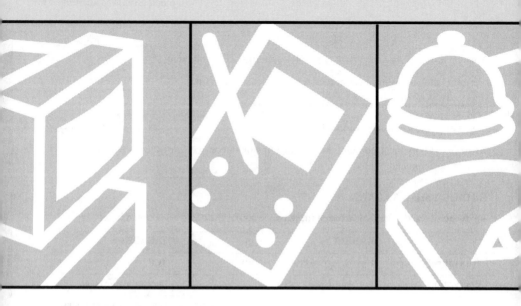

Section 9
Wireless

Wireless technologies are making their way everywhere computer networks might be found. Cisco is certainly making their mark in the industry, helping to further standards and release products for all aspects of this exciting new field.

As a CCIE candidate, you are expected to be familiar with the basics of wireless technologies in general, and you should also possess knowledge of Cisco's vast array of wireless networking products.

This section helps you to achieve these objectives and provides you with a feel for the types of topics you are likely to see in the CCIE certification environment.

Question 1

Currently, what is the most widely deployed IEEE wireless standard technology?

Question 2

What band does 802.11b operate in, and what is the maximum data transfer rate that this technology offers?

Question 3

What band does 802.11a operate in, and what is the maximum data transfer rate that this technology offers?

Question 1 Answer

The 802.11b standard is the most widely deployed wireless standard.

Question 2 Answer

This standard wireless technology operates in the 2.4-GHz unlicensed radio band and delivers a maximum data rate of 11 Mbps.

Question 3 Answer

The 802.11a standard delivers a maximum data rate of 54 Mbps and operates in the unlicensed portion of the 5-GHz radio band.

Question 4

What is the level of compatibility between 802.11a and 802.11b devices?

Question 5

What band does 802.11g operate in and what is the maximum data transfer rate that this technology offers?

Question 6

What is the additional functionality that a wireless access point must perform to implement fast secure roaming for the network?

Question 4 Answer

The 802.11a standard is not compatible with existing 802.11b-compliant wireless devices.

Question 5 Answer

802.11g operates in the same band as 802.11b (2.4-GHz unlicensed radio band), thus ensuring compatibility. The 802.11g standard delivers 54 Mbps maximum data transfer rates.

Question 6 Answer

Under fast secure roaming, the access point caches client security credentials as authentication to a centralized RADIUS server. When a client roams, keys are provided to the new access point by the fast secure roaming-capable access point.

Question 7

What major new technology did Cisco release in Structured Wireless-Aware Network (SWAN) Phase 1?

Question 8

Name at least four major considerations you must take into account when troubleshooting radio frequency (RF) connectivity issues?

Question 9

What standards-based IEEE authentication protocol is used heavily in wireless environments for the authentication of clients attempting to access the wireless LAN (WLAN)?

Question 7 Answer

The first phase of Cisco SWAN saw the release of Wireless Domain Services.

Question 8 Answer

You need to consider the following when troubleshooting RF:

Line of sight

Antenna selection, placement, and alignment

Transmission line issues

If the signal is passing through glass, metallic tinting on the glass degrading the signal

Rain, fog, and other environmental conditions degrading the signal

Question 9 Answer

Authentication in 802.11 leverages the 802.1X standard to authenticate users and to permit policy assignment to those users as a result of the authentication transaction.

Question 10

What new IEEE standard looks to redefine wireless security and introduce AES (Advanced Encryption Standard)?

Question 11

You are considering the use of a Cisco Aironet Series Wireless Bridge for bridging and simultaneous client access. Is this possible?

Question 12

What operational mode of the Cisco Aironet 1400 Series Wireless Bridge specifies that the bridge connects to a remote LAN and must associate with the root bridge using the wireless interface?

Question 10 Answer

802.11i is a new IEEE security standard that will encompass a number of security improvements, including those implemented in Wi-Fi Protected Access (WPA).

Question 11 Answer

This is not possible because the Cisco Aironet 1400 Series Wireless Bridge is used for bridging purposes only. It does not communicate with clients.

Question 12 Answer

Nonroot mode specifies that the bridge connects to a remote LAN and must associate with the root bridge using the wireless interface.

Question 13

Name at least five key features that the CiscoWorks Wireless LAN Solution Engine (WLSE) provides.

Question 14

What does the acronym CCX stand for in the area of Cisco wireless networking?

Question 15

What IEEE quality of service (QoS) draft standard do Cisco Aironet products support?

Question 13 Answer

Centralized mass configuration of Cisco access points and bridges

Centralized mass firmware updates

Cisco IOS conversion tool

Autoconfiguration of newly deployed access points

Security policy, fault, and performance monitoring of the Cisco WLAN infrastructure

Customer-defined, dynamic grouping

Client tracking and performance reports

Extensible Markup Language (XML) application programming interface (API) for data export and integration with syslog and Simple Network Management Protocol (SNMP) traps

Question 14 Answer

The Cisco Compatible Extensions (CCX) Program for WLAN devices provides tested compatibility with licensed Cisco infrastructure products.

Question 15 Answer

Cisco Aironet products support QoS based on the IEEE 802.11e draft standard specifications as of November 2002.

Question 16

What new technology is used in IEEE 802.11e to manage access to the radio frequency medium?

Question 17

What Cisco access point technology provides a modular design and allows single- or dual-radio configuration for up to 54-Mbps connectivity in both the 2.4- and 5-GHz bands and is fully compliant with the IEEE 802.11a, 802.11b, and 802.11g standards?

Question 18

Which Cisco Wireless Bridge technology is especially designed for harsh environmental conditions?

Question 16 Answer

The current IEEE 802.11e draft contains Enhanced Distributed Coordination Function (EDCF). The EDCF is an enhancement of the Distributed Coordination Function (DCF) process.

Question 17 Answer

Cisco Aironet 1200 Series Access Point

Question 18 Answer

Cisco Aironet 1400 Series Wireless Bridge

Question 19

Under IEEE 802.11e, what happens to traffic that is already classified with a class of service (CoS) setting?

Question 20

Name at least four roles supported by the Cisco Aironet 350 Series Wireless Bridge.

Question 19 Answer

Traffic that arrives at the access point over an Ethernet trunk, if already classified by its CoS settings within IEEE 802.1P, has that classification mapped to EDCF.

Question 20 Answer

The Cisco Aironet 350 Series Wireless Bridge supports the following roles in the radio network:

Nonroot bridge with clients

Nonroot bridge without clients

Repeater access point

Site survey client

Root bridge with clients

Nonroot bridge

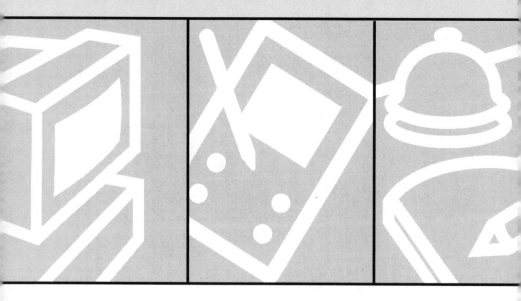

Wireless
Quick Reference Sheets

IEEE Standards

2.4 GHz (802.11b)

The 802.11b standard is the most widely deployed wireless standard. This standard wireless technology operates in the 2.4-GHz unlicensed radio band and delivers a maximum data rate of 11 Mbps.

Interoperability between many of the products on the market is ensured through the Wi-Fi Alliance Wi-Fi certification program. If you must support wireless equipment from a wide variety of vendors—802.11b is a choice worth considering.

5 GHz (802.11a)

The 802.11a standard delivers a maximum data rate of 54 Mbps and eight nonoverlapping frequency channels. Operating in the unlicensed portion of the 5-GHz radio band, 802.11a is also immune to interference from devices that operate in the 2.4-GHz band, such as microwave ovens, cordless phones, and Bluetooth devices.

The 802.11a standard is not compatible with existing 802.11b-compliant wireless devices. Some products support dual-band operation, and it is important to note that 2.4- and 5-GHz equipment can operate in the same physical environment without interference.

2.4 GHz (802.11g)

The 802.11g standard delivers the same 54-Mbps maximum data rate as 802.11a, but it backward compatibility with 802.11b equipment. Both 802.11g and 802.11b operate in the same unlicensed band. As a result, they share the same three channels, which can limit wireless capacity and scalability.

Fast Secure Roaming

Roaming is the ability to maintain network connectivity while moving from one access point to another. Roaming between access points that reside on a single IP subnet (virtual LAN— VLAN) is considered Layer 2 roaming. Roaming between access points that reside in different IP subnets is considered Layer 3 roaming.

Roaming at Layer 3 is currently addressed in the access point by Proxy Mobile IP (PMIP), which relies on software entities on the network routers known as home agents and foreign agents to tunnel traffic for a mobile device. Roaming at Layer 2 is managed by the access points using a combination of multicast packets that inform the switches in the network that the device has moved.

A Cisco Aironet client takes between 400 ms and 600 ms to roam at Layer 2. 802.1x authentication adds even more latency, while Lightweight Extensible Authentication Protocol (LEAP) adds anywhere from 200 ms to 1.2 seconds.

Fast secure roaming is a possible solution to the delays caused by roaming. Keep in mind that latency sensitive applications would be intolerant to such delays.

Fast secure roaming reduces the number of radio frequency (RF) channels that must be scanned and reduces the overall scanning time. Fast secure roaming also allows authentication to occur much more quickly by using an access point as a local authenticator.

Under fast secure roaming, the access point caches client security credentials as authentication to a centralized RADIUS server. When a client roams, keys are provided to the new access point by the fast secure roaming–capable access point. Roaming without the fast secure roaming feature requires a full reauthentication to a centralized RADIUS server on each and every roam. The result is a delay that can cause problems for any latency sensitive applications running during the roam.

Fast Secure Roaming

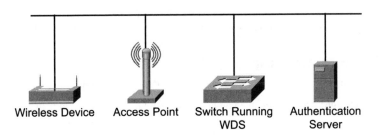

| Wireless Device | Access Point | Switch Running WDS | Authentication Server |

SWAN

The Cisco Structure Wireless Aware Network (SWAN) solution encompasses many components and was introduced in phases. The components include Cisco and Cisco-compatible clients, Cisco IOS access points, CiscoWorks Wireless LAN Solution Engine (WLSE), CiscoSecure Access Control Server (Cisco Secure ACS), and other Cisco IOS routing and switching products. Here are the two phases of SWAN:

- **Phase I**—Cisco IOS Software Release 12.2(11)JA introduced the concept of Wireless Domain Services (WDS). WDS includes fast secure roaming. Other relevant features in this release were local authentication service and Wi-Fi Protected Access (WPA) support. This phase also included a new CiscoWorks WLSE platform, the CiscoWorks 1130 WLSE, and Release 2.0 for all CiscoWorks WLSE platforms.

- **Phase II**—Cisco IOS Software Release 12.2(13)JA and CiscoWorks WLSE Release 2.5 introduced the concept of air and radio frequency (RF) management, which included rogue access point detection, assisted site survey, interference detection, radio management (RM) aggregation, and CiscoWorks WLSE enhanced reporting and visualization features, including Location Manager.

SWAN

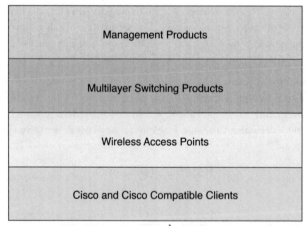

Swan also includes AirdeFense — an IDS
└ built into Aironet 1200 series
as std.

RF Troubleshooting

When you are RF troubleshooting, you need to consider the following:

- **Line of Sight**—Make sure that you have visual and radio line of sight between the devices.

- **Antenna**—Ensure that the appropriate antennas are used and that antenna placement and alignment are correct.

- **Antenna Placement**—Poor antenna placement (such as duct taped to a metal object) can cause many problems; make sure that the antenna support structure is solid.

- **Antenna Alignment Tool and Carrier Test**—Cisco has a light duty tool, the antenna alignment tool, built into the bridge operating system that helps align the antenna in the correct direction.

- **Transmission Line**—Avoid using long coaxial, antenna cables; make sure that the cable is not crimped in anyway; as the transmitted frequency (channel) increases, so does signal loss.

- If the signal is passing through glass, metallic tinting on the glass can degrade the signal.

- Rain, fog, and other environmental conditions degrade the signal.

Security *This book is late '04 / early '05 — find out latest.*

Authentication and encryption supplement basic 802.11 security mechanisms. Authentication and encryption check user credentials before granting access and to increase the security integrity of the user's session after association to the network. *— P49? (not very clear).*

Authentication in 802.11 leverages the 802.1x standard to authenticate users and to permit policy assignment to those users as a result of the authentication transaction. Basing the authentication transaction on user rather than machine credentials reduces the risk of security compromise from lost or stolen equipment. 802.1x authentication also permits flexible credentials to be used for client authentication. These credentials include password, one-time tokens, PKI certificate, or device ID.

Encryption for 802.11 is enhanced with multiple mechanisms, to aid in protecting the system from malicious exploits against the Wired Equivalent Privacy (WEP) key as well as protecting investment in the system by facilitating encryption improvements in existing hardware.

TKIP?
Temporal Key Integrity Protocol protects the WEP key from exploits which seek to derive the key using packet comparison. Message Integrity Check is a mechanism for protecting the wireless system from "inductive attacks." Inductive attacks seek to induce the system to send either key data, or a predictable response which can be compared to known data to derive the WEP key.

?
802.11i is the Institute of Electrical and Electronic Engineers (IEEE) security standard, which should be ratified soon. 802.11i will encompass a number of security improvements, including those implemented in WPA. In addition, 802.11i will standardize a new form of encryption for 802.11 wireless—AES or Advanced Encryption Standard. AES is recognized as a stronger security algorithm than the RC4 stream cipher used with WEP, although AES is more processor-intensive.

LEAP mentioned on p521!

Antennas

Cisco 2.4-GHz Standard Antennas

- The rubber dipole antenna is a standard antenna supplied with many Cisco Aironet access points.
- The multiband antenna, like the dipole, is an omnidirectional antenna (sending radio signals in all directions).
- The PC card integrated antenna is a low-gain antenna also having omnidirectional properties.

Cisco Aironet 802.11a Antenna

- This antenna supports both 2.4-GHz and 5-GHz radios, preserving existing IEEE 802.11b investments and providing a migration path to future IEEE 802.11a and IEEE 802.11g technologies.
- Its modular design supports single- and dual-band configuration.

Cisco Aironet 1100 Series Access Point Internal 2.4-GHz Antenna

- Cisco Aironet 1100 Series Access Point antennas provide coverage performance comparable to a pair of 2.2-dBi rubber dipole antennas.
- Cisco Aironet 1100 Series Access Points support either 802.11b or 802.11g radio.
- Cisco Aironet 1100 Series Access Points do not support external antennas.

Bridging

Bridges connect two or more wired LANs, usually located within separate buildings, to create one large LAN. A Cisco Aironet 350 Series Wireless Bridge can act as an access point in some applications by communicating with clients at the remote sites. This is accomplished with the Cisco workgroup bridge, PC Card, and PCI products. The Cisco Aironet 1400 Series Wireless Bridge is used for bridging purposes only. It does not communicate with clients.

Cisco Aironet bridges operate at the MAC address layer; they have no routing capabilities.

Cisco Aironet bridges offer many advantages over other more costly alternative connections. Some alternatives include T1 lines, cabling, and microwave connections.

The normal or operational mode for the Cisco Aironet 1400 Series Wireless Bridge is also referred to as the root and non-root mode:

- **Root mode**—Specifies that the bridge connects directly to the main Ethernet LAN network and accepts associations from other bridges
- **Non-root mode**—Specifies that the bridge connects to a remote LAN network and must associate with the root bridge using the wireless interface

The Cisco Aironet 350 Series Wireless Bridge supports the following roles in the radio network:

- Non-root bridge with clients
- Non-root bridge without clients
- Repeater access point
- Site survey client
- Root bridge with clients
- Non-root bridge

WLSE

The CiscoWorks Wireless LAN Solution Engine (WLSE) is a Cisco solution for managing the entire Cisco Aironet WLAN infrastructure. A single CiscoWorks WLSE gives administrators visibility into the WLAN without the need for any special sensors, add-on devices, or so-called wireless switches.

Key features include the following:

- Centralized mass configuration of Cisco access points and bridges
- Centralized mass firmware updates
- Cisco IOS conversion tool
- Autoconfiguration of newly deployed access points
- Configuration archive
- Security policy, fault, and performance monitoring of the Cisco wireless LAN (WLAN) infrastructure
- Customer-defined, dynamic grouping
- Client tracking and performance reports
- Extensible Markup Language (XML) application programming interface (API) for data export and integration with syslog and SNMP traps
- Integration with CiscoWorks LAN Management Solution (CiscoWorks LMS) and other network management systems (NMSs)

Client Form Factors

Cisco Compatible Extensions Program for Wireless LAN (WLAN) Devices

The Cisco Compatible Extensions Program for WLAN devices provides tested compatibility with licensed Cisco infrastructure products. Compatibility is assured through extensive, independent testing of third-party devices and can be found by looking for products displaying the Cisco Compatible logo.

QoS — *works with encryption?*

Cisco Aironet products support QoS based on the IEEE 802.11e draft standard specifications as of November 2002.

Data frames in 802.11 are sent using the Distributed Coordination Function (DCF). The DCF is composed of two main components:

- Interframe space (IFS)
- Random backoff (contention window)

DCF is used in 802.11 networks to manage access to the radio frequency medium.

The current IEEE 802.11e draft contains EDCF. The EDCF is an enhancement of the DCF process. The enhancement is the adjustment of the variable CWmin and CWmax random backoff values based upon traffic classification.

The WLAN infrastructure devices (such as an access point) advertise their QoS parameters. WLAN clients with QoS requirements use these advertised QoS parameters to determine which is the best access point to associate with.

The access point based on Cisco IOS software can prioritize traffic based upon a WLAN client's request for a particular traffic classification because of its appliance type.

Traffic that arrives at the access point over an Ethernet trunk, if already classified by its class of service (CoS) settings within IEEE 802.1P, has that classification mapped to EDCF and applied unless the Per-Appliance classification applies a subsequent classification.

Traffic flows are identified by IP TOS, DSCP, or protocol settings with class map–based prioritization. An identified downstream traffic flow is given a specific CoS applied over the radio interface. This process is consistent with current Cisco IOS software implementations.

Products

The Cisco Aironet product family is available in a variety of form factors to fit almost any application. The products include the following:

- **Cisco Aironet 1200 Series Access Point**—Modular design allows single- or dual-radio configuration for up to 54-Mbps connectivity in both the 2.4- and 5-GHz bands; fully compliant with the IEEE 802.11a, 802.11b, and 802.11g standards

- **Cisco Aironet 1100 Series Access Point**—Upgradeable 2.4-GHz WLAN solution that delivers enterprise-class security and manageability; available in the IEEE 802.11b or 802.11g standards

- **Cisco Aironet 802.11a/b/g CardBus Wireless LAN Client Adapter**—This product is for laptops and tablet PCs and complements the Cisco Aironet 1100 and 1200 Series Access Points; also IEEE 802.11a/b/g-compliant

- **Cisco Aironet 802.11a/b/g PCI Wireless LAN Client Adapter**—For slim desktop and point-of-sale devices; complements the Cisco Aironet 1100 and 1200 Series Access Points; IEEE 802.11a/b/g compliant.

- **Cisco Aironet 350 Series Client Adapter**—Complements Cisco Aironet 1200 and 1100 Series Access Points; available in PCMCIA and PCI form factors ; 802.11b-compliant client adapters

- **Cisco Aironet 5-GHz 54-Mbps Wireless LAN Client Adapter**—Complements the Cisco Aironet 1200 Series Access Point; 802.11a-compliant CardBus adapter operates in the UNII-1 and UNII-2 bands to allow 54-Mbps throughput

- **Cisco Aironet 1400 Series Wireless Bridge**—54-Mbps, license-free wireless bridge that uses Cisco IOS software; designed to be a cost-effective alternative to leased lines; engineered specifically for harsh outdoor environments.

- **Cisco Aironet 350 Series Wireless Bridge**—Enables high-speed building-to-building links of up to 25 miles (40 km) in U.S. Federal Communications Commission (FCC)-regulated areas, or 6.5 miles (10.5 km) in Europe; point-to-point or point-to-multipoint applications supported

- **Cisco Aironet 350 Wireless Workgroup Bridge**—Workgroup bridge quickly connects up to eight Ethernet-enabled laptops or other portable computers to a WLAN, providing the link from these devices to any Cisco Aironet access point or wireless bridge

- **Cisco Aironet Antennas and Accessories**—Antennas and accessories are available for client adapters, access points, and bridges to support customized wireless solutions